Victorian Revolutionaries

Victorian Revolutionaries

Speculations on Some Heroes

of a Culture Crisis

Morse Peckham

George Braziller   *New York*

STANDARD BOOK NUMBER: 0–8076–0543–3
LIBRARY OF CONGRESS CATALOG CARD NUMBER: 78-104701
FIRST PRINTING
DESIGNED BY JENNIE BUSH
PRINTED IN THE UNITED STATES OF AMERICA

O Mort, vieux capitaine, il est temps! levons l'ancre!
Ce pays nous ennuie, ô Mort! Appareillons!
Si le ciel et la mer sont noirs comme de l'encre,
Nos coeurs que tu connais sont remplis de rayons!

Verse-nous ton poison pour qu'il nous réconforte!
Nous voulons, tant ce feu nous brûle le cerveau,
Plonger au fond du gouffre, Enfer ou Ciel, qu'importe?
Au fond de l'Inconnu pour trouver du *nouveau*!

—Baudelaire

Contents

DEDICATED TO
ROBERT W. BUEDINGEN

Preliminary

THIS BOOK does not offer an argument, nor even an historical account, with a beginning and an end. Such endings as it does offer are principally questions. Yet the six essays have a number of themes in common. The most important theme is that of culture transcendence. All the men discussed here managed to get outside of their culture, to escape its presuppositions. The novel conclusions they came to may not seem particularly relevant to our times, though it is my opinion that they are highly relevant. But even if one finds their conclusions useful, it is the mode of their escape that is of greater importance.

The effort to achieve culture transcendence is a consequence of a culture crisis. Culture crisis is a term we are now familiar with. It is evident that we are living in a culturally critical period today. Any help we can get in understanding how to deal with it is bound to be of some value. Not the particular strategies of these men, but the general pattern of their strategy is probably the most useful thing they have to offer. Although it may seem that the culture crisis of Victorian England has little to do with that of Kennedyan, Johnsonian, and Nixonian America, it appears to me that ours is a continuation of the English one, now accessible only by historical reconstruction, unreliable as such

1

constructs must be. The strategies of the men discussed here to meet their cultural crisis by innovating various modes of cultural transcendence have, therefore, a double interest.

The values of a culture are necessarily incoherent. What we call the logic that holds the values of a culture together is itself but a cultural convention. What seems firmly mortared together falls apart under the pressure of a crisis. A culture is always in at least a mild state of crisis, for its values are never coherent and never adequate to meet the demands made on it from within and from without. Nevertheless, when a culture is in what we may call a non-critical or reasonably healthy condition, the incoherency of values is not observed, nor is there present an irony which juxtaposes obviously inconsistent values. In such an era a man says to himself, "Look before you leap!" when he wishes to postpone a decision. But when he wishes to make a decision in a hurry, he encourages himself and validates his act by "He who hesitates is lost." The sensible man never juxtaposes these two aphoristic devices for controlling his behavior. But in times of crisis, that is exactly what he does. The result is an irony which makes action exceedingly difficult and even psychologically perilous.

No one has analyzed the process more illuminatingly than Søren Kierkegaard, whom we may call a Danish Victorian. That stage in which a man moves easily from one value to another without ironic juxtaposition and to gain the maximum immediate gratification, whatever his gratificatory interests might be, he called the "aesthetic stage." But when his interests conflict, as Kierkegaard's did when he was in love and wanted to get married, and simultaneously wanted to continue his philosophical and religious pursuits with a devotion that meant the impossibility of a close relation with another human being, a man can become a Buridan's ass, unable to choose between two equally desirable stacks of hay. Kierkegaard called this crisis "irony." Then, he concluded, the only recourse is to step away from one's culture, to see that it is penetrated through and through with similar ironies, to grasp in its fullness the necessary incoherence of one's culture.

It is followed by what he called the "ethical stage," in which the individual attempts to find a metaphysical ground for existence, that is, for decision, a principle that will enable him to act once more within his culture, to be effective and to be ethically right, to be good. But just as irony dissolves the aesthetic stage, humor dissolves the ethical stage; one discovers that there is no ground to be reached. Ethical existence is suspended over nothing, and though any number of ladders reach down toward a metaphysical ground, all equally attractive, none of them have any lower rungs. They stop short and, whichever he chooses, a man is left dangling. To the man who has really understood what he has so far gone through, this situation is funny, is filled with humor. But it also means that there is no return to the culture that irony forced him into making the first step away from.

The only thing left to do is to climb to the final stage, the religious stage, since only this can offer him what he so desperately needs—a justification for existence, a conviction of meaningfulness, of value—since humor has swept away all available justifications, meaningfulness, and value. God, then, is the final terminus. But Kierkegaard's God was a very strange being indeed.

In moving from the aesthetic stage to the dissolutions of humor, the individual exhausts the resources of his culture. Among those resources are definitions and explanations of God. These are no longer available to him. In this Kierkegaardian religious stage, the word "God" can be used in no sense and in no situation in which the rejected culture uses it. In effect, in this situation the word "God" simply means that there is no farther to go. The end has been reached; the individual is now completely alienated, as Kierkegaard made abundantly evident in his final, savage attacks on Danish Christianity or, more accurately, European Christianity. Rejecting any cure for the culture by political or other revolution, and any action taken on the basis of the culture's existent values, he could only recommend that the alienated individual turn aside entirely from his society and culture and devote himself to creating a new possibility. To do so would be to achieve a true culture transcendence, a possibility that rises above and resolves the incoherence of the culture which is so filled with self-defeating ironies.

Can it be done? That is the question asked by the men with whom these essays are concerned. They understood the problem with various degrees of completeness; they offered answers of varying adequacy. None of them, perhaps, understood the problem so well as Kierkegaard, and he cannot be said to have understood it as fully as might be, for all of his enormous efforts to do so, so exhausting to himself and to his readers. These men can be placed along various stretches of the Kierkegaardian schema, though I have not attempted to do so. It may be that their analyses were better than his—his being superior only in elegance.

More interesting and useful than the content of Kierkegaard's analysis is what it tells us about the form of nineteenth-century thinking. By the end of the eighteenth century it had become established in European culture that abstract thinking, if properly performed, is parallel with the world. Abstract thought moves with the world. What is in our minds has its experienced origin in the world. The way we structure our experience corresponds to the structure of the world. This is still the most common way of conceiving the matter; few today have really left the eighteenth century.

Berkeley and Hume had their doubts about all this, but it was Kant who damaged this system irreparably. He pointed out that logically arrived at conclusions lead to antinomies, to antithetical but equally well-founded conclusions. Kant concluded that it is not the world which organizes our minds, so that the structure and content of thinking correspond to the structure and content of the world, but that the mind organizes the world. The categories which we use to cut up the world for whatever purposes we may have are not derived from the world, nor is the structure with which we organize those categories. The cutting up or categorization of the world he called the activity of the Understanding. The structuring of those categories he called the activity of the Reason.

There is much that is puzzling about Kant, much that is unsatisfactory, and much that will never be understood, probably because Kant did not understand it either. However, it is not what Kant said that is important for the present purposes but the form of his saying it. What he called an antinomy, Kierkegaard called an irony. Just as Kant moved back from the world to the Understanding and then back again to the Reason, and then back again to a God of whom nothing can be said, so Kierkegaard moved from the aesthetic stage back to the ethical and then back to what he so strangely called the religious stage. The structure of their abstract thinking is not an attempt to create a structure parallel with the world but rather one that proceeds at right angles to the world. It is not their philosophical correctness which is important here. As far as that goes, both were wrong, in that they thought they were talking about the "mind" but were in fact talking about language. What is important is that in response to a culture crisis they both radically revised the structure of the explanations of the world as established in their culture, and revised it in the same direction.

Hegel's philosophy shows precisely the same pattern or structure. What he called logic was utterly different from what the eighteenth century called logic and, for the most part, what is still called logic today. Though Hegel has been pretty well rejected, in the last few years a number of contemporary philosophers have begun to have a nervous feeling that after all

Hegel was saying something of great importance.

The traditional logic which he relegated to a minor task within his system may be called a one-level logic. Or better still, since excellence, in this kind of logic, depends on all terms being on the same plane of abstraction or concretion, it might be called a planar logic. But Hegel's was a hierarchical logic. Planar logic tries to move parallel with the world, and is often successful in doing so; Hegelian logic, which owes much to Plato and even more to the Neoplatonists, moves at right angles to the world. The one is concerned with explaining the world; the other, with explaining the structure of explanation.

This difference may be put in a simple, behavioral way. Traditional logic is interested in the fact that there is a tendency for all individuals faced with an identical stimulus field to respond in the same way. It is interested in the congruence of behavior and in the fact that, in spite of error, we all make our way around in the world with considerable success. Hegelian logic and nineteenth-century thinking in general are interested in the fact that, faced with an identical stimulus field, individuals can respond with a wide range of varying behaviors. They are interested in the incongruity of behavior; interested, as Kierkegaard put it, in irony and creativity.

It is not a question whether either system is right or wrong. Both, after all, may be quite in error, and probably are. That is not the consideration here. The point is that at times of cultural normalcy, awareness of incongruity of behavior is repressed in favor of awareness of congruity, while at times of culture crisis, the reverse holds: incongruity is what is noticed. When a culture's processes are smooth, the mind—whatever it is, or whatever the word refers to —is felt to be in harmony with the world, parallel with the world, structurally identical with the world. But at times of culture crisis, the mind is torn loose from the world; the world is felt to be in its essence inaccessible and the mind is felt to be without foundations—dangling. Traditional, planar, logic wants to get along with its culture, to improve it and at the same time adapt itself to it; nineteenth-century hierarchical logic wants to get away from its culture, to transcend it. Hegel is the greatest philosopher of culture transcendence. That is what his philosophy is all about, and that is why suddenly he is very pertinent once more.

It will be evident to the reader of these essays that they have been written from the position that the culture crisis of the nineteenth century was the greatest not merely in European history, but in human history, and that the crisis of the late twentieth century is a continuation of the crisis of the nineteenth, which actually emerged in the last decade or so of the eighteenth. It will also be evident that the speculative structure of this group of essays is typical of the structure of the explanatory response to a culture crisis. If there is indeed no culture crisis today, then these essays have nothing to say; if there is such a crisis, it is possible, though not necessarily likely, that they may speak to our condition.

M. P.

I

Escape from Charisma

ONE OF Tennyson's strangest acts was the publication of his first volume, *Poems by Two Brothers*, in which the three oldest of the eccentric and melancholy Tennyson brothers had a share. Alfred, the third son, born in 1809, not yet eighteen, had been a poet of professional technique for some years; yet most of his contributions to the volume—and he had written more than half of it—were not at all like his early surviving poetry. Most of his poems in the joint volume imitated Byron, Scott, and Moore. Many bore a distressing resemblance to the verse of Mrs. Felicia Hemans, "the female Byron," though not, unfortunately, a Byron in her personal life. Years later Tennyson called the volume "rot," though admitting that some of it was better than he had remembered. He never printed any of it again. In 1830 Tennyson published, as the first volume to bear his name, *Poems, Chiefly Lyrical*—the most accomplished first volume put out by an English poet up to that time, and arguably since. He had been writing this kind of poetry for years; it is hard to imagine why he never published some of his earlier pieces. Perhaps he did, for there is no reason to believe that all of the 1830 volume was written after *Poems by Two Brothers.*

This volume was published in 1827 at Louth, the nearest large town in the remote corner of Lincolnshire in which the dozen tall Tennyson sons and daughters were growing up in so restricted a house that their clergyman and alcoholic father had to add a dining room so that they could all sit down to a meal at once. The publisher was a Louth bookseller, but the book was also brought out in London; and this was no doubt part of the arrangement by which the publisher paid twenty pounds, half of it in books from his stock. Tennyson omitted from this first volume the kind of work he really cared about, because, his son tells us, it was "thought too much out of the common for the public taste." This gives us a clue to the anomalous place of the volume in Tennyson's career and tells us something important about him. The volume published at Louth and London was clearly aimed at the public taste. Most of the poems in it were written to make it a highly salable book. It was a time in which poetry sold well. Byron had but recently died; Moore was at his most popular. Scott's poems, though written long before, were increasingly well-liked because everybody knew by then that he was writing the Waverley novels. Even Wordsworth was approaching the height of his popularity in the 1830's.

Yet the market for poetry was soon to vanish, not to return for many years. The spread of literacy and the application of machine power to making paper and to printing and binding was about to create a vast new audience, too crude to relish the kind of literature published for a restricted and well-to-do public. Tennyson was out to make money, which he and his brothers needed if they were to attend the university properly, and the twenty pounds the publisher gave suggests that he too thought he had a potentially popular book. Well, everyone was mistaken; it received but one notice, not unfavorable at all, but it never sold well. It should have. The fault lay not, one suspects, with the poetry, but with a publisher who could not command enough attention from booksellers and the literary world. Byron's publisher, John Murray, could attract attention for almost anything he put out.

If the young Tennyson, as the venture leads one to suspect, deliberately set out to make a killing, it must be recognized that eventually he did. He was the last English poet to make a considerable fortune out of poetry, enough to build a spacious and beautiful country home and to live in it like the landed gentry. Faced with the problem of how to succeed professionally and financially as a poet and at the same time write the kind of poetry he wanted to, his first solution was the deliberate attempt to create what would sell, while holding back what he cared about and knew was of poetic value. It is easy enough to say today that his was a deliberate denial of his genius, but he was not the last artist to attempt to lead a double life. It is a problem many a serious writer has faced since the coming of Romanticism and the alienation of the innovative artist from his culture and his society.

Nor when Tennyson was a youth was the problem as easy to discern as now. In the 1820's the parents of a young poet could remember poets who wrote for their society and their culture, who were not alienated, and who were recognized and rewarded. Pope, before Tennyson the most financially successful of English poets, had died eight years earlier; in the boy's youth there had been Scott and Byron, and soon there was Moore. The spectacle of the artist without a public was still novel, and the tradition of how to play that role was by no means well established. Keats, only fourteen years older than Tennyson, had longed and planned for fame, and expected to have it. The neglect of Wordsworth was beginning to end. Coleridge's great poems, written thirty years before, had become part of the canon of English poetry; and though reputed to be sunk in opium, he was not only alive but surrounding himself with some of the most intelligent youth of the day, as Tennyson was shortly to learn when he went to Cambridge.

The peculiar separation between what Tennyson wrote for a

10

public which did not materialize and what he withheld was, in fact, an extraordinary insight for one so young and so isolated, one would think, in one of the remotest of English countrysides. Yet his oldest brother had already entered the great world of Eton and Cambridge. In those days the public schools and the universities were a part of the great world, as well as training grounds for it, and were to become even more central to the culture as the century went on. They may be in their decadence today, as many English insist, but in the 1820's they were just entering their takeoff period. Tennyson early recognized the situation, and prepared to arm himself for the struggle. A few years later the young Browning—bewildered and seduced by immediate success, the kind of success unknown to Tennyson until the 1840's—failed to see the problem and got himself into a terrible difficulty.

The question confronted Tennyson with a peculiar intensity when he went to Cambridge in February, 1828. He fell in with a group of young men who had formed the Cambridge Conversazione Society, known as the Apostles, a club which still survives. There he reached an astonishing conviction—that from this group would emanate forces which would redeem English society and culture from the materialism into which it had sunk, and from the revolutionary spirit which was penetrating the working class. The Age of Reform had begun, with its first great struggle—Catholic Emanicipation. The immense and dangerous powers of the middle classes to generate social and economic innovation were about to break through the walls with which the aristocracy had surrounded government, and to begin their extraordinary attempt to rationalize English and European and American social management. They had already rationalized the productive system and had made great changes in their effort to do the same with the economic system.

It must never be forgotten that the great nineteenth-century revolutionaries, Marx as well as Tennyson, Chopin as well as

11

Engels, came from the middle classes, and that their astonishing confidence was born and bred in the middle classes. From a wider point of view, they can be seen as engaged in the same role as their brothers, the hated bourgeoisie, who were about to conquer the world and reduce all but western culture to a sub-cultural status.

Nor were the young Apostles engaged in mere youthful illu-sionary idealism; almost everyone who was a member of the group with Tennyson went on to an important career. Each contributed significantly, either intellectually or in more direct ways of social management, to the social revolution of Victoria's reign.

The Apostles recognized the genius of Tennyson at once, and this is puzzling. He was all promise, not achievement; but that was true of all of them. Still, one wonders a bit at the adulation he received. Presumably he read to them the poems he was to publish in 1830. The man who was to become Tennyson's great-est friend, and whose early death was of the greatest possible importance and value to him—Arthur Hallam—was sure he was a genius. Did the Apostles see something in the poems of 1830 that we fail to see today? *Poems, Chiefly Lyrical* is not much admired now, except by a very few. In ascribing remarkable poetic value to it, I am much in the minority.

The truth of the matter seems to be that the Apostles needed a poet. It was not merely reform they were after, not merely political revolution. They were opposed to the latter, and per-haps rightly; by now it appears that after every revolution we end up with the same damned old society we started out with. They wanted a new kind of society, a new kind of culture; and for that a poet was necessary. Only a poet, according to the mode of thinking they were engaged in, could introduce into the empirical world that radiance of value to human existence which was once the task, the privilege, and the prerogative of religion. In Germany, only a few years earlier, Hegel had published the notion that the highest forms of human thought were philosophy, religion, and art, and he was still teaching this at the University of Berlin. Never before Romanticism had art been thus elevated above society; nor did Hegel mean that art should be subordinate to religion. It had its own unique mode of being which did not require either philosophical or religious validation, sanction, control; all three belonged, though hierarchically, to the realm of pure spirit. Nor was this German idealism, though not yet in its Hegelian form, unknown to the Apostles. They were reading Kant and arguing about him; moreover, though he had already left the University, John Sterling's spirit still inspired them and he still visited them—John Sterling, the follower and adorer of the sage of Highgate—Coleridge, the nearest thing the English had to a German idealist.

German Idealism has been half-forgotten for a long time now. For some decades professional philosophy has ignored it, even in the universities where, after all, one is supposed to be able to learn about the past, and so often one cannot. Walter Kaufmann has recently published a fascinating reinterpretation of Hegel. It is said that the contemporary English philosopher A. J. Ayer, when asked a few years ago if he still held to everything he had uttered in *Language, Truth, and Logic,* the great exemplar of logical positivism replied, "No, but I hadn't read Hegel when I wrote it." The real oddity is that the basic pattern of the speculations of the German idealists, particularly of Hegel—and also particularly of Coleridge—are beginning to be rediscovered by, of all people, American behavioral psychologists. One can never be sure that an idea is dead. Hegel's often derided, "What is real is rational; and what is rational is real," is turning out, in its epigrammatic way, to be exceedingly sensible and convincing.

Put in simple behavioral terms, Hegel was saying that response varies independently of stimulus, and that the meaning of a perceived configuration is not immanent in that configuration—it is a consequence of what happens between stimulus and response, that is, in the "mind," as we too blithely say. He was saying that mankind cannot help making sense out of the perceived world, and the kind of sense it makes is culturally established and transmitted, but that the mind is also radically creative, particularly in philosophy, religion, and art, and therefore the sense we make out of the world is emergent, historical, changing, and increasingly more adequate. This radically creative aspect of man is the spirit, which is meaning and value, and from which is derived both the meaning and value of the sense we make out of the world in everyday affairs. That sense is rational and it is what makes, for human purposes, the world real. The real and the rational are therefore identical. The spirit cannot come into existence without the phenomenal world; but the phenomenal world cannot be meaningful, or rational, without the spirit. To use other, and yet somewhat old-fashioned terms, the spirit is what separates and unites the subject and the object, and the relationship of subject to object is one of eternal and unresolvable tension.

This is the pattern of viewing man's relation to the world which lies behind the remark of one of the Cambridge Apostles, "The world is one great thought; and I am thinking it." In simple behavioral terms, any configuration is a sign, in the sense that the meaning of it is the response to it, but it does not dictate that response. It is a position confirmed again and again by contemporary psychologists in laboratory and clinic. But this idealism alone was not enough to make the Apostles affirm Tennyson to be the redemptive poet of the future. They needed a poet not because of German idealism but because of John Sterling and Coleridge, as well as Wordsworth and Shelley and even Keats, but especially Coleridge. It was he who enunciated in the form available to English culture the great doctrine of the Creative Imagination, which now has more than a stranglehold on the modern mind and which, it must be confessed, has done much to damage clarity of thought about both the arts and the sciences. From Coleridge's notion of the Imagination, more than from any other source, has developed the redemptive notion of art, so that without thinking about it most educated people simply assume that what is creative is art, at least if it claims to be art, and is therefore value-laden and of literally unspeakable significance. Looked at coolly, the proper substitute for "creative" is "socially validated innovation" and, as Hegel was well aware, innovation is the second thing that man cannot avoid.

When stripped to its hide, Coleridge's great notion amounts simply to this: The Imagination is responsible for the emergent in cultural history, as well as responsible for the order, meaning, and value we ascribe to experience. Since poets are obviously individuals particularly good at making things up or, more elegantly, inventing constructs of experience, more so, he thought, than anybody else, it follows that the poetic imagination is the most creative, the most innovative, and therefore the most valuable manifestation of the Imagination. It does not follow at all, really, but it seemed to. After all Coleridge was a poet and bound to be a little biased in the matter. The whole thing is uncomfortably like Orwell's "All men are created equal, but some are created more equal than others." At any rate, it is a notion infinitely seductive for poets and artists and lovers of poetry and the arts, and for anyone who has disengaged himself from his society and culture, who has achieved a degree of Romantic alienation, who is challenging his society and his culture, but who, at least as yet, has no notions of alternatives to the current culture and modes of social organization and management.

Before Romanticism, when a cultural crisis occurred and a new style of poetry emerged from it, it was the philosophers who defined the new orientations, and the critics who used the philosophical speculations to explain and justify the new poetry.

At the end of the eighteenth century, however, the cultural breakdown was so severe, the crisis was so intense, and the resultant loss of any sense of value so desolating, that the poets, particularly in England and Germany, had to be philosophers, critics, and poets, all at once, to be able to write at all. It is not surprising that Coleridge, himself a poet, and with the great example of Wordsworth before him, came to Wordsworth's conclusion, that they were philosophers and critics because they were poets. Their new vision of meaning emerged, it seemed to them, from the same mysterious depths of the mind from which poetry, itself so mysterious in its meanings and its effects on the individual, had always emerged.

To be sure, it is probably true that, no matter how guided by cultural conventions, every response to every stimulus, even a response a man makes to a stimulus generated by himself, emerges from the same mysterious depths; but though Wordsworth and Coleridge had gone a long way toward seeing that the everyday, the quotidian, is as mysterious in its generative emergence as any poem, they had not yet penetrated beyond the superficial similarity of most patterns of behavior to apply their insight to all human action, as their great inheritor, Wallace Stevens, was to. Even today it is hard enough, and for most human situations all but impossible, to be so discriminating in one's perceptions and cognitions. One may say, perhaps cruelly but not inexactly, that for Wordsworth and Coleridge and the Apostles and Tennyson it was mostly the grossly obvious innovation of the arts that could as yet be discerned as emergent and creative.

In any event it was this mode of thinking about poetry that made it so essential for the Apostles to have a poet that they made Tennyson an honorary member when he turned out to be either too shy or too lazy to give the requisite papers and too poor to give the substitutive dinner. And it was this conception of the poet and his redemptive task that Tennyson used to define himself. Above all, since Hallam asserted it, Tennyson accepted it; and hence something of the relation between the two young men must be understood both to grasp what was exciting about the 1830 volume and to comprehend the great importance and value to Tennyson of Hallam's death.

Arthur Hallam was the perfect upper-middle-class intellectual son of the perfect upper-middle-class intellectual father. Two years younger than Tennyson, he was far more sophisticated, having grown up in a London household frequented by the advanced and reformist thinkers of his time, whose conversation he was permitted to listen to from an early age, and eventually to join. Nevertheless, he was a member of a new generation, a Romantic generation. Taking from his father and his circle the middle-class belief in the value of innovation, he found, like so many of the Romantics, the authority for it not in the supposed logic and structure of Nature but in the Creative Imagination, the Imaginative Reason, the Spirit, that is, the unique individual. If the medieval style of thinking affirmed that the attributes of the object could be subsumed under the categories of the subject, and if the Enlightenment–Rationalist style believed the contrary, that the attributes of the subject could be subsumed under the categories of the object, the Romantic style assumed that both were, as we have seen, in an eternal interlocking tension; and at this stage of the development of Romantic thinking the authority for the meaning and value emanating from the Imaginative Reason into human experience was the Divine, was God.

This is only superficially in the medieval style, for the Imaginative Reason's dependence upon the empirical world was not, as in that style, a dangerous exposure to sin because the mind is a fallen mind. On the contrary, the release of the force of the Imaginative Reason into the world was analogous to the

Incarnation, was perhaps a repetition of the Incarnation. Perhaps the Incarnation was the continuous penetration of the divine into the human, of the infinite into the finite, of eternity into time. Perhaps, according to some thinkers more daring than Hallam, every human act, no matter how we judge it, is a new Incarnation. At any rate, with such an attitude Hallam, in spite of the deep affection between them and superficial similarity of many of their ideals, had departed from his father's world. He needed someone, preferably a little older, to whom he could transfer that emotional dependence; by defining him, he could define himself.

It was indeed, throughout Europe, a period of intense friendship between and among the young men who were entering with utmost enthusiasm upon the inheritance of orientations forged by their predecessors, the men of the generation of Coleridge, Wordsworth, and Hegel, of Beethoven and Caspar David Friedrich, the great German painter, and his counterpart in England, John Constable. Though inheriting the bourgeois drive to innovation, their justification was utterly different: they were alienated from their society and culture; deeply anti-bourgeois, transcendental, not rational—visionary, not empirical. The young needed to sustain each other, and intense friendships were the result, relationships deriving from an irresistible and terrible need for justification and self-definition. For Hallam the very brilliance and success and intellectual canonization of his father's historical studies made an emotionally loaded friendship all the more necessary, and as an Apostle he needed a poet, for he himself had experimented in that direction, enough to realize that the gift was not his.

As for Tennyson, he had a father who was as nearly satisfactory as a poet's father could be, and at the same time utterly unsatisfactory. All the sons and daughters were remarkable individuals, tall, handsome, looking more Spanish than English, exquisite speakers, capable of saying anything in any company, preferring genteel poverty to work, lazy, often religiously obsessed, and constantly a prey to almost psychotic melancholia. Some in fact reached psychosis. Their father was permanently embittered because his father had disinherited him in favor of his younger brother and had forced him into the church, for which he had no aptitude and in which he had little interest. But the Tennysons had always been called the black Tennysons, an allusion both to their complexions and to their transmitted weakness for melancholia and personality instability. The reason for old Tennyson's decision remains mysterious, but one suspects that he saw that the more stable younger son would be the right one to found the family fortunes, as he did.

George, Alfred's father, was certainly a man of unusual talents, learning, and powerful fantasy; but by the time Tennyson went off to Cambridge the family life, with his father's violence and drunkenness, had become barely tolerable. The poet, in short, was born into a family of powerful and dominating personalities; and his two older brothers were no exception. He needed a friend, a young friend for whom he could play something of the role of older brother, protective and loving and not dominating. At the same time, Hallam's superior sophistication made him as meaningful to Tennyson to satisfy the needs of justification and self-definition as Tennyson was to him. In visits to Hallam's home Tennyson found that rational and tranquil domestic life which he needed so desperately, as much of his subsequent poetry and eventually his own family life makes very clear. In the Tennyson-Hallam relationship the Imaginative Reason found its incarnation, the one representing the Imagination and the other, the younger youth, the Reason. The price was dependency; how to terminate that dependency became for Tennyson a central and ultimately illuminating problem.

Today it is not easy to respond with any adequacy to the 1830 volume, and much of the next volume—dated 1832 but published in 1833—nor to comprehend why Hallam and the Apostles were so enthusiastic about it. One mode of preparing oneself is to perceive a certain parallel between Tennyson and Chopin, born eighteen months after the Englishman. The extraordinary harmonic imagination and melodic daring of the composer can be traced back to his boyhood work with Bach's *Well-Tempered Clavier*; correspondingly Tennyson's father started him on Bach's virtual contemporary, Alexander Pope. He once told his son that the fault of his verses was an excessive smoothness; he must introduce rhythmic variety. For a long time Pope had been accused of exactly this fault, even by Keats; yet nothing is farther from the truth about Pope, whose style is infinitely and exquisitely varied. For professional mastery of versification the only equivalent to Pope and his only rival is Tennyson himself. Yet the salient importance of Pope to Tennyson, and of Bach to Chopin, was more than this, as we can see when to these we add the dependence of Delacroix, eleven years Tennyson's senior, upon Rubens. Three of the greatest artists who emerged in the 1820's and 1830's found their master, not in their immediate predecessors but in the baroque.

The importance of baroque art in the construction of the nineteenth-century styles has rarely been fully appreciated, yet even Wordsworth and Coleridge took many of their formal notions of how to write poetry from the seventeenth century, and not just from Milton. The problem for the Romantic artists was that by the end of the eighteenth century the ideal in all the arts had become what has been called neoclassicism. It is not a bad term, and it has some genuine justification, particularly in sculpture and architecture, though very little in music. Yet even in its classicism the eighteenth century was strangely pallid and to our taste without vigor.

The clue comes from the fact that it was the age which created what are still our ideals of domestic architecture and furniture, even when we do not imitate and copy its styles directly. The home is above all a place for physical and psychological comfort, the one place in the world in which it is of the utmost importance to have a perceptual field to which perceptual and cognitive adaptation is easy. And such adaptational ease was the cultural ideal of the late eighteenth century, and in all the arts; it found its philosophy, as we have seen, in the notion that the subject is properly subsumed by and incorporated into the object, that is, ultimately, Nature, in the grand eighteenth-century sense of that term. The perfect adaptation of the human organism to the environment—life, liberty, and the pursuit of happiness—was the cultural ambition. Romanticism emerged because for a few people in Europe that ambition had been so hopelessly frustrated as to reveal its epistemological inadequacy.

Tension between subject and object was the truth of the matter, they were convinced, and hence the task of the artist was to create a perceptual field to which psychological adaptation was anything but easy, a field which would permit and require and force the artistic observer to experience perceptual and cognitive disorientation and in grasping that field to engage the power of the creative imagination. The experience of the work of art, as well as its creation, was to be an incarnational act. To fulfill such an ambition the Romantic artist needed models, and the most recent and accessible models were the arts of the baroque. In his old-fashioned insistence that his son master Pope, George Tennyson was doing him, considering what his stylistic task as a poet was to be, the greatest possible service.

One of the best ways a modern can prepare himself to respond with some adequacy to Tennyson's first two volumes is to spend a little time looking at op art. Such an experience provides a useful cognitive model, for the quality to be responded to is visual and aural splendor. Tennyson was severely criticized at the time and has been ever since for such poems as "Claribel," and "Isabel," and "Madeline," and though other matters are at work in the masterpiece of the volume, "Mariana," that same splendor achieves its utmost beauty in "Recollections of the Arabian Nights." Tennyson gave the reader a clue in the subtitle to the first poem in the volume, "Claribel: A Melody." The comparison with Chopin is irresistible, for he too seems in his first work, which appeared at about this time, to have been concentrating on seductive and wholly novel melodies and harmonies. Poetry, however, has no such aural resources as music, and its "melody" and "music" are confined solely to a more frequent repetition of sounds than is to be found in any random selection of speech, whether of consonants or vowels. One may call this principle phonic over-determination, and the same term will serve to identify a great regularity and patterning of stress (or as it is still called outside of circles affected by modern linguistics, accents, or even beat).

In these poems Tennyson set out to achieve a degree of phonic over-determination, together with sudden violations of the patterns he presents, such as no English poet had attempted before. It was undoubtedly this that aroused the enthusiasm of the Apostles and of Hallam; yet one wonders why, for such over-determination, as in Pope, had previously been justified and sought for to provide an appropriate background or setting for the meanings of the words. One would think that with their deep earnestness, Tennyson's Cambridge friends would have rejected such an intense and energetic concentration on one aspect of poetry as a spiritual trivialization of poetry's high mission.

We may find clues to their attitudes from several sources. First, the language of some schizophrenics and other psychotics is characterized by quite this same interest in phonic over-determination with apparently little interest in the meaning of what is being said. There is a difference, of course. What Tennyson says in these poems is perfectly intelligible; it is merely that there seems little reason why anyone, with a few exceptions, should trouble to say it. Further, more often than not the language of the schizophrenic has a private meaning to him. As psychiatrists have frequently found out, if they can break the code of the schizoid's language, or of his painting, which is visually equivalent in its over-determination of patterning, they can frequently help the patient and even bring him to the point of a functional relation with the rest of the world. There is no denying that the position of the Romantics is in some ways similar to that of the schizoid.

The very term "alienated," comes, after all, from the legal language organized to deal with the insane. Both the insane and the Romantic have lost a certain degree of command of conventionalized interactional functions. The difference is that the schizoid suffers from a sense of internal breakdown which is quite out of his control. The Romantic, however, perceives that the metaphysical or explanatory systems which direct and control a culture's behavior—let us call these, in the manner of the sociologists, the belief-systems—are no longer adequate to the challenges which the current historical situation is presenting to the society's systems of social management, to its belief-systems, and to the individual's task of integrating his behavior with both. From this point of view the doctrine of the Creative Imagination, whether or not it is given a divine or transcendental origin and validation, is an assertion that the restructuring of social management and the reorganization of the belief-system can arise only from the imagination of the individual who sees the true state of affairs.

The difference between the schizoid's overstructuring and Tennyson's concentration upon a phonic over-structuring, innovative in the English poetic tradition, is that the one uses his structuring powers to keep himself from further cognitive disintegration, but that the other uses it to defend his powers of cognitive integration against what he perceives as the cognitive

23

disintegration of his society and his culture. This comes out clearly if we contrast the schizoid's meaninglessness, according to the conventions for responding to words, and another aspect of Tennyson's structuring or imaginative powers, his imagery. His power to sustain a consistency of visual images is as remarkable as his power to sustain phonic over-determination. These early pieces may be regarded as exercises, in a sense, in cognitive integration of a kind achieved in English poetry only by Coleridge in "Kubla Khan," occasionally by Wordsworth as sections of longer poems, and in a handful of lyrics by Keats, of which "To Autumn" is the most remarkable. But even that marvelous poem has three different modes of cognitive integration, while Tennyson in a number of poems in these first two volumes is able to sustain it over considerably longer stretches.

Considering their mode of defining themselves and their place in the world and in history, it seems reasonable to conclude that in these imaginative powers of cognitive integration, evinced in sustained phonic and imagistic over-determination, the Apostles and Hallam saw incontrovertible proof that Tennyson was the genius they needed, both to validate them as a group and to validate their enterprise and ambitions for social and cultural innovative reorganization.

But there was an even subtler appeal. An individual's knowledge of himself is for the most part no different from another's knowledge of him. We know what we are because of the way we see ourselves behave, and mostly this is the same kind of information we have of others, their overt, or observable behavior. Some information, however, is privileged, such as covert or unobservable verbal behavior, one of the categories of behavior we talk about when we use the word "thinking." Similar is covert nonverbal sign behavior, such as dreams, mental images, and visions. Still another is our observation of the emotional loading of behavior, the emotional intensity that accompanies, for example, our swearing at a dog for barking too long. Yet another is more subtle; such information pertains to what may be called feeling-states, of which the subtlest is the sense of identity, which ebbs and flows; it is no doubt the same feeling-state we refer to by such phrases as "the sense of meaning" and the "sense of order," or relatedness. Similar are other feeling-states, the sense of inhibition or of expression; of rejection or of openness; of energy conservation or energy release; of demand, the sense of controlling the environment; or of acceptance, the sense of letting some element in the environment assume control over ourselves; and so on.

For such feeling-states there are conventionalized sign systems, both outside the arts and in them. Of such sign systems the most readily obvious is music. It has been said that music does not have meaning, but this means only that it does not have the kind of meaning language does, for the simple reason that only language has that kind of meaning. Consequently, in spite of aestheticians, most music lovers and composers have been convinced that music is meaningful. When, therefore, the music of poetry is spoken of, the reference is not, as some have attempted to maintain, to some analogy between the formal aspects of music and poetry, but rather to the fact that poetry, though less richly, can and usually does present the signs of feeling-states which it is the semantic function of music to manipulate, as well as language signs. That kind of feeling-state which the phonic over-determination of alliteration and assonance signifies is, I believe, the sense of demand, the sense of imposing one's will on some aspect of the world; while rhyme, my researches into the matter strongly suggest, signifies the sense of being adequate to the demands of the situation; in western music the equivalent is the major key.

It is from this point of view that it is to be understood why Tennyson in several poems exhibits the most astonishing technical command over rhyme; in poems of some length he uses the same rhyme sound for every line. Responding to this, though not of course knowing why, Tennyson's friends would interpret him as a poet who was at once capable of imposing his poetic will upon his material and of being adequate to the demands of the poetic tradition and of the newly defined poet, and who also constructed sign systems of such feeling-states which served both as model and inspiration. Hence the sense of euphoric exhilaration in the language experienced by the early readers of Tennyson, as well as the Apostles and Hallam.

Yet still more is involved. As we have seen, Tennyson subtitled the first poem in the volume "A Melody," thus giving a hint that the important thing about the poem was its similarity to music. The values of the poem were to be conceived in terms of the values to be found in one's response to music. It has been pointed out a thousand times that the nineteenth century was the century of music; as Pater said decades later, "All art approaches the condition of music." That is, I propose, all art seeks to equal music in its power to present signs of feeling-states. At the beginning of the century, there was still a hierarchy of the arts; poetry was at the top, followed by painting, sculpture, architecture; music was considerably lower. There was some justification for this, since up to the Romantic period the emotional and feeling character of music was controlled by the situation for which it was composed. It was, in effect, a subordinate art, and the assertion that the first great Romantic composer, Beethoven, was the man who freed music, means that he wrote music the character of which was totally unrelated to the character of the situation in which the performance took place. To make such a separation is to assert that feeling-states transcend the values of smooth interaction.

An odd position, yet one so familiar to us that it takes some effort both to realize how novel it was and what were the interests that lay behind it. As we have seen, feeling-states are the subject matter of privileged information. They are directly accessible only to the individual who experiences them. To grant

26

them high status is to assert that the uniqueness of one's individuality is separable from the social roles conventionalized in one's culture. It is to separate the self from the role. Hence the importance of music in Romantic culture and its rapid rise to an equality with the other arts, and even, for many, to a position of importance and value above all the others.

The ways of experiencing music are manifold, but certainly one is to go through a sequence of feeling-states, more or less corresponding to those signified in the music, depending on one's unique personality and one's musical and semiotic sensitivity. It is to concentrate upon a flow of feeling-states, divorced from any action, any attempt to manipulate the environment. Perhaps no artistic experience is so isolating and so incommunicable as music, and in that lies its particular virtue for the alienated Romantic. It confirms his own identity by enabling him to contemplate his feelings without any social or environmental interaction, without performing any social role. For the Romantic at any rate—and an endless series of testaments by Romantic figures from the early nineteenth century to the present day affirm this—musical experience above all experiences confirms and reinforces the sense of identity. One literally feels one's self. And this was the profoundest appeal Tennyson's first volumes made to those who were adequate in their response to what Tennyson was doing.

In two poems Tennyson began to work out both the moral and social function of the creative imagination and its particular dangers. In "The Poet" is the claim that the poet, "born in a golden clime," provides the weapon with which Freedom, clothed in Wisdom, "shakes the world." Thus early do we begin to find what was implicit in Kant and became one of the great themes of the mainstream of philosophical thinking in the course of the century, culminating in Nietzsche, James, and Vaihinger—the instrumental notion of truth, truth as a weapon or tool rather than as a stable revelation—a position culminating, so far, in the modern notion that the truth value of a proposition is its value as a set of directions for managing both the linguistic and nonlinguistic worlds, rather than a proposition to be passively believed in.

Here again we encounter the assumption of a terrible idea which has so exalted and crushed the nineteenth and twentieth centuries, the redemptive function of art. On the other hand, Tennyson is also, as he was to be all his life, wrestling with an awareness of the dangers of exalting the creative imagination, the temptation it holds to the alienated individual to experience and justify his alienation by turning away from the empirical world, the world of fact, the world of modest failure, the necessary condition of man, and to enter instead a world of perfect success.

The more intensely one holds that reality is the tension between subject and object, the more unstable the sense of identity becomes, particularly for the individual whose rejection of the current modes of social management and belief forces him to question his adequacy to make that rejection. It was something Tennyson knew a great deal about, for he himself frequently had the experience of total loss of identity, of the merging of the boundaries of the self with the perceived world. The experience was both exalting, convincing him that the creative imagination finds its source in the divine, and frightening, for the loss of self meant a loss of any grip or foothold for action in the phenomenal world. Thus two themes emerge of the highest importance for his subsequent career, isolation, in which the poet's golden clime turns to a hell, and alienation, in which a creative tension is maintained between the self and the role, between the creative imagination and, particularly, the social world. But that in turn led to a further problem. How was one to reenter the world, to engage with it, without compromising with it and losing the self's tie to the creative imagination and the divine authority for it?

28

The danger of isolation is to be found in "Mariana," and "The Palace of Art," which appeared in the 1833 volume; the problem of reentry is also to be found in the later volume in that endlessly fascinating work, "The Lady of Shalott." To turn entirely in the direction of the structuring power is to risk either pure negative value or loss of selfhood in a destructive illumination; to turn in the direction of the world and social reality is to risk the loss and extinction of the structuring power. Likewise to find in a single individual a symbol of one's identity and thus to become dependent on that individual, to risk all on love, is to become both internally blocked, for the beloved threatens at once to become the sole model for self-definition, and externally blocked, for the beloved threatens to become the sole channel for reentry.

This was exactly the threat Hallam posed, and that is why I have suggested that Tennyson was lucky in Hallam's death. It forced him to examine the nature of dependency and the problem of how to resolve the fact that though one rejects socially validated roles it is impossible to act without a channeling mode of behavior, an anti-role. For nearly ten years Tennyson published nothing. The new poems of the 1842 collection of his work to that point and *In Memoriam A. H. H*[allam] are the record of these new struggles.

In "Ulysses," as he has recorded, Tennyson created, very shortly after Hallam's death in September, 1833, the courage to continue. It is the monologue of the island-king, threatened with a meaningless isolation, addressing the souls of his dead mariners, determined to encounter once again the sea-road of experience with its eternally promised goal, never arrived at. And in "The Two Voices" he sees that the death of Hallam makes it possible to channel his dependence on him into a love for those men fully submerged in existing social institutions, the family and the church, who cannot reciprocate, as Hallam had, the confirmation of identity. Psychologically, the problem of Hallam's death was solved—one might more correctly say, successfully exploited—almost without delay, certainly in a few months. The understanding of how that solution was arrived at and what was involved in the problem and its solution was to occupy Tennyson for nearly twenty years; it is the subject of *In Memoriam,* which is not so much the record of his love for Hallam as the examination of how he freed himself from him. Hallam alive was dangerous; Hallam dead threatened to become an incubus.

Tennyson's father died in 1831, but the new rector permitted the family to live in the old house until 1837, when the poet, who was capable of great practicality, moved his mother, and those siblings still at home, to the outskirts of London. This gave him not only access to the life of literary London, but also, and more important, the opportunity to explore the great and increasingly terrible city, as Dickens was recording at the time. Above all, it gave him the chance to become something of a Bohemian, to loiter in London bars and drink a great deal of brandy. One doubtful tradition has it that in subsequent years he got drunk on brandy every night of his life. There is perhaps a reason for the lack of intimate details of his life from this time until his death. At any rate, to become a Bohemian was to establish an anti-role, to learn how to become a foreigner in his own society. Certainly from this time his manners at dinners and evenings, even with ladies present, became extraordinarily free, even for a Tennyson, and increasingly direct and outspoken.

Part of his luck was to make a bad investment and lose the little capital he had inherited. Eventually he recovered it, because his brother-in-law, whose marriage he was to celebrate in *In Memoriam,* insured the life of the inventor who had taken Tennyson in. The death of that inventor made it financially possible for Tennyson to marry in 1850. It must not be imagined that this financial error marks him as a dreamy poet. It was a time of burgeoning invention and financial speculation; losing one's fortune was a common occurrence. There were, after all, innumerable instances of individuals who had made great fortunes by taking just such chances. The whole affair merely served to intensify and prolong his wandering, Bohemian life. Fortunately, there was enough money left in the family to make it unnecessary for him to work. When he was not wandering about London he wrote, mastering his problems and his technique.

One may speculate that had Hallam lived and married Tennyson's sister this Bohemian episode might not have occurred. Tennyson would inevitably have been drawn into Hallam's circle and into the respectable middle-class intellectual life of Hallam and his father. Great things were expected of Hallam, and it seems reasonably clear that he was career-minded, planning to take part in the middle-class capture of the government from the aristocracy, or at any rate of the economic powers that controlled the aristocracy and their governmental decisions. The upper-middle classes were making money, always an attraction to the English aristocracy. They seemed reasonably willing, indeed, to welcome the new fortunes into the government of the country so long as they could share in the plunder, which mostly took the form of investment opportunities. Bourgeois wealth and ancient name melted together in nineteenth-century England in the most comfortable manner imaginable, and Hallam's aimed participation in this process would very possibly have deflected Tennyson into an interpretation of his poetic task as more direct moral involvement with the immediate problems of the day. As it was, when he turned his poetic interest to writing about the contemporary world, it was usually to attack the values of the landed gentry and aristocracy, particularly those they shared with the middle classes.

The 1842 collection was most notable for the revision, polishing, and selection of the earlier volumes. In bulk what was added was little more than what was preserved from the volumes of 1830 and 1833, and for the most part what was new was less striking than the old. There were, however, several masterpieces, and of these the most significant was "Morte d'Arthur," the germ of the later *Idylls of the King*. It contained the famous lines, "The old order changeth / yielding place to new / And God fulfills himself in many ways / Lest one good custom should corrupt the world." These are the words of Arthur, and the *Idylls*, which dominated Tennyson's life from the late 1850's almost to his death, are an exploration of what they meant.

The significance of the corrupting effect of a good custom can be explored in several ways. While he was at Cambridge, Tennyson startled his companions by proposing that species were not fixed, nor were individual species created by God, but rather that the various species had emerged from preceding less developed species. It was not, of course, a novel idea to the more advanced scientists of Europe, though they were, on the whole, extremely discreet. At almost the same time Lyell, the founder of modern geology, was writing in a private letter that he held the same opinion, but since he could offer no explanation, when he published his *Geology* in 1830 he presented the traditional theory. Darwin did not invent the theory which we now call evolution. He merely proposed an acceptable biological mechanism which demonstrated that evolution was the only tenable hypothesis. The heart of that hypothesis is that adaptation of organism to environment is inevitably imperfect, that any adaptation is, to a certain extent at once and in the course of time inevitably, a maladaptation.

Darwin ended metaphysical or theoretical evolutionism such as Tennyson was thinking about and began scientific evolutionary theory. The notion of imperfect adaptation is so consonant with what I have called the Romantic irresolvable tension between subject and object that it seems more than likely that Tennyson thought of his evolutionary theory by analogy with the relation of the creative imagination to the world. Certainly a number of the German idealists, such as Schopenhauer, had, on epistemological grounds, thought of it, and on somewhat similar grounds Browning was to arrive at it a few years later.

Today we rather have a tendency to sneer at the Victorians for their facile belief in progress, and thus we often enough misinterpret the major figures. A distinction must be made. The common notion of progress was a rationalist-enlightenment notion, emerging in the seventeenth century. It was progress conceived as emergent over short time spans. But the Romantic notion of progress gradually separated itself from its predecessors and was a long-term notion, closer to biological time than historical time, and by no means certain at that. Tennyson, who often used biological and evolutionary language in *In Memoriam*, saw faith in progress as an imaginative construct and clearly could accept it only in terms of immense periods of time. Granted he said he saw evolution as teleological, moving toward some far-off, divine event. A good custom can corrupt the world, then, because, since it is good, it can be taken as final, as a perfect adaptational mechanism. The term "custom" appears to contain the corrupting element. For short historical spans Tennyson clearly believed in the value of traditionary good customs; just as clearly he saw them as corrupting in terms of evolutionary aeons.

But he also saw the good custom as corrupting because he had very nearly experienced such corruption. Ulysses, his island-king, saw the corruption of a good custom getting its grip on him, and the suggestion is powerful that Tennyson saw his dependence upon Hallam, defined as friendship and therefore, in spite of both of them, a social role with traditional protocol, or custom, a potentially and perhaps actually corrupting influence.

This is why, perhaps, Tennyson's grief was so rapidly overcome, and why *In Memoriam* begins with a poem that rejects violently the notion that personal tragedies make better men of us. Had Hallam lived, it is possible that Tennyson could never have faced the fact of his dependence and its attendant dangers, nor have achieved the extraordinary insight into his own personality, which is the material of *In Memoriam.*

There is yet another way in which the significance of the good custom that corrupts may be understood. One of the central themes in his work is the theme of doubt. It is too plain a word to get at what he was talking about. At the end of another poem of the 1842 collection, "A Vision of Sin," he cries, "Is there any hope?" There is an answer to the question, but it is indecipherable, "in a tongue no man could understand," a theme which emerges again in the *Idylls.* In Tennyson's poems, over and over again, it is the man of absolute and unquestioning faith who comes to grief, and the man who transcends faith, confidence, and belief who sees, as at the end of "A Vision of Sin," "an awful rose of dawn." Yet there is no question that Tennyson himself believed in God, the soul, and immortality. He said so, and he also said that without his faith in immortality he could not continue to exist.

Tennyson's thinking seems inconsistent or at best paradoxical, but it is neither. He could simultaneously hold a position, understand what interests, indeed what characterological weaknesses, led him to hold it, and thus doubt and even deny its validity, while continuing to hold it. Doubt, it is apparent, for Tennyson gave a position its vitality, its cutting edge, its dynamism. He was, after all, a poet, and for the Romantic poet, increasingly as the century wore on, explanation and conceptualization, the logical reason, became the enemy of the creative imagination, the imaginative reason. Explanatory propositions have a terrible power to block further exploration of the empirical world, to hypostatize or freeze the subject into a fixed orientation toward the object, the result of which must necessarily be the slackening and eventual failure of the tension between subject and object.

Tennyson disliked explaining his poems, and when he did, frequently made most elusive and ambiguous and puzzling remarks. It was a defensible and even salutary strategy. When a scientist's explanatory theory fails him he feels his way by analogy through a series of experiments, hoping to grasp some pattern which can correct or displace his failed theory. Tennyson's long poems, *In Memoriam, Maud*, the *Idylls*, are cyclical, a series of poems in which exploration is conducted by analogical permutation. What has been discovered is extraordinarily difficult to pin down and to conceptualize; that something of great significance has been glimpsed through a series of analogies, like the series of receding arches through which Ulysses proceeds toward the ever-vanishing limits of experience, is irresistible. To conceptualize, to explain, is to threaten doubt, for language in the form of a generally true proposition has a fearful finality. Tennyson was reluctant to explain even what he meant by "doubt"; but perhaps what he was after was most succinctly put by Darwin, in a later edition of his *Origin of Species*: a natural law is only a mental convenience. Tennyson's "doubt," then, was ultimately that epistemological and linguistic instrumentalism toward which the high culture of the nineteenth century steadily and majestically moved—or drifted.

If the new poems of the 1842 collection were, as a whole, less striking than those of its predecessors, the reason was that Tennyson's major effort was going into *In Memoriam*. It is not a planned poem. It accumulated itself over a period of about sixteen or seventeen years; when Tennyson started writing his brief elegies in odd four-line stanzas, he had no notion that he

35

would eventually turn out a cycle of 133 poems. We do not know the order in which they were composed, nor even though the manuscripts are to be accessible to study, will we probably be able to find out. Tennyson deliberately forbade examination of the manuscript; and though his will has now been violated, the manuscript has not yet been studied. It has been assumed that Tennyson forbade the examination to protect his private life, but it makes just as much sense to say that he did so to protect the reader.

In his later years Tennyson lived at a time when literary scholars were using poetry to reconstruct the intimate internal and external history of poets. What was being done to Shakespeare's *Sonnets* was a prime example. To examine the manuscript, to determine the dates of composition, would inevitably lead the reader to interpret the poem as autobiographical data, and that would be to mislead the reader. For *In Memoriam* is not an autobiographical poem. Tennyson frankly uses his own experiences and his own efforts to deal with the problem of the death of Hallam as the material of the poem, but it cannot be said that it gives or is supposed to give an accurate history of the poet's emotional life. He used his own experiences, as any artist whose subject is psychology must do, simply because he himself was the only possible source of the kind of information about the human psyche he wanted to write about. To use the term proposed above, privileged information was his theme.

The time scheme of the poem extends over several years, and in the poem it takes that long for the problem to achieve a resolution. But the problem of the grief was solved in a few months, while for Tennyson the problems that consideration of Hallam's death gave rise to continued for the rest of his life. Further, he clearly stated that the speaker of the poem was not himself, and that the speaker arrives at much more optimistic conclusions than he, Tennyson, ever did. The far-off divine event toward which the whole creation moves is a notion of the poem's speaker, not one Tennyson held except as governed by his peculiar and apparently instrumental notion of doubt. Insofar as the poem is a poem of consolation, the consolation arises from the emotional need of the speaker, and not from Tennyson's discovery of some cosmic truth. The need is Tennyson's subject, not the cosmic truth which is presented as hardly more than a strategy for satisfying the need. So far as Tennyson himself was concerned, the poem is not about how he consoled himself for the death of Hallam, but how he finally got rid of him.

Ultimately, Tennyson's problem was by no means an unusual one; on the contrary it is the most common of identity problems. When the individual leaves his family and enters onto the stage of the world, he needs models for the roles he must play, and for none so much as that role which carries for him the greatest emotional weight, in which his investment of emotion is heaviest, whether it be his career or his sexual life. The problem of how he should identify himself, that is, define himself as a social being, is a matter of learning the cultural conventions and then observing his necessarily unique way of performing them. To the degree to which he achieves success, no matter what the role may be, to that degree he places increasing confidence in variations of the role, in his innovations. Innovation there must be, since no behavioral pattern can be learned with exactness. Emotional dependency on the role model means that the individual suffers from two deficiencies, failure to observe his innovations and failure to place confidence in those he does observe. To the degree he corrects these deficiencies he becomes his own role model. But to accomplish that, the dependency on the role model must be lessened and finally extinguished, usually by transferring that dependency to himself. To the degree that he is no longer even dependent on himself but is free to manipulate his own unavoidable innovations and deliberately to innovate new modes of playing his role, to that degree he may be said to have achieved personal freedom; he has objectified his performance and perceives it not as sacred because emanating from a beloved other nor from a beloved self, but simply as part of the phenomenal environment, to be managed for his own benefit.

How many people actually reach this final stage, it is impossible to say; perhaps not so many as we imagine, perhaps more. Perhaps most people do. In any event, it is evident that the crucial problem is the emotional dependency on the role model, in that the role model is seen charismatically, that is, as a sign that if his way is followed, the tensions of uncertainty and lack of confidence will be relieved. It is, of course, a delusion; and there seems to be no question that Tennyson's vision of Hallam was thus charismatic and hence dangerous to his development as a human being and as a poet. His position, personally and culturally, was so extraordinarily difficult and culturally so novel that his investment in Hallam as a charismatic symbol was exceedingly heavy. This is why Hallam's death was a piece of Tennyson's extraordinary luck.

The very way *In Memoriam* is printed is itself deceiving, and consonant with the style of the poem. One difference between Browning and Tennyson is that it is obvious that the former is a difficult poet. Tennyson looks easy, and never so easy as in *In Memoriam*, but in truth Tennyson's style is, if anything, more difficult than Browning's, particularly in *In Memoriam*. It appears to be divided into 131 poems of varying length, preceded by a prologue and followed by an epilogue. The fact of the matter is that the 131 poems are subsumed under nine divisions. In later years Tennyson, typically, told this secret ninefold organization to a friend, who told it to a critic, who subsequently recorded it. This may seem unfair to the reader, and a literary trick, but it is more reasonably seen as a further instance of Tennyson's suspicion of explanation as opposed to experience. Perhaps like so many men of subtle minds, he thought that what was obvious to him would be obvious to everyone. (For the reader who wishes to try this for himself, the divisions are: 1–8, 9–20, 21–27, 28–49, 50–58, 59–71, 72–98, 99–103, 104–131.)

The first five are dramas of failure: the failure of the desire for death; the failure of the retreat to unreality; the failure of the illusionism of the past; the failure of immortality and the future; the failure of any justification of God's ways and of the meaningfulness of human existence and the universe. Only after these failures is the dependency discovered, and only then can the speaker affirm his difference and uniqueness from the charismatic role model, achieve equality, and displace the role model into the cosmic process. The marriage in the epilogue is a sign of the transcendence of a psychic state that has outworn its usefulness.

If there is a moral to *In Memoriam*, it is this: one can transcend a need only by discovering its function. Tennyson himself put it with great exactness: "Born of love, the vague desire that spurs an imitative will." Having discovered that his will was imitative, Tennyson could strike out on his own, to the manifestation of a unique will. That his unique will had already been manifested, the stunning quality of the 1832 and 1833 volumes had, one would have thought, already proved. But as we have seen, it is very easy to innovate and either not to realize that one has done so, or not to have confidence in it, or worse yet, to be unable to take any credit for it, to feel that somehow one had nothing to do with it. It is a very common feeling among artists and, for that matter, business executives of a highly and successfully innovative character.

In Memoriam is one of Tennyson's great achievements; the other is *The Idylls of the King*. It took him nearly twenty years to write the one; on the other he spent nearly thirty years. In the same conversation in which he said that the "I" of the first poem was not himself and had arrived at a more optimistic position than he himself ever had, he went on to say that he had wanted to write another work which would deprive man of any such consolation and throw him back on his more primitive instincts. It is typical of him, and of the defensive and self-protective stance of the alienated Romantic, that he neglected to say that for some years he had been working on such a poem and had published some of it. The twelve idylls were published in this order: 3, 4, 6, 7, 11; 1, 8, 9, 12; 10; 2; 5. Further, each of the five collected editions involved changes and adjustments in what had already been published. As with *In Memoriam*, no doubt composed in the same manner of addition, interpolation, and revision, only slowly did the pattern emerge—Tennyson again working like the scientist whose theory has failed him, finding his way by vague half-intuitive, half-logical analogies from experiment to experiment. As early as 1835 he composed "Morte d'Arthur," subsequently incorporated, in 1869, in the last of the *Idylls*, "The Passing of Arthur." Already, though obscurely, the theme of the Idylls was feeling its way toward him, the great king who attempted to establish the perfect society and failed.

Thus early, though probably he could not yet formulate it, he was beginning to doubt the feasibility of the aim of the Apostles, the redemption of society. He had grown fast since the death of Hallam. The distinction between historical progress and biological evolution was beginning to emerge. Further, a psychological theme of the *Idylls* was appearing, that the individual who is dependent upon a charismatic vision of himself is better off than one who is dependent upon a charismatic vision of somebody else—but not much. For such an individual, freedom has not yet been attained.

The ostensible theme of the *Idylls* is baldly set forth in the epilogue, "To the Queen"; it is "Sense at War with Soul." This seems to have little to do with forcing man back on his more primitive instincts, but it is deliberately ambiguous, in Tennyson's usual manner. Not that there was not a very practical function to that ambiguity. He was, as I have pointed out, capable of being a very practical man. He wanted success, and he wanted financial success, and he got both; he did not sell out. He created works which a superficial interpretation, though correct as far as it went, would make appealing to a wide and relatively unsophisticated middle-class audience, one of the new audiences of the nineteenth century—the result of increasing wealth and the communications revolution. He wrote a number of competent and some very charming and even beautiful poems for that public, just as many a nineteenth-century composer wrote both serious music and light, for amusement and dancing. Thus Queen Victoria, culturally in many ways part of that audience, though in so many others an aristocrat of the Regency, could be consoled by *In Memoriam*. It was beautiful language about the death of someone beloved, and that was all she needed, especially if her Poet Laureate read it to her in his wonderful and always slightly provincial voice. Her Poet Laureate was a sensible man, and a patriotic one, and obliged. But that does not mean that his major works were incapable of more subtle and disturbing interpretations, more adequate than the superficial interpretations because they took account of more of the data and more of its interlocking connections.

Sense at War with Soul can mean immorality, which is sensual pleasure, at war with morality, which comes from God. Thus the failure of Arthur's kingdom is the result of Guinevere's adultery with Lancelot. Even Arthur thinks so for a time, but eventually he learns better; and Sense at War with Soul comes to mean the eternal warfare, or tension, of subject and object. Arthur, then, is the full-blown Romantic transcendentalist of the 1820's and 1830's who seeks to redeem the world, a role in which Tennyson once saw himself and which he had been urged by the Apostles and Hallam to assume. Tennyson's morality is a middle-class Christian morality, and to the degree that he assumes the stance of moral prophet, this is the substance of his prophecy.

The Idylls, however, are so constructed that the fault for the failure of Arthur's kingdom lies with Arthur, who attempts to impose the vision of the subject upon the recalcitrance of the object, and who, psychologically, is dependent upon his own charismatic vision of himself. His blindness to Guinevere's adultery is entirely his own fault, and arises from his mission; while the adultery itself is, to put it as baldly as possible, the result of the fact that Guinevere found Arthur a wholly impossible husband. Yet Arthur's fault is still a superficial explanation, though less so than that of Guinevere's. Tennyson's point is that the imagination enters the world, through its power constructs its vision of experienced reality, fails to see that vision as an illusion, and thus destroys itself and its power and its cohorts in an attempt to realize an illusion. Yet Tennyson strikes deeper yet, for it is apparent that neither Arthur, nor any man, nor imagination, has a real choice in the matter. To act we must act on illusions. Illusions are the basis for action, the only basis. Historically, then, there is no progress, only—it is implied—an endless cycle of visions converted into illusions converted into failures. The last lines of the poem are incomparable:

> Thereat once more he [Bedivere] moved about,
>   and clomb
> Ev'n to the highest he could climb, and saw,
> Straining his eyes beneath an arch of hand,
> Or thought he saw, the speck that bare the King,
> Down that long water opening on the deep
> Somewhere far off, pass on and on, and go
> From less to less and vanish into light.
> And the new sun rose bringing the new year.

Concealed within the charm, the beauty, the splendor, the sentimentality, the moralizing of the *Idylls* lies a bleakness that makes it quite understandable that Tennyson felt he could not live were it not for his belief in the immortality of the soul. That continued belief marks him as one not yet fully modern. To the end he was convinced that there is a meaning in human existence, and a divine meaning, but also that that meaning is, for man, utterly inaccessible, and that further the belief itself exists to satisfy a human need for meaning—a need that may or may not be divine in origin. In his psychological understanding he had again moved toward the modern.

Who that is genuinely modern can have the charismatic vision of any man, or of himself? Perhaps to have transcended the need for the charismatic vision of oneself is to be as psychologically modern as it is possible to be. What Tennyson worked out psychologically in the *Idylls* was that such transcendence is possible. Had he achieved it for himself? Perhaps he had not gained for himself that final freedom—though one of his last poems, "Akbar's Dream," suggests that perhaps he had—or that if he had, he did not know what to do with it, as that poem also hints. But who even today wants this freedom? Surely very few. And who, having it, knows what to do with it? Is there anyone?

2

We Are Insane

A RECENT English critic called Carlyle's last and largest work, *A History of Friedrich II of Prussia called Frederick the Great,* "unreadable." In the best edition of Carlyle it is printed in eight volumes, nearly 4,000 pages; it was more than twelve years in the writing and eight years in the publishing, from 1858 to 1865. It is longer than Gibbon's *Decline and Fall of the Roman Empire.* It is also just as readable; to be sure, Gibbon is more entertaining, but then his history is perhaps the most entertaining book in the world.

Still, the critic was on safe ground in calling Carlyle's masterpiece "unreadable." Who living has read it? I have met no one besides myself, except one friend, a music critic, who found it as fascinating as I did; and I know of no Victorian scholar who has done so. When it was being published it certainly was not considered unreadable; it was Carlyle's most successful work. The first printing of the first installment, 2,000 copies, sold out in a few days, and a second printing went almost as fast. Within weeks a third printing was called for. In those days that was a large sale for a serious historical work; and today, too, it would be. Swinburne, who disliked Carlyle, particularly his politics, could hardly wait for each additional volume to come out, he found it so intensely interesting. If the London *Times* critic found it unreadable it can only be that he had read very little of it.

Yet, among other treasures, it offers in the portrait of Frederick's father, Frederick William, the only literary portrait in English that can come close to challenging the portrait of Uncle Toby in Sterne's *Tristram Shandy*; after finishing that novel one is desolated to realize that now one has learned everything about Uncle Toby it is possible to know. The comparison was made often at the time. Truly, it is not often that so thoroughly deserved a contemporary reputation has been so completely eclipsed by modern taste. Carlyle is the most vivid of historical writers; yet *Frederick*, his masterpiece, is totally neglected, even by scholars of Victorian literature. It must be confessed that the one scholar I know of who has read much of it thinks it a "literary failure." In truth, *Frederick* calls for readers who can still perform on the grand scale, and such seem to be rare. I have met any number of people who have started what everyone admits to be one of the great masterpieces of the twentieth century, *The Remembrance of Things Past*, but very few who have finished it. *Frederick* is for readers whose equivalents among musical enthusiasts find Bruckner's symphonies a little short, and experience Wagner's music dramas as models of classic proportion and artistic self-restraint, as indeed they are. Carlyle was a heroic writer; he demands heroic readers. Who finds *Frederick* unreadable and a literary failure does not judge the book; the book judges him, and finds him severely wanting.

After casting about among various subjects Carlyle finally chose Frederick. Even Froude, Carlyle's excellent and honest biographer, felt the choice was a mistake. Frederick, he felt, was insufficiently heroic for Carlyle's prophetic

45

purposes, and the one recent Carlyle critic who has read in it agrees. Both appear to feel that Carlyle should have written about a successful hero, one whose heroic qualities and accomplishments were not so equivocal as Frederick's. This is to miss the point. Frederick had a double appeal for Carlyle. He had always been most intensely interested in heroes who were failures, whose accomplishments were equivocal, damaged; for he was interested in why heroes could not be heroic. Heroism damages the hero, sometimes destroys him. Few writers have led so heroic a life as Carlyle himself, and few have felt themselves so damaged by their efforts, and finally few have felt such utter failures. Who, he once asked Froude, had ever really paid the slightest attention to what he had to say, or had heeded his message, or had taken seriously his warnings? No one. He has been compared far too often—and too unwisely and incautiously—to Old Testament prophets. Yet he and they are alike in this: did the Jews or anyone else ever take them seriously, before it was too late? Or even thereafter?

Carlyle is notorious for his attacks on liberal democracy, particularly as it was practiced in England at the time. Parliament he saw as a talking machine, the only function of which was to create a legal and governmental smoke screen while the real rulers of the country, many of whom were, naturally, members of Parliament, properly elected, plundered the working classes of the growing wealth of England which they were creating. He saw in that working class a steady and monstrous accumulation of injustice which one day would demand retribution. If the English working class refuses, as we are told by all the best economists, as well as by the heirs of those who plundered that class in the nineteenth century, to be as productive as their fathers and grandfathers and great-grandfathers, is it not because of what happened in the nineteenth century? They know of what little profit to themselves was the labor of their predecessors. Their revenge is now, in the form of the minimum expenditure of energy and the maximum of reward. It is up to the managers of society to see that such expenditure of energy as the worker is willing to grant results in a vastly increased output per man hour; and that those managers have obviously failed to do. The first task of the hero, according to Carlyle, is to look at the facts of the matter; obviously there are few heroes today among the social managers of England.

Carlyle went to Ireland during the great potato famine, planning to write a book about Ireland. But he abandoned the project. What was obvious to him, what he would have to say in the book, was something he knew that nobody could either grasp or, if they did, would assent to. It was simply that the manner in which England had governed Ireland for a thousand years indicated that the real rulers of England were quite incapable of grasping the fact that a system of social management successful in England was not and could not be successful in a nation alien in culture and religion. The Irish were not the English, nor would ever be, nor could anything make them be. Yet the English persisted in acting as if neither of these necessities existed at all. English culture, Carlyle saw, was constitutionally, irredeemably, incapable of perceiving that it was not the only possible culture. The English were, then, basically incapable of facing facts. Their Empire was still growing, but Carlyle was convinced it would not last, that it was accumulating a weight of terror and injustice, of plundering in the guise of management, that would sooner or later destroy it.

For the admirer of Carlyle little is so hard to accommodate oneself to as his attitude on black slavery in the English colonies and in the United States, and little has done his reputation so much damage. He thought the freeing of the slaves in Jamaica would be immensely damaging both to the slaves themselves and to the economic structure of the island. To him the American Civil War was a smoky chimney; both sides talked intolerable cant to conceal their true piggish interests. Certainly today a good many modern historians are convinced that in the South the war was fought by the non-slave-holding poor to protect the wealth of the exceedingly small white minority of the population that owned large numbers of slaves. Many a white Southerner is convinced to this day that the Confederacy was an utterly meaningless enterprise which has kept him as poor after its defeat as he was before its founding.

It was not that Carlyle was in favor of slavery. Rather he saw that the establishment of slavery in the New World had led to problems which the simple freeing of the slaves would do nothing to resolve, would make worse, for after such freedom the exploitative minority would feel no responsibility for the welfare of the exploited, whereas a slave owner *might* feel some responsibility for the welfare of his property. Gurth, the serf in *Ivanhoe,* Carlyle reiterated often enough, was better off than the nineteenth-century factory laborer. To Carlyle, noble talk about the freeing of the slaves was cant that concealed a desire by the plunderers to free themselves of all responsibility for the plundered.

And he was pointing to another problem. His declared enemy was the Enlightenment conclusion that if the individual took care of his own economic interests, an invisible hand would automatically take care of the economic interests of the society and all members of that society. "What's good for General Motors is good for the country" was even more an article of unquestioned belief than it is today in the United States, and that is saying a good deal. Carlyle called it the "Pig-Philosophy." George Orwell's *Animal Farm* says much the same thing; perhaps he got the idea from Carlyle's most vituperative writings, the *Latter-Day Pamphlets.* Carlyle was convinced that those who wished to free the slaves were not interested in freedom but in their own particular trough. Hence they completely ignored the problem of what to do with a large population which was torn from its natural and social environment and placed in an absolutely alien one in which they were the victims of exploitation but not the beneficiaries of acculturation. What good was freedom without acculturation, except to condemn them to the most abysmal poverty? No promise the American government has made to the ex-slave, from the time of Emancipation to the present moment, has been kept. Perhaps Carlyle in his grim and brutal way—and his brutalities are, like Schopenhauer's, unusually refreshing—would say that one modest consequence of merit has been forthcoming; we are now aware that there *is* a problem. This has been little enough, but it is not nothing, though a hundred years late in emerging.

No, Carlyle was a man lacerated by his compassion for human suffering, and exasperated beyond endurance by the bland indifference of the possessors to the tragedy of the dispossessed, and by his inability to do anything about it, or even get himself heard. He saw man as a creature plunged into an alien environment, and he saw man's religion, his philosophy, his values, his whole belief-system as having but one aim—to conceal that fact from himself. His compassion made him realize that human beliefs exist to cover man's nakedness, are protective, and enable him to act and to live. But that did not prevent him from perceiving with an astounding sharpness the necessary inconsistencies and incoherences and dishonesties within any belief-system. Further, the higher the social level, the greater the inconsistency, the incoherence, and the concealing dishonesty. He would have agreed with Wagner's Rhinemaidens, who sang as they watched the gods cross the rainbow bridge into Valhalla

> The true, the trustworthy
> is only in the depths;
> false and cowardly
> is what rejoices up there!

In the early 1850's Wagner was just discovering that to human problems, and above all to the problem of problems, social power, there is no answer. Carlyle had known it for a long time. Yet Wagner, at least when he wrote the *Ring*, was more despairing than Carlyle, who although he detested the unjustified confidence of hope nevertheless detested equally the abandonment of courage. Frederick, then, was heroic because he maintained his courage in the face of innumerable defeats and humiliations and established Prussia as a European power. But that, as Carlyle saw it, was not his real achievement. His real genius lay in finally coming to understand the nature of power in spite of his initial efforts to solve the problem by avoidance and sentimentality. That is why Carlyle carried Frederick in great detail through his wars, but sketched the rest of his long life in but a few hundred pages.

In circulation nowadays are two generalizations of the utmost idiocy. One is Blake's, "To generalize is to be an idiot." The other is Lord Acton's, "All power corrupts." To Carlyle only power can be responsible, only power has the opportunity not to be corrupt. Looked at coolly, power is the attribute of the individual in the decision-making role of any institution; that attribute requires him to decide how the resources available to that institution shall be used. Two forces hinder just and adequate decisions. One is, as Carlyle pointed out early in his career, that the desires of every human are literally infinite. The resources of eternity could not satisfy the desires of a shoe blacking boy. An institution, moreover, is made up of individuals. That is, there is no such thing as an institution; it is merely a word by which we categorize a certain range of human behavior. Institutions exist no more than do societies. Both are terms which if we reify or hypostatize them lead us into the delusion that we are talking realities when we are only talking. Consequently all the resources of the world cannot fulfill the aims or achieve the goals or accomplish the mission of any institution, which are only the aims, the goals, the missions of individuals interacting according to certain culturally validated and transmitted patterns of behavior.

So the first problem of the man in the position of power is that the resources available to the institution never are and never can be enough. Second, his decisions are necessarily governed by the belief-system of the culture of which he is a part; and these, as Carlyle saw with savage clarity, are riddled with inconsistencies and absurdities, and furthermore, as they are used, are constantly wearing out. A desperate innovation is required of the man in power; but that innovation, to be meaningful, must be directed by his perception and comprehension of the actual state of affairs he is dealing with. However, his culture's belief-system is devoted to making it virtually impossible to see what the state of affairs really is. The responsible man of power, who is the only man who can be responsible, though, as Carlyle knew better than most people, he rarely is, penetrates through his belief-system, sees the realities, and uses power, naked force, to carry out his decisions. He is the hero.

Frederick, to Carlyle, saw that for the welfare of the people who had been entrusted to him, the establishment of Prussia as a socially disciplined, economically strong, and—under the circumstances of European international politics—feared nation was the only possible decision; and to effectuate that decision he had to use naked power, force, the foundation on which society rests.

The events of the twentieth century have undoubtedly made Prussia a name of infamy. In the 1840's, however, Prussia had not yet assumed the aspect it did in 1870. On the contrary, it seemed to a great many observers that no nation had recovered so intelligently, so liberally, and so promisingly from the onslaught of Napoleon and its near-destruction. In the 1860's Matthew Arnold thought it matched and in some ways surpassed

51

France in the rationality of its internal management. Undoubtedly much of the current denigration and neglect of Carlyle
arises from the conviction that his teaching in *Frederick* was
ultimately responsible for the rise of Prussia into German imperialism, for the first and second world wars, and for Hitler.

It is perhaps not very important that *Frederick* contains less
teaching, or preaching, or ideology, or moral meditation, or
lesson-drawing than anything that Carlyle ever wrote. It is almost pure history. Perhaps it is not important, since his other
books provided the guide for interpreting it, but it is worth
recording. At any rate, if Hitler was indeed influenced by his
misunderstanding of Carlyle, it is hardly Carlyle's fault, since
Hitler misunderstood just about everything he read or heard
about. He is the perfect example of the man of power who
innovates not as one who penetrates through the smoke screen
of his belief-system but as one who is totally the victim of it.

Moreover, as we have seen, Carlyle was not interested in
Frederick because he succeeded in what he set out to do but
because what he did was all he could do under the conditions
of the European culture he lived in. Nor does Carlyle spare
Frederick in his fashionable dallying with the trivialities of that
culture, nor for the quarrel with Voltaire and his treatment of
him. Carlyle's real interest in Frederick arose from the insight
the whole terrible story gives into how the responsible exercise
of power is limited by the belief-system of the culture in which
perforce it must be exercised.

An example from our own times will show what Carlyle was
after. We have two interrelated problems of great moment, the
Negro problem and the urban problem. What should be done
is perfectly obvious.

First—the marshaling of the immense resources now being
squandered on such matters as multiple wigs for women, male
cosmetics, motor boats, snowmobiles, pornography, incredibly
elaborate and expensive churches in which architecture is con-

fused with millinery, and funeral services, plus all but five percent of what is being spent on the arts, which includes spectator
sports, professional and academically "amateur," and television
and cinema and theater.

Next, the destruction of our megalopolises, the erection of
clusters of new cities of not more than 100,000 each in the
immense waste of our country, most of which is empty.

Finally, the cultural and economic upgrading of at least
twenty-five percent of our population.

Once all that is done the majority can return to or for the first
time enjoy multiple wigs for women, male cosmetics, and all the
rest. (It is possible, though not likely, that after such an effort
some might enjoy something a little less trivial.) As it is, our
belief-system prevents even responsible men of goodwill in positions of great power from doing much more than dabbling.

Carlyle is accused of believing that might is right, that the
decisions of the man in the position of power are right because
he has the power to enforce them, of a fascistic conception of
proper social organization, of the cult of the hero as tyrant, of,
in short, belief in power for its own sake. Not one of these
accusations is justified, though it is true that the violence and
the savagery of his highly metaphorical and emotional language
led him on occasion to make statements which detached from
their context appear to justify, slightly, some of the abuse that
has been directed at him. He did believe that power, rightly
grasped, is indeed the basis of society, for he was convinced
that man needs order in a world which, for him, is chaos; that
the proper end of man is reducing this chaos to such order as
he can achieve, and the only right is the right of men engaged
in such effort to discipline those who seek only to exploit that
effort for the sake of their own piggishness. Nor did he make any
general recommendations or recipes about how society ought to
be organized. He only pointed out that there have been men
who have made sense once again out of a disintegrated social

situation. Even his wildest ravings, in the *Latter-Day Pamphlets*, are but vituperations of the rulers of Europe for not understanding the nature of the social protest of the year of revolutions, 1848, and for refusing to see what was right in front of them, the accumulation of injustice for which someone, someday, would have to pay.

Seeing all men as divine, he gave generously and almost always to beggars; they were victims of a situation which he himself had just barely managed to escape being utterly victimized by. Power, ultimately, is the limited power man has to impose his will upon the environment, and social power is but the collectivization of that individual power. Slavery, it must always be remembered, was in its origins an important human invention for coordinating large masses of individual labor. Metaphorically, to be sure, all men are slaves to a chaos, internal and external, subjective as well as objective, a madness of mankind and an invincible resistance by the environment to man's wishes. (What Carlyle did not think of, what possibly he never understood, was that of all the systems of slavery that have existed the version established in the United States was the most vicious.) The coordination of human effort, then, to struggle to impose man's will upon the ever-changing world is the great human task, for only thus can man exist. What prevents that coordination? That was Carlyle's problem. And his answer was—man's beliefs.

This sense of man's inalterable inadequacy is what gives Carlyle's writings their bite; this is the source, too, of his wild humor, a mingling of contempt and compassion. It is also what lies behind his theory of history, which in turn is the foundation for his recommendations for practical action, proposals so often confused with theories of ideal social structure, something which on his own principles Carlyle could not have created, and did not. Even if we today cannot accept his explanation of history, within it lie intimations of great relevance.

At least early in his career, in the 1830's, he saw history from archaic Greece to the nineteenth century as oscillating in a great rhythm between organic and inorganic periods. Of the former the Middle Ages was the commanding exemplar. In an organic period a belief-system was experienced as coherent, and hence the value of human life and struggle was not questioned. To link the modern term "belief-system" with Carlyle's thinking and to rescue what is still useful we may use a middle term, one that takes something from his period and something from ours—cultural metaphysics. Although Carlyle rejected Darwin's proposal that man is descended from the primates, nevertheless his notions of cultural metaphysics are by no means out of line with Darwinian thinking when it is applied to culture. The metaphysics of a culture may be conceived of as an adaptational mechanism which functions by explaining the relation of man to environment and by providing what to men is a meaning for their adaptational efforts. And here "meaning" is the selection of propositions that give instructions about how to deal effectively with the environment and the structuring of those propositions into a coherent system, or at least a system which is felt to be coherent.

It is not important that such a system be "true." Indeed, it cannot be true. It is only necessary that the second-order system give instructions about how to relate and interlock the propositions of the first-order system, the system, so to speak, closer to reality, since it tells us how to deal with it. Controlling the structure of the second-order system, moreover, is a system of propositions that gives instructions about how to handle it. Apparently the highest man can go is a fourth-order proposition which subsumes all the lower systems. Thus belief-systems, or cultural metaphysics, are arranged in what we may as well call a hierarchical logic. This is the kind of logic Hegel was talking about, and of a Hegelian character, too, is Carlyle's conception of cultural metaphysics as a consequence of and guide for man's interaction with the world. It is what Hegel called "Geist." It is the boast, and the justified boast, of the cultivated German that his culture exhibits a sensitivity to cultural metaphysics, or Geist, unknown to other nations. It is to be expected, therefore, that Carlyle's foundations are to be found in his understanding, not always accurate but always penetrating, of the idealistic philosophy of German Romanticism.

Nevertheless, in spite of what he learned from the Germans, especially Goethe, Carlyle was also a product of his own culture, English and Scottish empiricism. The weakness of the Germans is that they are too impressed with the *structure* of Geist, which they seem to believe gives it a transcendental authority, a validity not to found in any dealing with the empirical world. Not so Carlyle. As a peasant, as a Scot, and as an Englishman he was capable of a suspicion of the adequacy of any system of cultural metaphysics. He saw beliefs and values and ideals and metaphysics as instruments, as tools. Man, he said, is a tool-making animal, a definition that anthropologists have taken from him and have liked for a long time. The current emphasis in anthropology on language and in French anthropology on myth has tended to obscure this definition, but it should not be so, for to Carlyle, man's prime tool was language itself, and the capacity to create myths, symbolic rather than abstract explanations of human interaction with environment, was man's primary tool.

The symbol and the myth, however, were to Carlyle two-edged weapons. One edge deals with the world; the other with man himself. It makes him capable of action by making him capable of belief. The distinction between belief and beliefs is crucial in Carlyle. Not liking the German tendency to hypostatize cultural metaphysics and render them absolute, Carlyle invented a brilliant metaphor—clothes. Myths, symbols, beliefs are clothes, which at once protect and arm. A belief-system may consist either of verbal signs or of nonverbal signs. Thus Carlyle proposes that for the prisoner at the bar the authority of the judge is his wig, his gown, his bench. For all his transcendentalism ·Carlyle had what we would call today an unflinching behavioristic bias. It is not the wig, the gown, the bench that are symbols of authority to the prisoner; they are the authority itself. Hence the peculiar twist of Carlyle's notion of symbol. A symbol does not stand for some transcendent, nonempirical value. Were it to do that, it would be merely a substitute for a proposition. It *is* that value. Hence words and sentences which control behavior and nonverbal signs which control behavior are both beliefs. They are on the same level. The latter are symbols. Both are clothes.

One of the peculiar advantages of a metaphor, which Carlyle, like so many Romantics, thought, perhaps correctly, to be the basic principle of language, or at least of language meaning, is that it can impart to a discourse all kinds of notions, which are not the principal reason for using it but which can often be very useful and instructive. It is for this reason that metaphor is a prime instrument of intellectual exploration and innovation, perhaps, as the Romantics thought, the only instrument. To Carlyle the best metaphor for a culture's metaphysics is clothes, and having adopted it, he explored its possibilities. Clothes are man-made; so are beliefs, cultural metaphysics. Clothes are inseparable from the total culture; so with beliefs. Clothes and beliefs are both products of unique historical situations. Clothes wear out with use and exposure to the elements and man's passions; and so do beliefs.

Carlyle long planned to write an essay to be called, "Exodus from Houndsditch." Houndsditch was a section of London where poor Jews dealt in old clothes; and Exodus of course is the escape of God's people from their oppressors. To Carlyle all people are God's people, and all nations God's nations. "Exodus from Houndsditch" meant the escape of the modern mind from the oppression of Judaeo-Christian religion and cultural meta-physics. His bitterness impelled him to write it, but his compassion bade him forbear; and in the end his compassion won. In fact for any careful reader of Carlyle his collected works are an "Exodus from Houndsditch." His private opinion was that Norse mythology made a great deal more sense and that if people must have a mythology it was more suitable for the nineteenth century than Christian myth. The need of the oppressed and exploited, and of the oppressors and the exploiters as well, was courage to face the facts of the nineteenth century, not spineless and supine submission to worn-out beliefs.

So much for beliefs. "Belief" was a different matter. It has been said cruelly of Carlyle that he praised silence in thirty-four closely-printed volumes. Man without beliefs is a naked two-forked animal; pitiable, but a fact. Man without his clothes is a creature bereft of speech and symbol. Pitiable again, but again a fact. For this is his natural condition, as God made him. When Adam and Eve reached for fig leaves they had become human, and not as God made them. Silence, then, is man's natural condition; in silence he is as God made him. Hence belief, which is God's, and the only thing in man which is God's, emerges from silence. Beliefs are only clothes, desperately made and defiantly worn, and always falling to rags. But belief is a condition of the spirit. Belief may be clothed in beliefs, but they are not an integral part of belief. Belief is what holds beliefs together. Contrariwise, when beliefs begin to tatter and turn into rags and disintegrate, belief is threatened. The reason is that beliefs, though created by man, are experientially part of the phenomenal, the empirical world.

Beliefs belong to the realm of the object; belief to the realm of the subject. Hence to commit belief to a body of beliefs is to move away from the subject into the object, to move away from the noumenal, the divine, into the phenomenal. Further, to commit beliefs to action is to subject them to the gritty recalcitrance of the world; it is to wear them out, like clothes. This is why Carlyle was interested in why the hero is damaged, disintegrated, destroyed by his heroism. The hero is one who can maintain his belief while his beliefs disintegrate, even to the point, with some heroes, in favorable historical circumstances, of leading his people not only into an Exodus from Houndsditch but even to the Promised Land, a new system of beliefs and cultural metaphysics which will, for the duration of an organic period of history, be appropriate to their unique historical condition. Thus Mohammed was a hero, though the beliefs of Mohammedanism, like all beliefs, including Jewish and Christian beliefs, have turned into rags, into nonsense, into what no sensible man can now commit his belief to.

This scheme left Carlyle with two problems: What is the source of belief? Can it be specified more exactly than simply silence? And, what was the historical situation as regards beliefs in which he found himself? As for the first, Carlyle's answer will not surprise a modern, but it may surprise him to find it in the 1820's. The source of belief, Carlyle was convinced, is the unconscious. "Mechanical" was his scornful term for the attempt to renew beliefs by putting them through logical and metaphysical permutations. A machine is an elaborate tool, and Christian theology to him had become an irresponsible public entertainment of toying with the tools of belief—clothes, in his other metaphor. That is why he affirmed that John Henry Cardinal Newman had the mind of a rabbit. He was merely frightened by the fact that his tools no longer could cut anything, and avoided his fear by building elaborate tool kits, not to speak of ultimately accepting a ready-made one. By placing the source of belief in the unconscious Carlyle was asserting that it is inaccessible to verbal tools and manipulation. But he was saying even more than this.

That one's life is impregnated with value, that it is meaningful, that it is filled with an infinite significance, that as the instrument of the divine or that as the divine itself, one's task and one's glory is to create in the wilderness of the universe a human order which incarnates the divine—who would not like to believe this? Who, really, does not? Even those who have rejected the notion of the divine have devised a functional substitute for it. And who cannot give reasons for such convictions, reasons which he has learned from his culture? Or if he has no such convictions, who does not struggle to generate reasons, to explain his existence in such a way that the value of that existence is affirmed? But what reasons, asks Carlyle, are more than artifacts, verbalisms, cultural metaphysics? None, was his answer. Consciousness, thought, cannot provide such reasons. On the contrary the utterly irrational *conviction* that life is valuable and significant and order-creating and perhaps divine, the experience that it is so, is necessarily prior to the ability to generate explanations, to entertain beliefs, whether old or new, and to grasp them as coherent. That conviction emerges from the unconscious.

Carlyle undoubtedly thought that the source of unconscious conviction, of belief, was the divine, though he was also convinced that nothing further could be said on the subject. We may call Carlyle's thinking merely an explanation, merely clothes, and now very old and ragged clothes. We fancy, indeed, that Freud has given us a true explanation of the unconscious. Some may even fancy Freud discovered the unconscious. He did, of course, nothing of the sort. In 1804 Wordsworth wrote Coleridge that we need a new word, something like "under-consciousness," and by the 1860's the unconscious mind was parlor chitchat. Freud's was an attempt to turn Romantic metaphysics into psychology, but his achievement, it is not too much to say, was a vulgarization of it. In cooler, more modern terms Carlyle was asserting that in humans response varies independently of stimulus, and that between stimulus and response lies an abyss which we can never explore; for the only tools we have to explore it with are responses to stimuli. That condition of human existence can never be transcended. Freud's attempt to bridge the gap was based on a couple of biological platitudes, already moldy in his own day, a few old clothes, already rags—aside from the fact that he was not investigating the unconscious at all but only certain patterns of verbal behavior. What he said about symbols was said better and more penetratingly by Carlyle, as Ernst Cassirer, the twentieth-century continuator of German Romantic philosophy, has pointed out. Freud's impressive system of explanation is beginning to wear out. Even he was getting a little impatient with it before the end. Yet Freudianism has penetrated at least the top half of American culture. Perhaps we need a new Exodus from Houndsditch.

In the individual's life, then, as beliefs wear out, belief emerges from the unconscious and weaves organic threads into new clothes. Yet the individual is part of his culture; indeed his personality is culture; and his experiences cannot be separated from his culture and its processes, that is, its history. To understand his own situation as one who has found himself in disintegrating metaphysical rags, Carlyle had to weave together and see as part of a single process personality, culture, and history. Only thus would the relation and lack of relation between belief and beliefs come clear. Only by locating him within these three dimensions could a man be defined. To understand Carlyle's position, therefore, one must understand how he thus defined himself, and why. One must turn to his life, not only as biography has recorded it but also as he perceived it.

To begin with it must be understood that Carlyle was a man terribly in earnest. Such men are rare, perhaps because they are always sad. Even when they are happy, their happiness is only superficial, though always welcomed. Inevitably, even their laughter rises from the contrast between man's trivialities and his fate. Everyone who encountered him has testified to the radiance of Carlyle's laughter, and particularly his laughter at his own lamentations, woe, vituperations, and most extravagant jeremiads. It was Carlyle's conviction that only the desperately earnest can laugh, and he judged a man by the character of his laughter and what he laughed at. Is it not true that most men are engaged with trivialities, or as much as they can possibly manage? Female wigs, male cosmetics, religious rituals, funeral services, snowmobiles, sex, and pornography, and all the rest—if the overwhelming majority of men were not committed to the trivialities of life, would there not have been far more revolutions than there have been? For Carlyle the only important event in recent history was the French Revolution. It was the subject of the book that made him famous in England. (Thanks to Emerson he was already famous in America.) And if we examine the range of his writings, all the figures he was most intensely interested in and devoted his greatest energies to comprehending were revolutionary figures. Revolution was his theme; to understand revolution was his central and perhaps only ambition. His model for that understanding was a revolution in himself.

Carlyle was born in southwestern Scotland into a peasant family. It was one of those parts of the world which is in reality in the dominions of the Red Queen; you had to run as hard as you possibly could to stay where you were, and even then there were very good chances that you could not even manage that. Work, thrift, an implacable sense of duty were required. But not all peasants in such dominions develop these virtues. The Scot also was a Presbyterian. Presbyterian theology is a highly sophisticated matter, and to have a proper ministry the Scots had established, long before England did, a system of public education. Carlyle complained about it, as he did about everything, and no doubt, like all educational systems, it left a great deal to be desired. Still, unlike certain educational systems in our country in the twentieth century it did not leave everything to be desired. Quite the contrary. Partly because of their education and partly because Presbyterianism makes every Presbyterian naturally contentious and properly equipped to be contentious, for nearly a century the Scots had been overrunning England. In an expanding commercial system and a developing Empire, they were simply better equipped than the average Englishman to make the most of every opportunity.

Carlyle, however, turned neither to the soil nor to business, in Scotland or England. He was the oldest son and he was highly intelligent. Even for a Scotsman he had unusual verbal gifts. He was obviously destined for the ministry, the noblest occupation a Scottish family could imagine. When he was fourteen he was sent off to the University at Edinburgh to begin his preparation to enter the kirk. His values were, at their most recent, those of the seventeenth century, but essentially were medieval. Only insofar as Presbyterian theology incorporated something of the rationalism of the seventeenth century could he be said to be, historically, so recent. At best a university education can be said to give man the opportunity to become an autodidact; at least that is the best it did for Carlyle. Not so much because of his teachers but rather because of the general atmosphere of Edinburgh, which in 1815 was one of the most cultivated and intellectually brilliant cities in Europe, he encountered the Enlightenment, particularly in the form of Gibbon, but also in such men as Dugald Stewart, half of whose philosophy was traditional Christian rationalism, but the other half Kantian. It was this split, in fact, that propelled Carlyle into a yet more modern historical condition.

It cannot be said that 1815 was late for Enlightenment thinking. After all, the vast majority of middle-class Americans today live almost entirely in terms of Enlightenment metaphysics and values, and quantitatively the most important thing that hap-

pened in the nineteenth century was the spread of Enlightenment thought and its consequences. For Carlyle, however, as for
many other young men then and since, the sudden plunge from
a late medieval world into the Renaissance–Rationalist–Enlightenment tradition was so unsettling that he could not come to
rest, as have the majority of people with a similar experience.
Why this should have been so, it is impossible to say, except that
he was a genius. Once the process of self-examination had
begun it could not be stopped. What he experienced was the
fusion of culture, personality, and history which became his
central concern.

History showed him, as it showed a number of other people,
that the Enlightenment values had not stood the test of the
French Revolution. What Carlyle perceived with an intensity
very few then or since have equaled was that the French Revolution had released forces which the Enlightenment had not
reckoned with, even at its most pessimistic—for there was a
pessimistic strain or wing to Enlightenment thought. The forces
which the Enlightenment had released were not forces it could
control. Its vision of human existence was after all shallow, and
social coherence had to be reestablished by force, by Napoleon,
who himself was defeated only by superior forces.

This established for Carlyle two propositions: one, that the
forces of the human mind were such that only naked power
could subdue them into social coherence; two, the most interesting man in the world is the revolutionary, and Napoleon was
such a man. Later Carlyle compared him to the American
woodsman who clears the forests so that the sun can be let in
and agriculture established; the woodsman makes room in the
natural world for man. Thus Napoleon cleared the European
forest of fifteen hundred years of accumulated social over-
growth; he rationalized government, and he made room for
human existence. He let in the sun. Because in nineteenth-
century England—and Europe—revolution was a very danger-

ous word, Carlyle called the revolutionary the Hero. It was a more respectable term, but make no mistake; it was the revolutionary he was interested in, and revolution. At the end of *Sartor Resartus*, Carlyle's hero and his symbolic representation—or ideal role model—Diogenes Teufelsdröckh—leaves his sleepy German university town, where he is Professor, without salary, of Things-in-General, and heads for Paris when he hears of the outbreak of the French Revolution of 1830. It had begun, he felt, the continuation of the abortive Revolution of 1789, the effects of which would not work themselves out, Carlyle thought, for a hundred and fifty years or more.

Also in *Sartor Resartus* an important incident in Teufelsdröckh's development is his love affair with Blumine. He is rejected, and he begins his wanderings. In his autobiographical scraps Teufelsdröckh records that it was a sentimental affair, and on the word hinges much. There may have been a Blumine in Carlyle's life, and we probably know who she was, but she herself is unimportant. What is significant is that in this incident Carlyle selects one of the most striking discoveries of the Enlightenment and reveals its inadequacy. "Sentimentality" is a term which has a good many meanings, like all terms, but historically the most important can be grasped only by seeing its place in Enlightenment thinking. It cannot be said, of course, that the Enlightenment either invented or discovered sentimentality. It is a universal mode of behavior. But it was raised to a position of the highest importance, almost of redemptive power.

In the Enlightenment sense of the term—and it is still perhaps the most important sense today—to be sentimental is to ascribe value to a stimulus because the response to that stimulus results in a discharge of tension and anxiety. In the late eighteenth-century novel, particularly in the Gothic novel, which is not in the slightest degree Romantic, the heroine goes through a regular cycle of emotional states almost like a piece of clockwork, something else the Enlightenment valued to a degree virtually incomprehensible now. Subjected to terror, fear, anxiety, or tension, she withdraws to her chamber, or to a garden or garden house, and dissolves into tears; and with absolutely predictable regularity she feels sufficiently better to turn once again to the realities of her problems. However, she is eternally the victim. Her problems once again arise; terror, fear, anxiety, or tension recur; once again she withdraws and weeps. Sentimentality keeps her going but it does not get her anyplace.

Now certainly the establishment of sentimentality as an emotional mode of great importance was one of the lasting benefits the Enlightenment has bequeathed to us. Psychiatrists tell us that everyone should have a good cry at least every six weeks, and that the ability to cry easily at the movies is the indication of healthy personality, presumably because the emotional life is not deeply repressed but is near the surface and ready to release energy into the adaptational enterprise. They certainly seem to imply that it is far better to cry over something trivial, especially if the weeping can occur in a completely irresponsible situation, such as the artistic situation. On the other hand it is clear that the heroine of the Gothic novel wept over serious matters, not trivial matters, matters that were intensely serious and of great importance for her welfare and even her life. This of course is the weakness of sentimentality and doubtless why it has earned for itself a bad name.

In any case, the reason the Enlightenment exalted sentimentality is that the Enlightenment ideal was the perfect adaptation of organism to environment, of personality to society. Epistemologically it meant the perfect fusion of subject into object. The Enlightenment invented upholstered furniture and discovered sentimentality, and did both at about the same time. Psychological comfort and physical and metaphysical comfort form the Enlightenment ideal. Thus there was a conservative line to Enlightenment such as that of Edmund Burke's and the Gothic novelists', who wrote for the possessing classes. Society, according to this way of thinking, is an organism, doubtlessly of divine origin, but certainly of slow and complex growth. It is the task of the personality to adapt itself to that society and its institutions. The other line of Enlightenment thinking was radical. Society is the creation of the possessors, of what we call today the Establishment, for its own selfish reasons. Thus the task of the mature, to incorporate the young into the Establishment, is in fact exploitative; and the task of the young is to rebel against the Establishment, to overthrow it, and to establish a just social order.

This is what the German *Sturm und Drang*, which is mistakenly considered a Romantic phenomenon, was all about, and one of the best places to see it at work is in Schiller's play of 1784, *Kabale und Liebe*, which could well be translated today as *Love and the Establishment.* There one sees laid out as in a blueprint the values not only of the radical late Enlightenment, but also of the New Left of today, particularly the student New Left. It is not surprising, since sociologists have shown us that such students come from affluent middle-class American homes, the embodiment of the middle Enlightenment. At least our young rebels have gotten to the late eighteenth century. Given time, they might get to the nineteenth.

At any rate this conservative-radical split in the late Enlightenment has left us with a pseudo-problem which has bothered people ever since. It is this: Given the task of reforming society, should one reform institutions in the radical manner or reform individuals in the conservative manner? Floundering around in this morass, we have not seen much change in either. It is a pseudo problem because both "individual" and "institution" are hypostatizations, verbal categorizations of certain ranges of human behavior. "Institution" refers to historically persistent structures of social roles, that is, socially validated patterns of behavior explained and metaphysically justified by the cultural belief-system. The word points out that among other factors in human behavior are these factors. "Individual" refers to the observable phenomenon that every human organism performs his social roles—of which he has a very large repertoire, particularly in high, complex civilizations—in a unique manner. He cannot help that uniqueness because response varies independently from stimulus, and thus it is impossible to learn with absolute precision any social role, or indeed anything else.

Further, in learning a social role the individual generally speaking has a variety of role models, and in his own behavior he abstracts and synthesizes various role features and factors in a necessarily unique mode. "Individual" categorizes certain factors in human behavior. The reason, then, that the problem of whether to reform men or institutions is unsolvable is that neither men nor institutions have, in this sense, other than a verbal existence. The question is a perfect tautology, properly expressed in the form: Should we reform human behavior, or should we reform human behavior?

Every cultural metaphysics has within it a basic incoherence which is bound to emerge, and this is what happened to Enlightenment thinking, which offered either sentimentality or rebellion, neither of which was to the point because each selected opposing and inconsistent strains in the same belief-system. So Teufelsdröckh tries sentimentality in his love for Blumine, and is rejected and sees her marry for money and position; and then he tries a *Sturm-und-Drang* rebellion, and that doesn't work either. The two cancel each other out and he is left with nothingness. The stage is now set for the great triadic sequence of the Everlasting No, the Center of Indifference, and the Everlasting Yea. These are the central chapters of *Sartor Resartus*, and they constitute the fullest and most precise account in English of the entry into Romanticism, and that amounts to the entry into the modern vision.

What had happened was that Carlyle had experienced with

that extraordinary intensity of his a complete sense of isolation, and in his symbolical autobiography, *Sartor,* he describes the collapse of all cultural metaphysics, the total failure of all belief-systems, particularly those of the Enlightenment, which initially had freed him from his Presbyterianism and had led to his decision not to enter the kirk, not to be a Presbyterian minister. In and about Edinburgh, by teaching, by tutoring, by translating from the German he managed, one way or another, to make a poor living; but he was a Scottish peasant and his needs were not great. Even so, in proper peasant fashion, especially notable in the closely intimate Carlyle family, he helped his brother become a doctor. He was scrupulously repaid, but not for many years. His asceticism and his willingness to accept poverty freed him to concentrate upon his spiritual problem and gave him time to read immensely and omnivorously. All, indeed, he had left to sustain him was his ability to work, and it is reasonable, therefore, that work should have been subsequently given a central place in his mature thinking. He called that capacity "the infinite nature of duty," but it was not in any sense a duty to "society" he was talking about, but a duty to oneself. Only by refusing to surrender to the meaninglessness of life, only by courage, not hope, could a man hope to survive such a crisis; but the only conceivable manifestation of that courage was action.

From Goethe he took "The end of man is not a thought but action." And he denied that "know thyself" was a possible precept, "till it can be translated into this partially possible one, *Know what thou canst work at.*" The "partially" in that sentence is not to be neglected or minimized. It is central in importance, because it emphasizes the uncertainty both of the value of any given piece of work and of its achieving any desirable aim. Both value, in this sense, and aim are given by cultural metaphysics, and that had become for Carlyle entirely unreliable. Thus he had entered, perforce, upon one of the most perilous of enterprises, to see with how few values it is possible to

69

live. It is perilous because to accomplish it one must examine the values made available by one's culture.

Carlyle had already seen that every belief-system is necessarily incoherent, just as Hegel, though twenty-five years older, was in the 1810's arriving at the same insight. Granted that insight, if one examines the values of one's culture, it is impossible that any value can sustain itself against analysis. This was the source of Carlyle's notion of organic periods of history, periods in which values are not subjected to analytic disintegration but are simply acted upon. Since action is the end of man, it follows that organic periods are superior to inorganic periods, which are, moreover, marked by extreme suffering in those sufficiently sensitive and by extreme social dislocation among the dispossessed masses, who lack insight but respond symptomatically to a disintegrating culture, turning, as they had at the time of the French Revolution, to an unimaginative violence. Carlyle had made the first step toward defining himself historically.

The Everlasting No, then, is an interpretation of man's existence which denies the explanatory power of any and all cultural metaphysics. As he tells us, only a certain afterglow of Christianity kept him from suicide, and suicide has been a common fate of those who have made Carlyle's dangerous experiment. A few years before, in Germany, Schopenhauer had managed to defeat suicide only by essentially denying his whole system. Carlyle was more honest, as in his life he was more earnest. He recognized that at least two cultural values continued to have force for him, work and the sense that suicide is disgraceful. But in so honestly accepting this, he was able to get closer to the irreducible surd in human existence.

Though more complexly and clumsily, Schopenhauer was not perhaps after all too far from the same position. We commit suicide for reasons, the most common being revenge; "They'll be sorry they treated me as they did." Certainly very common is also a fear based upon reasons, loss of faculties; for studies have shown it is this the majority of men fear, not death. All of us spend a certain amount of time longing for death. We are all half in love with it, for to love is to interpret a real or potential stimulus as offering the reduction of all tension, and death is necessarily imagined as a stimulus. Suicide, then, is a rational act, invariably based upon the values of the belief-system, invariably justified by cultural metaphysics. After all, some cultures approve of it most heartily, perhaps with wisdom. No, it is not suicide that is irrational, but the determination to live, in spite of all reasons to the contrary. Thus Carlyle presented his determination to live, his refusal to succumb to the Everlasting No, as a new birth, as a fire baptism, as an act of "indignation and grim-eyed defiance." He was not a Scotsman for nothing.

The experience, in which Carlyle was involved for most of the 1820's, is not easy to grasp. Teufelsdröckh is presented as wandering throughout Europe, viewing and observing both ancient ruins and modern societies but becoming involved in no activity. He had been a wanderer before the fire baptism, but then it was as a driven, despairing, guilt-ridden wanderer. An important element in the new birth was in fact throwing off the sense of guilt which arose from his lack of engagement with the social order and institutions. But now that lack of engagement is entirely without guilt. In Carlyle's own life this sociocultural exploration of Teufelsdröckh was equivalent to Carlyle's vast reading, his investigation into the nature of cultural metaphysics, and particularly his development of an historical orientation.

The historicization of Romanticism is one of its most interesting but puzzling factors. What its function was cannot be seized at a glance, and it can only be understood as a strategy for dealing with a problem Carlyle faced. To mark the difference between his wandering before and after the fire baptism, let us use his term and call the first kind, "isolation," and the second, "alienation." As the word is commonly used today it has far less radical meaning than when applied to Carlyle, for when we speak of the "alienated" New Left or "alienated" students or even the "alienated" blacks, the word indicates individuals who have attempted to solve the emerging incoherence of their cultural metaphysics by selecting one strand and rejecting another. It is a matter of simplifying choice, the function, biologically, of all belief-systems or cultural metaphysics.

Carlyle, however, had rejected not only both strands but even the notion that any belief-system can be trans-humanly valid, or absolute, a position reserved only for belief as pure affirmation, unconditioned by beliefs. He had arrived at an even more radical position than Kierkegaard was to. The latter rejected system building; the former rejected the validity of the metaphysical impulse. His was an anti-metaphysical metaphysics. This true alienation, in which only life and work remained from the ruins of his cultural values and were themselves as yet unjustified, does nothing to simplify the problem of choice; it makes choice virtually impossible. And this is why Teufelsdröckh is presented as wandering from country to country, taking an inventory, as it were, of cultural possibilities, and why Carlyle himself wandered across the present and through the past, for the same purpose.

To live and to work, however, require action, as Carlyle had already seen, and action requires choice. If the cultural bases for choice have collapsed, the only possible strategy is to achieve some kind of cultural transcendence, some means of arriving at a genuine innovation which, though it might eventually be doomed to incoherence itself, at least for the time being could serve as a basis and justification for choice and decision. Once again Carlyle found a further impulse for his intense interest in the hero, the cultural revolutionary who achieves cultural transcendence; such a hero was of infinitely greater significance to him than the political revolutionary, who merely selects one strand of the existing belief-system and weaves his way to power out of that.

History is more than a mere cultural inventory. What it does is to show how values and beliefs emerge in a culture as a consequence of its response to the situations it finds itself in. Thus explained, values are displaced into nature, into the phenomenal and away from the noumenal. Beliefs are seen as the products of interaction of man and environment. Society is seen not as something instituted by God but as something created by man as a tool for dealing with the environment. This was the logical path to one of Carlyle's most striking insights, already mentioned, culture as symbols, as opposed to symbols as the expression of culture. The drive behind this logical step was his insistence upon fact, observable fact, of which the new birth was the prime exemplar and model. Before Romanticism history had been seen as a collection of good and bad models; significant actions were significant because they were examples of absolute and usually divine metaphysical truths. But to the anti-metaphysical temperament of Romanticism, particularly powerful in Carlyle, there are no statable divine or metaphysical truths. No proposition can be divine, only a fact, and indeed only one fact, the fact Carlyle had experienced in his fire baptism, his new birth.

The alienated Romantic, then, used history not to justify his beliefs but to disengage himself from beliefs. Further, having understood that beliefs are "natural" historical products, he can conceive the possibility of arriving at new beliefs; if he understands the historical process of the emergence of beliefs, he can innovate by transcending the current beliefs, perceiving the situation and its character in such a way as to arrive at beliefs valid for that situation. Since, to Carlyle, the early nineteenth century was an utterly inorganic, mechanical period, the attempt to innovate appropriate beliefs was the only task a serious man could properly address himself to, since only in this direction lay the possibility of providing a basis for action and decision, an unavoidable necessity if he was to live.

Culture transcendence means not only rising above one's own

culture but in addition consciously entering the historical process and directing it, riding the whirlwind indeed. Hence continued progress in cultural innovation requires the prophetic individual, the hero, to interact constantly not with his culture but with the history of that culture. Above all it requires him to grasp the character of cultural crisis, and the character of the true hero (not the political revolutionary) who responds appropriately to the situation by generating new beliefs. The Center of Indifference, then, is that period in the development of the alienated Romantic in which he sees that he must achieve cultural transcendence and that his principal tool for doing so is the comprehension of history as the history of cultural metaphysics, of which the central problem and fact is crisis and innovation.

One can say this with all the greater confidence because so many figures in the Romantic tradition of the nineteenth century arrived at virtually the same conclusion. This strategy of turning to history as a means of comprehending crisis and innovation and therefore as a means of self-definition can be found from beginning to end of the century, from Coleridge to Spengler and beyond to today. In our present cultural crisis a good many of our historians are quite consciously rewriting history, particularly that of this country, while world history is at last beginning to be established as a discipline and as an historical mode in its own right. Such historians frankly admit that their historiography is tendentious, and justify themselves on the grounds that all historiography is tendentious. They are correct. What they are seeking to do is exactly what Carlyle was after, to discover analogies in past cultural crises which will give us some understanding of our own.

For instance, it has been said endlessly that American society is basically revolutionary in character. Was it not started by a revolution? It gives considerable insight into the excessive social stability of American society to assert that the American Revolution was not an affair like the various French revolutions or the Russian revolution. On the contrary, it was a conservative revolution, engineered and capitalized by the possessing classes. It was England, responding to the emergence of its first world empire, that proposed revolutionary innovations in the relations of the English government to the American colonies. The colonies, or rather the wealthy in the colonies, responded by refusing to accept innovations which they saw as revolutionary in character; they fought and won the American revolution to maintain and improve the status quo. It was a conservative revolution, one that refused to admit that the crisis in English government, caused by the emergence of empire, had anything to do with the North American English colonies. It was a revolution by which those in effective power remained in legally stabilized power. That American culture ever since has been devoted to maintaining social stability rather than correcting obvious social defects is not at all surprising, nor is it surprising that now when so many, even in government, wish to correct such defects it is so difficult to do so. The correction of social defects has never been a forte or interest of American society, only the bland and reiterated assertion that we have none.

The study of history and the emergent character of beliefs was the *work* of Teufelsdröckh—and Carlyle—during the period of the Center of Indifference, the task of which is full cultural disengagement and the reward for which is the realization that "all speculation is by nature endless, formless, a vortex amid vortices: only by a felt indubitable certainty of Experience does it find any center to revolve round, and so fashion itself into a system." This position has been made possible by what Carlyle calls the Everlasting Yea, the necessary precondition to which is renunciation, *Entsagung*, or self-annihilation, *Selbst-Tödtung.*

This is a difficult point, for it seems to contradict the assertion of the self at the moment of new birth. However, the general picture is clear enough; Carlyle is distinguishing between the self and the personality. The former is the "felt indubitable certainty of Experience," belief; the latter is beliefs, those speculative systems, or cultural metaphysics, which are part of the historical process which Carlyle has transcended. "Love not Pleasure; love God. This is the Everlasting Yea." What he is out to destroy is the Enlightenment ethic of gratification responsible for both sentimentality and non-disengaged rebellion; it is the notion of final satisfaction in the perfect adaptation of organism to environment, or of fulfillment in personalized love, the dependence of one's own personality on another personality and on one's own.

The historical condition, then, manifests itself in the personality, and since it is impossible to act except through the personality, it must be regarded as "but the Stuff thou art to shape that same Ideal out of: what matters whether such Stuff be of this sort or that, so that the Form thou give it be heroic, be poetic?" That is, true innovation, like true poetry, emerges from the unconscious and can be the creation only of one who has achieved the position of disengagement not only from the metaphysics of his culture but also from the kind of symbol, or clothes, which are the most intimate manifestation of that culture, one's own personality, which must be viewed as everything else is, mere phenomena, at once material to be shaped and instrument for the shaping.

The profoundest and most common misunderstanding of Romanticism is to interpret the great Romantic figures as in the ordinary sense intensely individualistic, and their self-centeredness as the charismatic perception of their own personality. Carlyle wrote about himself for the same reason Tennyson wrote about himself in *In Memoriam*; Tennyson's poem and *Sartor Resartus* are alike in that each uses autobiographical material only because for their purposes it was the only material that could be used. Renunciation, or self-annihilation, is the refusal to devote one's life to the gratification of one's personality, the determination to regard such gratification as no different from the same devotion to the gratification of another's. Above all, and most subtly, it is to refuse a gratification which hypostatizes or reifies that personality by establishing and justifying it by some speculative system. Romantic individualism is not, in the ordinary sense of the term, individualism at all. The extreme self-centeredness of everyone from Wordsworth to Wallace Stevens means only that the personality is the one possible area of research into those problems Romantics are most interested in. In the Everlasting Yea Carlyle achieved that three-dimensional self-definition through personality, culture, and history which is his most remarkable achievement.

The last part of *Sartor Resartus* is understandably a kind of adumbration of what he was to spend the rest of his life doing, the study of cultural innovation, the identification of historical crisis and the historical hero, and the prophetic assertion that nineteenth-century culture was in a condition of inorganic cultural crisis. It must not be imagined, however, that Carlyle defined himself as the prophet who would or could be the hero of his times. He thought of himself, always, as an Ishmael, as a voice crying in the wilderness, not as an announcer of the new dispensation. It was complained of him by the young that he had led them into the wilderness and had left them there. The necessity for the Exodus from Houndsditch he had announced, but he was like Moses in that he never attained the Promised Land himself, nor had more than a Pisgah-Sight that such a land —a condition of organic culture—was more than an historical possibility. As with the Jews, he seemed to have thought that those who entered into the wilderness would die there, and that only their descendants would see the new world.

In his life Carlyle remained a man whose alienation was so thoroughly confirmed that he was convinced that in becoming a man of letters he had taken a wrong direction, though he could not see any other possibility. In his social role he felt misplaced, and it is probable, really certain, that he would have felt the same way in any role. Modesty and conviction of inadequacy were for him proof that his renunciation and self-annihilation of personality gratification was not a pretty bit of theorizing but something completely sincere. For such a man the sense of failure is what he has to endure. If one renounces the gratification of stabilizing one's personality through accepting the culture's belief-system, one necessarily renounces the pleasure of success in a social role justified by that belief-system.

This was true even of his relations with his wife and was responsible for the disabling sense of failure he experienced when, after her death, he went through her papers and discovered for the first time the suffering, both physical and psychological, which she had endured and which she had successfully concealed from him. She too was a Scot and not a complainer, and she conceived her task as facilitating the unfolding of the great gifts she perceived in him long before anyone else did. It was indeed those gifts she was in love with, rather than his personality. She was in love with Edward Irving, a gifted preacher who eventually founded his own sect and came very close to madness if indeed he did not become psychotic, as he may have. And Irving was in love with her, but a prior engagement, by Scottish custom, was considered as binding as marriage unless both parties withdrew from it, and Irving's fiancée refused to. Since Jane herself was an individual of significant literary gifts, this sacrifice of herself to admittedly greater gifts would have to be lamented were it not for her letters; she is one of the best letter writers in the language. Carlyle himself wrote marvelous letters, and when the project is accomplished of publishing both of their letters in a single series, which will run perhaps to thirty volumes, we will have one of the most thorough and intimate personal glimpses of nineteenth-century culture it will be possible to have.

How then did Carlyle conceive of himself? Oddly enough it

was as a journalist, and his immense and thoroughgoing labor as an historian was more the kind one expects of a journalist than of an historian. In *On Heroes, Hero-Worship, and the Heroic in History*, based on a course of lectures the immediate predecessor of which was, significantly enough, *Revolutions in Modern Europe* (never published), he asserts the hero of the present day to be the journalist, the man who collects and distributes that information which is necessary to understand the current state of the culture. Carlyle was indeed one of the few to realize that perhaps the greatest revolution of the nineteenth century was the revolution in communications. It is typical of him that his sense of fact was strong enough for him to perceive that the tool of the revolution was the mechanical printing press, and that that had been made possible only by the invention of machine-made paper in the first decade of the century. Again we find the emphasis on tools and on language as man's greatest tool.

As a journalist he entered into his literary career, writing not news of events but news of cultural developments. One of the most brilliant of his early essays, "Signs of the Times" (1829), was what modern journalism would call a "think piece." His careful survey of every battlefield on which Oliver Cromwell fought and every one of Frederick the Great's battlefields, as well as the geography of his campaigns, was modeled more on journalism than it was on the then current technique of historiography. *The French Revolution*, undertaken only a little more than forty years after that crisis had begun, is the kind of work a supremely gifted product of the *Time* school of journalism might produce. It is *Time*, with taste and genius and as much interest in the factual as in the vivid; and though not the most reliable, since research into the French Revolution was just then beginning and will never be complete, it is still the most exciting and lively history of what Carlyle conceived of as the most important event in European history.

Carlyle conceived of himself as a failure. And thus Frederick is nearly as much Carlyle as Teufelsdröckh himself. The long, wearisome years of grinding struggle that Carlyle began when he was nearly sixty and finished when he was past seventy were possible only because he saw in Frederick's struggle his own. The great king was, after all, only that; in an increasingly inorganic culture all he could do in the phantasmagoria of European eighteenth-century politics was to extend and strengthen his kingdom and discipline his people into work. Of quite genuine heroic temper, as Carlyle himself was, in the end he could only lead to the French Revolution; for in reading Carlyle's biography of Frederick, that oncoming event is always to be remembered. Further, the French Revolution itself was a failure. Carlyle's vision of that terrible event was of an abyss opening up and forces issuing thence which could only be controlled by Napoleonic strength.

Teufelsdröckh also is a failure. Professor-of-Things-in-General (without salary) in the University of I-Don't-Know-Where, he spent his life on top of a tower overlooking the city or, at night, in a cloud of tobacco smoke, issuing, almost like Coleridge, mysterious but infinitely pregnant remarks and judgments on the affairs of the day. At the end he disappears toward France at the outbreak of the Revolution of 1830, and Carlyle hints that he is now in London, suggesting that the Professor is himself. But even by the time Carlyle finished the work it was apparent that that Revolution had again failed; nothing had changed; the nineteenth century continued on its mechanical way, without belief, victimized by its disintegrating cultural metaphysics. Cromwell's revolution, too, was a failure.

Nevertheless Cromwell, Frederick, the French Revolution, Napoleon, the Revolution of 1830, all were indications of the immense forces, principally of accumulated injustice, concealed to all but such an eye as Carlyle's by the trivialities of official beliefs and by a disintegrating cultural metaphysics. It has been said, of course, that Carlyle's bilious outlook on the world around him was just that, bile, indigestion, from which he certainly suffered. It was the physical price he paid for the enormous risk he ran. To use his own formula, he attempted to increase the value of life to infinitude not by increasing the numerator but by decreasing the denominator, that is, the demands one makes on life, which is but another name for one's values.

But a superficial notion of personality projection will not work on this man. His three-dimensional scheme of personality, culture, and history meant that he had three paths by which to get to the heart of any matter. If he defined his personality culturally and historically, then personality in turn could properly lead to a comprehension of culture and history. This was, in fact, the very opposite of psychic projection, for it was a consequence of disengagement from personality, of seeing personality, history, and culture as but three ways of perceiving and talking about the same phenomena. Revolution and cultural crisis and heroes fascinated him, not merely because they were all part of a situation of crisis in which terrible forces emerged. Those forces were terrible only because men had lived by lies and injustice; and these eruptions, particularly the French Revolution, revealed that beneath those lies lay the force ultimately responsible for crisis, the truth, the only truth man can know, the truth Carlyle himself had discovered and experience i. And that truth is that belief, the sense of value, is man's only reality, is therefore divine, is the entrance of the eternal into the temporal. These last two propositions we now may regard as consequences of Carlyle's failure to be completely free of his own culture, to achieve a total cultural transcendence. Divested of that, however, perhaps Carlyle was right. In any case he was also convinced that belief, that a sense of value, can never be embodied in beliefs, in personality, culture, history.

To man the solid world itself is but a symbol; his only effective pseudo realities are his beliefs, his clothes. The intensity, the fulminations, even the violence with which Carlyle asserted that ultimately the belief that produces and sanctifies beliefs is divine is but the counterpart of his equal conviction that personality, culture, and history—that beliefs—are lies. "We are such stuff as dreams are made on," and such stuff as the imagination is made on, and such stuff as insanity is made on—for all these are also in Prospero's great speech in *The Tempest*. The increasing despair of Carlyle as he grew older, reaching a climax in the *Latter-Day Pamphlets*, forced him into symbolic reconsideration of his life in terms of Frederick's. And what did Frederick's great and heroic efforts result in for him? The trivialities of flute playing, writing platitudes in French, and conversing and quarreling with Voltaire. So Carlyle felt that his heroic efforts had ended in but the trivialities of literature—and the realization that he had, through his own willful blindness, caused his beloved Jane endless suffering.

In *Sartor Resartus* an extraordinary passage reveals man issuing from mystery, storming across the earth in a frenzy of meaningless and insane activity, and disappearing once again into mystery—"from god and to God." But if God is here, so is the frenzy, the madness. Carlyle had risked everything; he had transcended his culture; he had achieved an extraordinary intellectual comprehension that history, personality, and culture are each concerned with the same thing, the one thing the human mind can know, the symbol. But beyond this lay a further vision, an appalling vision, one that he brought to the surface only occasionally, a vision responsible for his brutality and his compassion, a vision that the one human truth cannot be embodied, except in insanity. "We are such stuff as dreams are made on," and most of our dreams are nightmares, and those that are not are self-indulgent deceptions. We are such stuff as lies are made on, and insanity. Between the sane and the insane the difference is only definitional, only cultural, only a matter of beliefs. This was the ultimate insight that only rarely he permitted himself to articulate, or even to recognize, but it was the direction in which his thinking necessarily moved. We should not speak of the Carlylean pessimism but of the Carlylean terror.

One man since then has, it seems to me, had the same insight, and in his work also the result was a tortured, distorted, and fragmented syntax and the same extravagant, exalted, and ter-ror-ridden rhetoric. To him also was given the vision—is it the only true one?—that the human mind is literally insane. It was William Faulkner.

3

Personality and the Mask of Knowledge

ONCE, WHEN Browning was asked why he wrote in so difficult a style, he replied that it was to warn people off his grounds who did not belong there. If that was indeed his purpose, and not the defense of a man who had once hoped for and expected and briefly tasted a wide readership, he has been successful. It is hardly an exaggeration to say that most of Browning is unread, except for the few remaining spiritual survivors of the old Browning societies, once so common; even scholars of Victorian literature are unfamiliar with the bulk of his work. *Sordello* is virtually unknown, except by a very few determined critics; the series of plays beginning with *Strafford* and ending with that Shavian comedy, *A Soul's Tragedy*, is neglected, dismissed as purely experimental work; it is the general opinion that everything after *The Ring and the Book*, except a few short lyrics, is hardly worth examining—twenty years of works and seven volumes in a seventeen-volume edition. "Browning" means ordinarily at most a third of his work, and half of that is *The Ring and the Book*, which is more admired than read, though one of the most endlessly fascinating poems in English, the *Ulysses* of the nineteenth century, as *Sordello* is the *Finnegans Wake*.

It is instructive that the scholar responsible more than anyone for the dismissal of the later Browning himself wrote a long book on Browning's last major work, *Parleyings with Certain People of Importance in Their Day*, and hopelessly misunderstood it. A young and more recent critic, who has made his reputation with quite a good book on a little of Browning, has now informed us that it is not true that everything after *The Ring and the Book* is poetically worthless; *Balaustion's Adventure*, the next work, is, it appears, also very good. Presumably this gentleman will work his way through the rest of Browning, announcing with each work he encounters that it too is good.

To those few who have troubled to acquaint themselves with the later Browning, this will not be news; but certainly to most people who pretend to a knowledge of Victorian literature it will come as a surprise, and probably an unbelievable one at that. Let me say at once that to my mind Browning's four greatest works are *Sordello*, *The Ring and the Book*, *Fifine at the Fair*, and the *Parleyings*, something like 30,000 lines of poetry, in itself one of the more formidable bulks of poetry in English. Together they are approximately equivalent in volume to Edmund Spenser's *The Faerie Queene*, one of the greatest poems of western culture, and like Browning unread by the vast majority of those who publicly announce themselves as devoting their lives to the study of English literature. One sometimes wonders about the morality of the academic world. Admittedly the life of academes is indeed morally very difficult. But need they be quite so lazy?

Certainly some of the current neglect of Browning by the nonacademic as well as the academic intellectual is the effect of the Browning societies. These curious organizations of earnest and well-meaning people, a few of whom did permanently valuable work, were for the most part devoted to extracting from Browning's poems innumerable moral plums. That was easy enough, for Browning is full of them. Unfortunately, they are not quite such plums nor so moral as they seem. "A man's reach should exceed his grasp, or what's a heaven for?" is uttered by a man whose reach came far short of his grasp, Andrea del Sarto, and who knows it. It appears to be a truth uttered out of a man's profound self-knowledge of his own weakness, but the situation is not really so clear as that; for the poem is a study in facile self-contempt, and Andrea's self-knowledge is not nearly so searching as he and the reader are tempted to imagine. "God's in his Heaven / All's right with the world," is sung by Pippa before a house in which, as she suspects, adultery is the theme, and her innocent little song precipitates a murder and a suicide.

Beginning with *Sordello* all these moral jewels are presented in an ambiguous light which steadily becomes more doubtful. The *Epilogue* to the *Parleyings* seems to imply that the invention of printing was an unfortunate historical error, for facile reproduction of truth can only multiply error. Or does it? On numerous occasions Browning appeared to explain his poems, but as these records are investigated with care, it turns out that his explanations are as equivocal and ambiguous as the poems themselves. He gave his *imprimatur* to his friend Mrs. Orr's handbook to his works, but her book is full not only of inadequate interpretations but even of factual errors. He did nothing to correct these, but he did quietly omit the dedication to her of one of his volumes when he republished it in a collected edition.

Still, the well-meaning efforts of the Browning societies can be understood and even forgiven. In the terrible complexities of a mature Browning poem, anyone can be forgiven who latches on to some sentence that clearly means something and rescues it from a context ambiguous, half-lit, and confusing. And what was rescued, of course, were precisely those portentous moral statements which are like the statements of critics who dismiss most of Browning, and for much the same reasons. It is easy to decide what a poet ought to do, as easy as it is to settle a moral problem. One need only adopt firm critical principles and apply them without hesitation or mercy. The firmer one's principles and the more merciless the application the greater one's reputation.

Aesthetics and criticism are indeed for the most part a branch of morality, and not a very interesting branch. To tell a poet, especially if he is dead, what he did right and wrong, where he made his mistakes, and where he was on the right track is easy enough. To discover what he really was doing is a much more difficult task, and far more time-consuming. How can one bother to do that when one has a reputation to make? Reading the mature and more demanding Browning is like having one's brain squeezed by a gigantic hand. The easiest escape from that humiliation is to deny the validity of the squeezer. Browning is truly one of the toughest of poets. After twenty years of reading him I can but propose that what I shall say here is, I *think*, aimed in the right direction. Reading Browning is not different from reading Wittgenstein, and their conclusions are remarkably similar, as are their methods.

Of the events of Browning's life there is little to be said. Its most notable event was the famous elopement with Elizabeth Barrett. Life with a morphine addict can be trying, but both were reasonably sensible about the matter and it seems to have made little difference, though occasionally giving rise to difficulties. There was the problem of money, of course, since Elizabeth's father refused to help—or even open her letters. Browning's father was quite a successful employee in the Bank of England. He lived well and never required his son to do anything, but supporting a second ménage, even in cheap Italy, was more than he could manage. However, an old friend of both husband and wife came to their aid, and in time, by a generous death, relieved them of all problems. Then, too, Elizabeth's poetry began to bring in respectable earnings; it was not until after her death that his own poetry began to earn something for him. For a time they were confined to Florence, but shortly began to spend long winter months at Rome and long summer months at Siena. Occasionally trips home intervened, with pleasant stays in Paris. Once in a while financial disaster threatened, but things always straightened themselves out.

Browning's marriage, his one event, was part of the general pattern of his life, a life characterized by rigid self-indulgence. That self-indulgence was writing poetry, and preparing to write it by reading. The extraordinary and out-of-the-way learning of Browning is one of his difficulties, but it is not surprising that he acquired it. Almost from childhood it was planned that Robert should be a poet. His father was a kind of poet manqué, as well as a draughtsman of some charm and competence. But above all he was a passionate bibliophile. He had a library of some ten thousand volumes, and it is said that he knew it so well that he could find any book he wanted in the dark.

The family lived in a then pleasant London suburb, with meadows and woods and rural roads to walk and the rich plant life of England to study. Nearby was the Dulwich gallery, a small and fascinating collection of paintings in the Dulwich School, housed, when Browning was an infant, in one of the most charming of art museums, designed by the fantastic Romantic architect, Sir John Soane. His mother was a fine musician, and music, too, became important and remained important all his life. In nearby London were concerts and theater. But for the young Browning it was the books that mattered. He tried the new University of London for a week in 1828, but decided, as he had earlier discovered in another school, that there was really nothing he could learn there. His father's books were his education, and he seemed to have read them all.

From 1812, when he was born, to 1846, when he left London with Elizabeth, thirty-four and a half years old, he seemed to have spent most of his time reading and writing. One of the great feats of scholarship of the early nineteenth century was the immense *Biographie Universelle*, begun by French scholars with Napoleon's blessing and as a contribution to his glory, but finished, not counting supplemental volumes, several decades later under the Bourbons. It is still a work of considerable usefulness, and Browning is believed to have read it all. He is also believed to have read all of Dr. Johnson's dictionary. He read, too, not merely in English but in Greek, Latin, Italian, French, and German, with, it would seem, a little Hebrew thrown in. Even so, he was less multilingual than his father, whose contributions to the infinite historical detail in *The Ring and the Book* were, it appears, considerable.

The result of all this reading is a mystery. Everything conspired to make him a literary poet, as Swinburne was to become. Swinburne had but one line of psychological insight, but that was terribly deep and terribly disturbing, and extremely personal. He was, however, capable of writing a long poem about Victor Hugo alluding to almost every one of his multitudinous works, and all are fully footnoted, a frustration for future scholars. Browning's learning was used differently. A knowledge of his innumerable historical allusions adds immensely to the understanding and enjoyment of his work, but the poems do not need that knowledge; the reader can get along very well without it. To be sure, Browning did annotate one poem, *Paracelsus*, but so little necessary are the notes, mostly quotations in barbarous Latin, that until recently no edition troubled to translate them, or provide further annotations of much information. Properly annotated, the poem is seen to be embedded richly in the history of the early sixteenth century, and notes add much to comprehending what Browning was up to. Yet readers have gotten along perfectly well for a hundred and thirty years and more without them; the notion that there is no true historical dimension to *Paracelsus* is standard, and not entirely wrong. You can go with Browning as far as you want to, and the results are rewarding, but there is always further to go.

A young man who admitted to his future wife that he had been spoiled by his parents, who apparently knew nothing of the world except books, who lived with his parents until he eloped to Italy, whose whole environment seemed to conspire to make him a bookish, cultivated dilettante—this young man developed the most astonishing sympathy with an immense range of personalities, from saint to sinner. His delight was to have villains defend themselves. Self-deception is his theme. Rationalization is his subject. In later years nothing so delighted him as to be taken for a well-to-do retired man of business, and after Elizabeth's death and his return to London he continued a pattern begun in Italy, a pattern that often involved leaving the ailing Elizabeth at home. It was the pattern of the profes-sional diner-out, the social lion, the delightful talker. Apparently he gave the impression of such superficiality that Henry James wrote one of his strange ghost stories on the matter, in which Browning is seen as a *doppelgänger*, or possibly twins, since the oddity of seeing a man working at his desk when you have just seen him drive off in a carriage for an outing with the ladies is never explained. And that was James's point. Browning seems inexplicable. It has even been suggested that the social Browning had no comprehension whatsoever of what the poetic Browning was saying.

This is unacceptable. Browning was like the characters he created. Both presented to the world a favorable projection of themselves, but his characters knew not what lay underneath, what levels of duplicity are necessary for existence. Only a man who knew that, only a man who knew what he himself was up to, who had penetrated his own duplicity, could create such characters. Somehow, somewhere, Browning had discovered

90

that men wear masks not merely to conceal their true characters from the world but for a better reason, to conceal their true characters from themselves. He had penetrated the secret of human interaction; it is founded firmly on the bedrock of insincerity, hypocrisy, duplicity, and self-deception. A wicked man can make as good a case for himself as a good man, perhaps better, because he has better reason to. Freud's greatest service to his fellow man was to expose the mechanics of rationalization; now we can all rationalize better. It is a platitude that self-knowledge paralyzes; it should be a platitude that rationalization, and only rationalization, enables us to act. Platitudes are, after all, our only reliable guides to life.

Browning's immense and varied reading led him, not as it does with most literary types to a sanctification of language, but rather to the insight that of men's masks the most important one is language itself. The mask of language, or language as a mask, is his theme; and this is why his characters tend to speak at such length. It is as if Browning had been aware that it is impossible to maintain a coherent and consistent verbal construct over any great length of discourse. Even Kant could not manage it. To talk at any length about anything is to give oneself away, particularly if the discourse is extemporaneous.

I. A. Richards has called the process the interinanimation of words; but it would be more precise and correct to say that once one has uttered a statement that statement is now part of the phenomenal world, at least insofar as we remember it, as is true of everything else. And even if we do not, the very process of listening, even with poor attention, to what we say changes this verbal response into a stimulus. This is the feedback phenomenon, and Browning's men and women respond very fully to what they say. The peculiarity of his dramatic monologues is not so much in the interaction between the speaker and situation in which he is speaking, but rather that the flow of utterance becomes part of and changes the situation, and thus changes the character of the interaction. This is why Browning's characters tend to be highly dynamic, why their personalities show such a high degree of the discontinuous, the unexpected. For Browning, in the beginning was the word, and at the end shall be the word, and everything in between will be words. One may put it in a not exaggerated quip: It is not that man uses language; rather, language uses man. Or better, man is language. The Greek and Roman philosophers of rhetoric were right. Everything reduces itself to language, and the management of language is the management of everything. Rhetoric is the key to social management, and the statesman must first of all be a rhetorician. We should never speak of *mere* rhetoric. Thus, at the end of the *Parleyings* Browning can imply that the invention of printing was anything but an unequivocal blessing.

Browning and his characters are alike in this. To manipulate language is to manipulate one's mask, and therefore is the prime method of manipulating others. And Browning's characters are above all interested in manipulating the responses of others and controlling them so that they take the speaker's mask at face value. Yet if the speaker talks long enough, like the rest of us, his manipulative control begins to break down; and he reveals not the reality behind the mask but the mask behind the mask. It is almost as if Browning conceived of the personality as an infinite regression of masks, and perhaps he did.

However, the other side of the coin is equally important. It is the mask of language, and language as mask, that not only facilitates but permits interaction. Manipulation of one's self and others in the furtherance of certain life-essential interests is the way we live, and what makes it possible for us to live. Browning's pleasure at being taken for a retired well-to-do businessman, or a social lion, or a quasi-professional diner-out was a mask behind which he could pursue his interests with that self-centeredness which properly understood is not pride but humility. To present publicly one's self-conception, the mask behind the mask, is on the one hand to force one's attitudes on others and on the other to expose oneself to unnecessary challenges. The full development of subtle and profound concepts requires protection. Without that protection either one's confidence is shattered or one becomes engaged in contention, and the worst kind of contention, sincere contention. Browning needed to maintain his insights, to develop them in silence, secrecy, and cunning, that they might reach their ripeness. To be sincerely contentious is to lose one's insights in sincerity, for the development of insights requires that one uncover, in secrecy, one's own insincerity, something impossible to do if one is busy defending them. The defense of a position hypostatizes it, reifies it, commits one to it, and ultimately leaves one stuck with it. The kind of conceptual fluidity Browning needed for himself if he was to be a poet of conceptual fluidity required defense by the deliberate and salutary dishonesty and ambiguity of which Browning became in time such a master.

A couple of examples, one from his poetry, and one from his life, will show this. The villain in *The Ring and the Book* is Guido Franceschini. He marries a child for the sake of money, persecutes and drives away her parents, persecutes and drives away his wife, and then kills his wife and her parents for the sake of settling an infinite complexity of legal suits and counter-suits, all resolved now in favor of his and his wife's infant son, now the heir and, as a minor, under Guido's total control. In his first defense Guido presents himself as the supporter of the prerogatives of the male, the defender of the rights of husbands, the supporter of the social order, one who accepts with full responsibility his position as a nobleman. When this does not work he presents himself as a wolf, one who preys upon mankind, ruthlessly and savagely. And this is the conception of Guido that Browning critics have accepted. Here is the real Guido at last. But the fact is that when he is faced with execution this mask evaporates and Guido is revealed as nothing, one who implores

Pompilia herself to save him. He is not even a wolf, and that self-conception was again a rationalizing strategy to provide himself with self-respect. Reduced to extremity, Guido can maintain no mask and reveals himself as merely an organism struggling only for continued existence.

Does Browning mean that any man so reduced would reveal the hollowness of his masks in the same way, that there is a point in human extremity in which the distinction between hero and villain, the good and the bad, evaporates? He should mean this, since both use the same linguistic strategies to support themselves. Perhaps it is impossible to be sure, for Browning often enough leaves us with a puzzle, runs us into a blank wall and abandons us. Yet it should be said that the hero Caponsacchi, who rescued Pompilia from Arezzo only to have her killed in Rome, is also at the end of his monologue reduced to a cry. The mask of language then, does not merely protect the man within, or the mask within; we are language, and language is a mask, and it is masks that hold our personalities together. Without masks, it may be Browning's implication, we are nothing.

From his own life one may choose another oddity. After the Lily Tower of Giotto, the most spectacular sight in Florence in the late 1850's was Pen Browning, the child of Robert and Elizabeth, playing in the gardens of the Pitti Palace, which were just across the street from the famous Casa Guidi, their home. His costume made Little Lord Fauntleroy seem a Boy Scout prepared for a month in the wilderness. His long curls hung below his shoulders, his shirt was all ruffles, his jacket and voluminous knickerbockers were satin, and his satin cap was a great artist's beret with an ostrich plume.

Elizabeth died on June 29, 1861; within a month Browning had left Florence forever. He headed straight for England, but stopped long enough in Paris to get Pen's hair cut and have made for him some proper English boys' clothes. Within a few years he had published a poem attacking one of Elizabeth's most cherished fantasies, spiritualism, and a few years later yet another, Napoleon III. Not long after, he attempted to marry again, only to discover that his love affair with Elizabeth was too famous; he was stuck with it.

It was certainly one of the most famous love stories of the nineteenth century, a period replete with grand passions, so replete that a certain suspicion is occasionally aroused. I confess that this particular grand passion arouses such suspicions in me. Browning's share of the famous correspondence between himself and the bedridden Elizabeth is too much like his poetry to make one entirely comfortable with the legend. The first time Elizabeth thought he proposed she was mistaken, and they were both rather painfully embarrassed. Did he fall in love with her *because* she was bedridden? Was it that as a poet he needed a grand passion and she seemed a reasonably safe object? Was he thus early snared by a too successful legend? It may be true, as Dr. Johnson has proposed, that people fall in love only because they think they ought to; fortunately, except for those who have been completely and forever taken in by the erotic propaganda of our culture, marriage reveals that an infinitely more interesting and satisfying relationship between men and women is possible than love.

Browning, however, may have been a special case. To know that one falls in love in order to obey a behavioral paradigm of one's culture, and to set about to fall in love in order to obey that paradigm—these are far different from simply obeying it. Browning's poems show such intimate knowledge of self-deception that it seems possible they could have been written only by a man who knew so much on the subject that he could deceive others but did not have to trouble to deceive himself— except, of course, that a self-conception built upon a refusal to deceive oneself is but another mask that holds one together and makes interaction possible. And Browning may have known this too. Everything points to the proposal that Browning knew that self-deception is as essential to life as the deception of others. Human freedom means merely that man has a choice of self-deceptions.

As Browning very nearly put it himself, our perception is governed by Will, or more precisely, Perception is Will. The Will, however, has but one aim, a viable self-conception that is necessarily a self-deception. Yet further, cognition, true knowledge, knowledge of the truth, is dependent on perception, and thus dependent on the Will. Will, perception, cognition, truth —they are inseparable—indeed they are one. But if that is the case, can truth ever be separated from the interests, the Will that leads us—or perhaps seduces us—into using the word "truth"? "What is truth?" asked Browning at the beginning of his poetic career; and at the end he was reduced to asking, "Under what circumstances and pursuant to what interests do we use this word?" In thus finding an unbroken and unbreakable chain between the Will and what we decide to assert to be truth, Browning participated in the epistemological puzzling of Romanticism; his position, like Carlyle's and Tennyson's, can be put in the form that our decisions about what to ascribe truth to are adaptational. The drama of Browning arises from emphasis on the decision itself, rather than on the resultant truth or its reliability. And in that drama his emphasis is on the moment of decision.

Like so many of his contemporaries, Browning held, at least for a time, a quasi-incarnational concept of the relation of divine to human. He was not among those who held the notion in its extreme form, that every act is an incarnational act, the entry of the divine into the human, but that only at certain moments, perhaps once in a man's life, is the gulf between the infinite and the finite, between the eternal and the temporal, bridged for a flashing second of illumination. Such a moment can occur, according to the line of inquiry so far pursued, only when the last mask has been stripped away, when the ultimate self-deceptions which make action possible have dissolved. Contrariwise, what leads to such moments is the gradual closing off of possible routes of action to the point at which no action is possible. Browning's villains fail precisely because their powers of self-deception, rationalization, and action are inexhaustible. They can always manage some further viciousness, if only a viciousness of thought. Those, however, who have the capability of coming to the end of their rope, experience the moment of pure value, which Browning calls variously "truth" and "love." Thus truth and love are particular kinds of experience, and it is the character of that experience with which Browning is so intensely concerned.

In a Balcony, a short play published in the *Men and Women* volumes of 1855, is one of his clearest presentations of this. The two lovers have involved themselves, each other, and their queen in conflicting and mutually incoherent networks of deception. Each of the lovers has made certain predictions about the queen's behavior, based upon an interpretation of her personality utterly distorted by their interests, their Will. The result is that the queen believes that the man is in love with her, as she is with him. Disabused, she leaves the lovers on the balcony to await her decision. In the moments awaiting them, not knowing what message the guard will bring—imprisonment, banishment, reward, permission to marry—they are reduced to total surrender of any predictively valuable knowledge of the queen, of each other, or of themselves. Thus stripped of all basis for action, and of all confidence in their comprehension of human personality, including their own, their love for each other is at last permitted disinterested expression and emotional fulfillment. The curtain falls and the work ends before the decision of the queen is revealed.

Now this looks like a paean to erotic love, and up to a point such an interpretation is adequate, but Browning is really interested in the psychological process of, to use a barbarous term, de-deception which makes it possible; and he is further interested in one form of erotic love as a representative or exemplification of something far more vital to human existence. As far as the process itself is concerned, Browning's position is analogous to, and virtually identical with, that of those psychiatrists who maintain that it takes high courage to permit oneself to have a really thoroughgoing nervous breakdown, one pregnant with the possibilities of genuine development.

As he grew older and studied and thought and wrote more, Browning became increasingly aware of the nearly endless variety of meanings men attach to the word truth; but almost from the beginning he was aware of the difference between the truth of a proposition and truth as a psychic experience. In this he resembles Carlyle, with his distinction between belief and beliefs, and Cardinal Newman, with his similar distinction between certitude and certainty. Yet he differs from both of them and makes his unique contribution to Romantic thinking in his concentration upon the role of personality in the problem of knowledge. Personality, to Browning, was self-conception as self-deception for the sake of arriving at a strategy for action; and propositional truth is but a factor in that strategy. Since each man is unique, in that he warps the general pattern of self-deception into a necessarily unique style of life, each man has a different notion of propositional truth; for the function of propositional truths is to facilitate and justify action directly or else indirectly by justifying the self-deceiving self-conception which is the ground of action. Hence the word "truth" has as many meanings as men who use it.

Anyone who reads Browning with an awareness of this problem learns to respond to the appearance of the word "truth" in his poetry as to a flag of warning. Never is this better illustrated than in the first book of *The Ring and the Book*, in which Browning himself is purportedly the speaker. He sets out bravely to discover the truth in the collection of documents on the forgotten murder trial he has accidentally discovered in the Florentine flea market, but by the end of this long book the word has been subjected to a terrible buffeting. It is only reasonable that at the end of the twelfth book, at the conclusion of the poem, when he is again the speaker, he should deny the possibility of propositional truth, and assert that the value of art lies precisely in the fact that art is not committed to truth. To understand what he is after it is necessary to go back to a much earlier point in his development, to his first important work, *Paracelsus*, in which the problems of truth and of its relation to personality and love are first explored.

Paracelsus was inspired by the life of the famous alchemist, proto-scientist and, by subsequent reputation, charlatan who lived in the first half of the sixteenth century. His achievement in medicine and science, though faulty in details, was notable in its general principles; however fantastic and now completely obsolete his explanations, he discovered the medical value of chemical substances. To say that he founded biochemistry is an exaggeration, even a falsification, but it is not incorrect to say that his innovation in medicine was the crude and unscientific application of the principles of biochemistry. It is almost impossible to say whether or not he made an important contribution to the development of medicine and chemistry, but that he was an extraordinarily courageous innovator cannot be doubted. His historical importance perhaps lies in that; he was model for the scientist who denies the validity of the scientific culture dominant and unquestioned in his society, starts afresh with the basic problems, and attempts to think through his science from fundamental principles and empirically verified propositions. The *legend* of Paracelsus as the revolutionary innovator is his true historical significance, and it was this that attracted Browning to him. The subject of Browning's poem, written in dramatic form and perhaps inspired at least a bit by Goethe's *Faust*, is the psychology of the revolutionary innovator. What does such questioning of received opinion do to a man, what is the self-conception that supports it, and what are the consequences to that self-conception of his failure?

His initial self-conception is that he is fated to know all, to learn the secrets of the universe, and thus to learn the attributes of God. He conceives of himself as the vessel of truth, and that that truth will issue forth from him and reveal the uttermost truth of the world. Yet that truth will also be natural truth. In this Browning was historically correct, for undoubtedly one of the most significant achievements of the historical Paracelsus was his conclusion that the secrets of nature were to be discovered from those who habitually dealt with nature—miners, for example, not from abstract speculators. Thus, for all of Paracelsus's failure, we find the secret of the peculiar success Browning eventually grants him, the determined and unshakable sense of fact which is central to the Romantic tradition. Fact, empirical fact, was to draw from Paracelsus the inner light.

When we see him again, some years later, he is involved in the deepest self-contempt, consulting an astrologer, the very type of nonempirical wisdom monger which initially he had spurned. What has him hopelessly puzzled is the reason for his failure, for his original ambition has been a disaster, in spite of the fact that he has learned all kinds of secrets of nature no man had ever known before. Nevertheless it is a heap of shards, disconnected curiosities. To him a poet comes, Aprile, whose message is that the desire to know is not the secret of life, but the desire to love. In Browning "love" has almost as many chameleon colors as "truth," and for much the same reasons, but here it means the power to value the world for its own sake, not as a repository of secrets which are to be seized upon by an intellectual raid or rape. Further, Aprile has a vision of being every kind of artist, the highest kind being the poet, who is capable of valuing human personality disinterestedly.

Here is the germ of Browning's later conception in *The Ring and the Book* that the very value of art is that it is not committed to efforts to utter the truth but presents the world in such a way that one's vision of it is not controlled by the interested will. The point of his sharp distinction in *Paracelsus* between knowing and loving is that cognition is always interested, and is always therefore subject to the limitations of the self-deceiving personality. Consequently loving is not a cognitive activity; it cannot give knowledge of the world, truth, but it can transcend the personality. And such self-transcendence Paracelsus now attempts.

But in this too he fails, for his self-conception of one who can know all is not essentially changed by conceiving of himself as one who can love all. The result is disastrous, for his attempts to teach mankind what he knows are repelled, simply because he requires that to learn what he knows they must abandon the received wisdom which he long since rejected. And this they cannot do. To his self-contempt is now added a contempt for others. His bitter prediction that he will be driven from his professorial post at Basel comes true, and he sinks into drunkenness and a redoubled self-contempt. When we last see him he is dying, but in a final burst of energy he rises from his deathbed and utters the vision he has at last achieved, a vision of evolutionary development, in which the present condition of man is but a stage to be transcended. He sees himself at last as but a part of that process, and his failure the consequence of his self-deception that he could complete that process in its twin aspects, knowing all and loving all. He dies content, redeemed by the acceptance of his failure.

Browning was twenty-two when he wrote *Paracelsus*. No other English poet has shown himself capable of such a sustained achievement at so early an age. Yet it is by no means the mature Browning either stylistically or intellectually. Most of it does not even sound like Browning. The impressive thing is the richness of invention, of argument, and insight which may be summed up as: the only failure is success; and the only success is failure. Yet the position he had arrived at left him with a new problem. It was all very well to abjure finality, as he had, and to recognize that no human problem is ever solved, since it is either displaced by a new problem or is incorporated into a new problem, or its apparent solution on application reveals new problems. It is not, of course, that this abjuration of the possibility of finality was not a signal achievement. The tolerance of uncertainty is not yet so common an accomplishment that Browning's grasp of it at the age of twenty-two and in the 1830's need be minimized.

We never know what we are doing. It is only after it is done that we can create constructs which are themselves in the service of our interests, whether our interest be at the moment self-justification or self-condemnation. The trouble with *Paracelsus* was that it was a denial of its main point. Paracelsus is not really driven to an extremity, for he can still explain where he went wrong and can still provide an explanation for his failure. To provide in terms of an evolutionary metaphysic a satisfactory explanation for one's life is not really to abjure finality; it is only to postpone it. Any such abjuration that is truly thoroughgoing must contain within itself a denial of the adequacy of the explanatory justification of that abjuration. Paracelsus gave with one hand what he took away with the other. A true denial of finality must undercut the reasons for that rejection of finality as well as the reasons for postulating that final answers and an ultimate explanation of man's place in the world are available. Like Carlyle, Browning had raised a problem that propelled him toward instrumentalism, but it was not yet clear to him how to disengage himself from metaphysics. He had seen the possibility of grasping the irresolvable tension between subject and object, but he had not yet grasped it.

It was to be many years before he did, and his path to it was tortuous and not at all philosophical. The argument in *Paracelsus* between the hero and his two friends, Festus and Aprile, swirls always around a single center, self-definition, conceived as the key to action. How a man defines himself determines how he acts and determines his particular mode of failure. Will, perception, cognition, truth are, in the final reaches of Browning's thinking, identical, four different ways of talking about the same phenomenon, though it is not exact to maintain that he said precisely that in so many words. As a young man, however, he had by no means reached anything like such a position. However, he had arrived at the realization that what unifies will, perception, cognition, and truth is personality, and that the problem of epistemology, that is, of knowledge and of what can be known, is inseparable from the problem of personality. The peculiar thrust of Browning's thinking, its oddity, the thing that makes it so difficult to grasp, is his vision that epistemology is a personality problem, not a philosophical question. What he had learned in writing *Paracelsus* is that the key to the problem is self-definition. His next major work, therefore, is even more directly concerned with that than was *Paracelsus*.

On no poem did Browning spend so many years or so much rewriting as on *Sordello*. When it was issued it destroyed his reputation at once and virtually deprived him of an audience for decades. There are good stories about it which are always worth repeating. Jane Carlyle said that she read it and at the end still did not know whether Sordello was a man, a city, or a book. Douglas Jerrold read it when he was recuperating from an attack of what the Victorians called brain fever. He thought that his brain had been permanently damaged until his wife confessed herself as confused as he was. It has, for the most part, except notably by Ezra Pound, remained unread ever since. In the late nineteenth century, an enterprising clergyman published a prose version of it, which might be called a prose translation.

In *Sordello* Browning created his mature style, but the result was so impossible for the readers of his time and most readers since, that for the next thirty years he wrote in what is best called a simplified version of the *Sordello* style. Only in the 1870's did he return to it, and the rejection of his later work has paralleled the rejection of *Sordello*. Yet Browning himself, once he had mastered the style, wrote it with an almost incredible ease and rapidity when he returned to it. It was not difficult to him, nor is it likely that initially he planned to write a difficult style. Rather his linguistic sensitivity and mastery were such that he played with syntax and elision with the ease of a master juggler. If his theme was the mask of language, it is because no English writer, not even Joyce, has had such a grasp of the possibilities of English grammar. And in this style he wrote a poem concerned with one of the most abstruse and difficult of psychological themes and set it in an historical period, the origins of the struggle between the Guelfs and the Ghibellines, which is one of the most confusing periods of Italian history, and that is saying a good deal.

As one looks through the range of Browning's writing career, it is apparent that the creation of the *Sordello* style, its abandonment, and its reemergence correspond with several other watersheds in his writing and his thinking. Up through *Balaustion's Adventure*, which is mostly a translation of a Euripidean play, most of Browning's poems and all his major poems except *Pippa Passes* and *Christmas-Eve and Easter-Day* have historical settings, studied and realized with the greatest historical accuracy. After *Balaustion's Adventure*, however, he embarked on a series of what has been called his Balzacian poems, poems based on true events of the nineteenth century, though occasional minor poems continued to be historical. His last major work, the *Parleyings*, was his first fully philosophical work since *Paracelsus*, just as it presented the uttermost range of his thought on the problems which that poem raised. Further, it was in *The Ring and the Book*, as we shall see, that Browning at last arrived at a solution to the relation of personality and knowledge which was the central problem raised in *Paracelsus*; he achieved a full grasp of what the irresolvable tension of subject and object really means. It was only after that poem that he turned to modern material for his major efforts.

In the discussion of Carlyle it was pointed out that to the Romantics history became the principal strategy for achieving culture transcendence. The prime value of historical knowledge is that it is so wonderfully efficacious for disengaging the individual from his own culture and its values. The great weakness of American education is its insufficient attention to this possibility of history, for on the whole it uses history very much as it was used in the eighteenth century, as a storehouse of moral examples. It is used to inculcate and reinforce the values of the culture. This is one of the reasons why the nineteenth-century function of history as a strategy for disengagement has been assumed in this century by Freudian psychology, which is itself an historical discipline. True, it is rarely used for disengagement, though that is how Freud intended that it be used. The same function is also performed by cultural anthropology, which as an intellectual discipline emerged in the second half of the nineteenth century from a fusion of historicism and evolutionary thinking, itself of course an historical matter.

The effects of such disengagement through history can be seen in the emergence of the realistic novel. Such a novel was clearly a new kind of fiction. It is not that there had not been novels about the contemporary world before the 1850's, when this new novel emerged. Thackeray and Dickens, among many others, wrote such fiction, although the historical novel bulked large in total publication. Yet the novels in contemporary settings of Thackeray and Dickens are quite different from the realistic novel as developed in France by the Goncourt brothers and Flaubert and in England by George Eliot. When critics call a novel a "realistic" novel and assert that it is a fictional genre

105

of a recognizable sort, they are certainly responding to something distinctive. Such a novel embodies a peculiar distance between the interests of the author and the interests of his characters. There is a coolness, a disengagement from the values being worked out in the novel. The author presents his characters almost as laboratory specimens. He analyzes them, but he does not take sides. His attitude is very nearly that of the cultural anthropologist studying an alien and hitherto unknown society and its culture.

The source of this technique was enunciated precisely by the Goncourt brothers, who created the realistic novel and its theory. The realistic novel, they said, is an historical novel about the present. Flaubert's famous remark that Emma Bovary was really himself is an instance of that disengagement and detachment, of that culture transcendence, which is the peculiar mark of the realistic novel and which has made it so important in the general culture of the past century or so.

The technique, then, of the realistic novel is the technique of the historical novel applied to a contemporary scene. But it would be something of a mistake to think that the historical novel differs from the realistic because the latter is concerned with a contemporary problem. On the contrary, the historical novelist is concerned intensely with contemporary problems. What he does, following the lead of the first great historical novelist, Walter Scott, is to find an historical situation with a sufficient analogical similarity to a problem in his own world so that he can isolate that problem for the purposes of examining it. The principle comes out in a correct interpretation of Zola's assertion that the naturalistic novel, a logical development of its predecessor the realistic novel, was the experimental novel. If this is interpreted to mean that the novel is properly an instrument for sociological investigation the weakness of the claim is at once apparent. How can one investigate the invented? On the other hand, if the claim is asserted that the naturalistic novelist, like the scientist in his laboratory, can control the variables, the claim is more respectable. For that is what the historical novelists were attempting to do, to control the variables.

To attempt to write about the problems of the contemporary world without a technique for creating a defined field of investigation meant that you would get something like the novels of Dickens and Thackeray, vast sprawling edifices in which every factor introduced drags along with it a chain of related factors stretching back into the world until it disappears in distance and confusion. For this reason the novelist is very much at the mercy of accident and therefore of entrapping his own interests and personality, of getting caught in his own machinery. This is not to imply that the Dickens novels are inferior to the subsequent realistic novels. If anything they are greater, perhaps far greater. The Dickens technique is admirable for savage satire on the culture. But the trouble with satire, if one is interested in disengagement, is that the values which make the satire possible are part of the culture which one is attacking. The disengaged man may feel compassion for men caught in their culture, as Paracelsus just before he dies at last feels compassion for the men he has contemned, but satire is neither one of the things he can do nor one of those he wants to do. The satirist is not disengaged.

In an historical setting one can control the variables of one's imaginative discourse. It is the technique of the fairy story and of the joke, particularly of the dirty joke. "Once upon a time" means that the writer can bring in factors on the basis of decision rather than compulsion, on the basis of knowledge rather than the conditioned response. Hence Browning investigated and explored his problem in historical settings, saw the solution, wrote a gigantic historical work which, as we shall see, develops a thoroughgoing skepticism about historiography, and then, except for two poems which are mostly translations from the

Greek, a dragging of the past into the present, turned to contemporary material. Like the realistic novelists before him, he wrote historical poems about the present. Working with historical material was his strategy for achieving culture transcendence; having codified that strategy as a technique, he was able to maintain his transcendence while dealing with the material of the world around him.

The play he wrote because of the great success of *Paracelsus* —*Strafford*—which started him on his rather bitter and very frustrating career of trying to write for the stage, may have used historical material out of current fashion, but *Sordello* was a different matter. There was sufficient analogy for him to work with. The historical Sordello, of whose life Browning uses very little, was an innovative poet, a precursor of Dante, without whom Dante could scarcely have done what he did. He was, as it were, at the archaic stage of a new style, and the first generation of the Romantics felt themselves very much as artists who were laying the foundations for a wholly new style of art and poetry—and life. Carlyle's notion that organic filaments were invisibly weaving a new stage of western culture was a spelling out of a very common feeling. The problem of the radical innovator, so radical that he must necessarily be misunderstood by most of the public, was present to them. Further, the early thirteenth century in Italy was an immensely confusing period in which the followers of the Pope and the followers of the Holy Roman Emperor were polarizing themselves not around the issues of Pope and Empire but around the issues, first, of imperial control of politics, economics, and culture, which was the ambition and the practice to his utmost ability of Frederick II, the Hohenstaufen, the greatest of emperors and one of the most fascinating personalities in the history of Europe; and, second, of local economic, cultural, and political development. Emperor and Pope, Ghibelline and Guelf, were but the names of issues as yet but obscurely felt. In the event, the Guelf principle was to win, and out of it was to emerge that marvelous Italian city-state culture which remains the central miracle of European civilization, from which nearly everything valuable in European culture has come.

In the early thirteenth century the issues were neither clear nor decided. The 1830's in England were similarly confused. The great Reform Act of 1832 which it was hoped would settle a major crisis did so only at the cost of opening up an awareness of an infinitude of problems which the English had scarcely known they had. The Reform Act of 1832 initiated the Victorian confusion, and in fact historians are still trying to figure out what happened. Certainly the legend of the Reform Act's having established Liberal England and having spread democracy is but a legend. It restricted democracy, but even that was not clear at the time, except for a few very acute observers like Carlyle, whom Browning had come to know and whose *French Revolution* had a great effect on him, and on his style. It is doubtful if Browning could have or would have developed his great *Sordello* style without the example of Carlyle's fantastic and brilliant prose.

Sordello is not the archetype of poet in Browning's poem, for he tries poetry only briefly, and abandons it when it crumbles beneath the strain he puts on it. He is the innovator in a time of great cultural and political confusion when the issues are not clear. Browning uses one of the most ancient themes in the world, the theme of the long-lost son restored to his father. In the two most popular solutions to this situation the son is incorporated once again into the family and the society or culture, or he picks up the sword from his father's failing arm and succeeds triumphantly in the enterprise in which father had failed. But *Sordello* concludes with neither of these hoary denouements. The son dies, but the father lives—and deteriorates into a meaningless and self-indulgent existence terminated by a humiliating but comfortable captivity.

In *Sordello*, in order to study failure, Browning combines an ancient fictional pattern, which implies a conclusion of either reconciliation or triumph, with the cultural and political situation of the 1830's, and the personality of the innovator, and places the combination in a remote and little-known and confusing historical period. The difference from *Paracelsus* is clear enough. In the earlier poem the innovator snatches intellectual and personality triumph from failure, but the result embodied a ruinous incoherence. It is not an illogical triumph Browning had to examine, but a justified failure. It was evident that in *Paracelsus* he had explored self-definition superficially and inadequately. Into self-definition as self-deception, into the Will as the source of self-deception he had to burrow more deeply. Only thus could he move toward his as yet unenvisioned goal of epistemology as a personality problem, not a philosophical one.

To push deeper he placed Sordello initially in a more extreme situation than he had Paracelsus. Instead of sending him to school and having him penetrate into the hollowness of received wisdom, he isolated him from the very beginning, half-abandoned, except for some old women, in an old castle. To indicate that his character is to be thought of as at the deepest personality level of creativity, innovation, and emergence, at the heart of the castle he places a fountain which is also the tomb of Sordello's mother, supported by caryatids. Orphaned, neglected by his proper guardian, who has in fact spread the lie that he is but the son of an archer instead of the son of the great warrior Salinguerra, as he really is, he thus is the completely alienated personality whose task is self-creation. His role models for life are not real human beings but figures in tapestries, hunters and warriors. Thus drawing his conception of life from art he does not learn that in life the will is necessarily frustrated and that joy comes from facing that frustration. Rather, after each effort to find a role he is aghast to discover that total fulfillment of the will is impossible.

His two major efforts are in poetry and in politics. Each, especially the latter, spurs him to new self-definitions, and new self-deceptions. Thus the problem Tennyson explored late, the charismatic self, Browning explored early in his career. At the end, faced with the temptation of abandoning one self-definition, the champion of the people, and establishing another, the accomplice with his father in establishing a realm in northern Italy strong enough to be independent of pope, emperor, and people, he finds that his self-fulfillment might be possible were he to accept the role of being the tool of another, were he to abandon both his poetic and his political principles.

Why not? Ordinary men can conceive only of partial fulfillment, and that contents them; but Sordello could conceive of total fulfillment. He can conceive of a complete theodicy, a complete justification of God's ways to man, and grasp the notion that all action, being the incarnate Will of God, is justified. Dostoevsky was to explore the problem of how all is permitted if there is no God. Browning turned in the other direction and raised the problem of what is the appropriate action if one's self-definition and definition of the world is the equivalent of God's. His answer is that if all is permitted, then there is no reason for action and no foundation for choice. And so Sordello dies.

Browning has thus traced the way from complete alienation from one's culture to total transcendence of one's culture. The problem he has emerged with is how one who has achieved culture transcendence is to act. Once the individual achieves that transcendence, the common bases for men's actions have evaporated. Whether there is a God or not, the conceptions available of God are part of the culture transcended. It was to be ten years before Browning, who appeared briefly at the

111

beginning and end of *Sordello*, was to step out once again on his own public stage, his poetry. At Elizabeth's urging he wrote in his own person, and wrote about Christianity. In *Christmas-Eve and Easter-Day* he ended the poem with the equivocal "—and who can say?" He reappeared only to disappear more thoroughly than ever—and for good reason. To believe in God means that as the explanations and justifications for action crumble away there is an ultimate ground for action to which one can retreat. Language functions by controlling action, and ultimate verbal explanations, such as a propositional affirmation of God, control our behavior only by affirming that we shall act. All mythologies, including the Christian, provide an ultimate reason for acting. By expelling Adam and Eve from Paradise God forced them to act. Through Sordello Browning had arrived at a position in which he neither believed in God nor disbelieved. Thus there were no grounds for action, but also no grounds for not acting.

It is not surprising that he should have adopted another mode of interpreting the term "acting," not mere behaving but acting in the theatrical sense. He had already made one effort to write for the stage in *Strafford*. The results were indecisive. It had a short run and was revived once a few months later, but then disappeared. Still, it had not been an entire failure; there was enough success to urge him to try again. He spent five years trying, and then gave up, after six plays for the theater, though one was clearly designed for the kind of theater that did not then exist. It was not to come into existence until the appearance of Bernard Shaw. The theater was a great attraction to Browning, and he did not give up easily. The reasons for his persistence are complex. Some reminded him too strongly of the relation of personality to knowledge. He began to suffer extreme headaches and, as he later told Elizabeth, the deepest recesses of his feeling about himself were such that he could define himself only in terms of coldness, of ice. From *Sordello* he had learned that to live meant to act. The form of his action was no problem—poetry; but the direction in which his poetry was to move, what he was to say, was another matter entirely. He needed both a justification for action and a theme for his poetry.

He needed a way back into society, and into his culture, while simultaneously maintaining his transcendence of that society and culture. The 1830's saw a good many individuals, some of them thinkers of remarkable power, who thought the way back into society was the development, in a condition of culture transcendence, of principles which, if successfully introduced into the society, would totally redeem it. For a time it was Sordello's dream, but it turned out to be another self-deceiving mode of self-definition which had to be discarded. To reenter society by totally redeeming it was something even Carlyle toyed with, and Balzac, and later on, Wagner, but at the time the most notable vision of totally redeeming society was Marx's, the only one that has survived as an active cultural and social force.

Marx saw the worker as alienated, and as the man who could take over society and redeem it. The pattern of this stage of Romanticism suggests—indeed affirms—that the worker was but a surrogate for Marx himself, a mode of self-definition such that the alienated and culturally transcendent individual might be incarnate, like Christ, in the body of the proletariat and so redeem the world. Browning, who was beginning to see more and more clearly the relation between knowledge and personality, could envision no such solution, for he was aware through *Sordello*, though invertedly, that any redeeming notion, like satire, to be possible, let alone effective, must derive its values from the culture it has rejected and proposes to penetrate and redeem. From Feuerbach Marx had grasped the notion that every man is the incarnate Christ, and this was the bridge of self-definition between himself and the proletariat. Sordello,

113

Browning wrote, needed a force more powerful than himself, but which could in no way be a rival. His theodicy identified himself with God, just as Marx's did, which also sought a justification for action that is the Christian pattern of redemption. For Browning a direct mode of action was impossible, for like Marx's it would have had to be derived from the culture it had transcended.

Indirect action was the only possible answer. Through *Sordello* Browning had learned that the reverse of the coin of totality is nothingness; to explain everything is to explain too much; a valid explanation must be partial. But any valid explanation he might arrive at—and the notion that there is a God and the notion that there is not are both invalid, since they are total —could only be derived from the culture. It would then be ineffective action since it would reinforce attitudes already available in the culture. The theater was the perfect mode of action, since it was, as it was then understood, necessarily indirect, and in Shakespeare he had the perfect model of the man who had successfully disappeared behind his work. Such disappearance was, then, possible.

In *Pippa Passes*, his next work after *Sordello*, Browning explored the possibilities of indirect action as a necessary preliminary for attempting to master the theater, which for him, as *Pippa Passes* shows, had become and was to remain for many years the metaphor for his relation to his culture. The actor is the man who knows that he is playing a role, and who knows that the world in which he plays it is a construct, a fiction; and the whole theater emphasizes the point that knowledge and personality are inseparable. That, really, it could be said with some reason, is what the theater is about.

Pippa is a little silk worker in Asolo, a hill town northwest of Venice which Browning had visited when he went to Italy to orient himself to Italian geography, landscape, and culture that he might complete *Sordello*. On her one holiday of the year Pippa wanders around Asolo and some miles off to another little town, envying, she says, the happiest people and hoping to infect herself with some of their happiness by sauntering in front of their houses and singing. Her songs have an extraordinary effect. It is not that they impel the people who hear them to wise or unwise, to good or bad, decisions, but rather that each song is interpreted in a way inseparable from the problem which they are involved in, a problem which has reduced them to inaction, since the alternatives are such that they can choose neither, or since no alternatives seem available.

It is instructive to think of those innumerable people in our own culture who, like Paracelsus, cannot act until they read their horoscope in the morning paper, or those worse off who cannot make any decision without consulting their personal astrologer—or psychiatrist; it makes little difference. It is possibly not inappropriate to remark that the theatrical professions include far more than their proper share of such people. It makes no difference, really, what the newspaper or the consulting astrologer suggests; it is always excellent advice, no matter when you were born. The real function of such astrology is to get people moving, and how they interpret the advice makes little difference, for the interpretation is governed by their own conception of their interests. Such is the effect of Pippa's songs on her listeners. She is a catalyst for action, though not for any particular kind of action.

Thus Browning worked out his relation to his culture. At the end of *The Ring and the Book* he says as much. Art is blessedly irresponsible; it does not and cannot, insofar as it is true art, give specific instructions for behavior. It can only incite to action by presenting vividly in the form of a thoroughly explored example of action the irrational conviction that wise and good action is possible. It is up to the perceiver of the work of art to interpret it according to his own interests, his own personality, his own mode of self-definition. From this time forward, with the exception already noted, Browning conceals himself. He is always behind the scenes, pushing his actors out on the stage, but in fact each of his actors is himself, acting indirectly, or the whole work is himself, acting indirectly. For Browning the theater was the mode of action in which he could act without acting, in which he could play a role in the culture without reinforcing any of that culture's values, in which he could contribute indirectly and unknowingly to his culture by showing the moment of decision, the moment of illumination, the moment of action, the moment in which the masks of self-deception briefly evaporate, the moment in which, therefore, a new mode of self-conception can be forged, deceiving to be sure, but less deceiving, truer to the actual needs of the man in the situation, than the previous one.

The moment of illumination is like the moment in which a man's heart skips a beat and for the first time his own death becomes something to be believed in, when that faith in one's own immortality which sustains most people until their late forties evaporates, and the knowledge of death is upon them. And he could also act indirectly by showing how people miss such moments, how they use events which should have illuminated them merely to confirm and reinforce their self-conceptions. This is the failure of the duke in the most famous of Browning's dramatic monologues, "My Last Duchess." He is appalled because he has missed the opportunity to abandon his self-conception and penetrate at least part way into his self-deception.

From this time forward Browning himself starts living that peculiar mode of life, the surface of which was only rarely interrupted, which led him later to take pleasure in being mistaken for a retired well-to-do and successful businessman, which permitted him to let Mrs. Orr's blunders go uncorrected, which inspired him to explanations of his poems as equivocal as the poems themselves, and which permitted him to attend meetings of the Browning society and listen to fantastic distortions of his work with the utmost blandness. Just as the theater had become his metaphor for the world, now the world became a kind of metaphor for the theater. Between the theater and the world he made no observable distinction. Even before he gave up the attempt to write for the stage he had perfected a device first tried long since—the dramatic monologue. It is Browning's substitute for the theater. He could perfect it because he defined himself as actor, and the heart of the dramatic monologue is that the reader perceives the speaker as actor, self-conceived, self-defined, and self-deceived. One feels that each speaker is but a mask for Robert Browning, even though his attitudes and values cannot be identified with Browning's, since what they were no one knew and we are still uncertain. The reason for the feeling that Browning is the real speaker is that in the dramatic monologues every man is revealed as a poet, one who invents himself. Only a poet, one thinks, can have thought of such a personality, and so the speaker must be a mask for Browning. But no, that is not the case. It is the case, however, that every man in inventing himself is as much a poet as any man who writes "poetry."

It is this sense of the speaker's self-invention and the connected sense of the speaker's knowledge and interpretation of the situation in which he is presented as being in the service of that self-invention, which is so disturbing about the dramatic monologue, which makes one so eager to search the poem with the utmost care to find what the truth of the matter is, and which makes critics so passionate in disagreeing with each other about what that truth is. But the monologues themselves always survive triumphantly this critical battering. They are, in Oscar Wilde's famous phrase, truly sphinxes without secrets, for the secret of the Browning dramatic monologues is that there is no secret. Behind the speaker is everything, and nothing.

Henceforth in public Browning himself becomes a dramatic monologist, even, I feel strongly, in the famous courtship of Elizabeth Barrett. The style of his contribution to the famous letters is uncomfortably like the style of the poems, particularly *Sordello*. It is not that he was insincere or that, in time, he did not come to love her very much. It is rather that he had seen that sincerity is possible only when one is playing a role, that insincerity is the only sincerity, because insincerity is the only possible basis for action. The sensation of insincerity arises, at least in Browning's life and in his poems, not from the perception that men are not what they seem to be, but rather from the feeling that they are only what they seem to be; beyond that they are nothing. The mask is human existence; hence men's fascination with masks, which goes back so many years that it seems that the invention of the mask must be coeval with the inception of human self-definition.

Browning's apparent position is that man is an animal who has invented himself, and his inventions are always threatening to dissolve into thin air. "We are such stuff as dreams are made on." Browning's insight was remarkably like Carlyle's that it is not that we wear clothes, we *are* clothes, and Carlyle very well may have influenced his thinking. But his conclusions are even more devastating than Carlyle's, for Carlyle had never seen that epistemology is a function of personality.

So far had Browning come in his grasp of the irresolvable tension between subject and object. Through volume after volume, with the dramatic monologue as his tool, he explored the way men interpret their experiences to confirm or to abandon their self-definitions. This was the source of his astounding psychological penetration, and the explanation of why his villains are as convincing as his good men and why both use the same mode of interpreting their worlds.

There remained, however, a conundrum. What was his own relationship to the speaker–plus–situation constellation of the dramatic monologue? If every man is a poet, both in his self-conception and in his conception of the situation with which he is interacting, then every man is invented and every situation is invented. In both the material is the same, what the man observes in his own behavior and what he observes in his situation, but those observations are in the service of his self-deception. What is the difference between the experienced situation and the imagined situation of literature if both are invented? The only difference—that in the experienced situation a man must act in his own interests but that in the imagined he need not act at all—Browning had already grasped. Thus the difference between experienced situation and imagined situation breaks down. Both, in Carlyle's terminology, are symbols, which is why *Sartor Resartus* is at once a novel and not a novel, a reliable autobiography and an unreliable metaphor for an autobiography. Moreover, once the distinction between experienced situation and imagined situation is obliterated, then the relation between a real man and an experienced situation, and between an imagined man and an imagined situation, which are identical, must imply that the same pattern applies to the poet and his dramatic monologue.

The monologues Browning had so far written had implied that he offered the truth of an imagined situation, and the further implication was that it was therefore possible to utter the truth about an experienced situation. But this was not the direction in which Browning was moving or needed to move. *Sordello* had left a problem unresolved. Sordello became morally omniscient, and thus unable to act. In that poem Browning had given in his own words the proper interpretation of Sordello's life. He had presented himself as omniscient in this matter at any rate, and though he had turned from narration to various kinds of drama, for the closet, for the theater, and in the dramatic monologue, he had not yet fully divorced himself from the attitude that he *could* tell the truth about a situation he had after all invented. Clearly some way must be found to compromise the validity, the truthfulness, of an invention. The way he found was extraordinarily ingenious.

He did not find it until after Elizabeth's death, the immediate aftermath of which was so equivocal. The material for *The Ring and the Book*, a collection of documents about a long-forgotten Roman murder, turned up in the flea market of Florence, on the bench which runs on two sides of the Medici-Riccardi palace. Browning discovered the Old Yellow Book, as he called it, before Elizabeth's death. Only after her death did he figure out how to make use of it. In this poem he really does what she had asked him to do and what he did not do in *Christmas-Eve and Easter-Day*. True, he did say, "—and who can say?" thus implying that it was possible to say that much. It was a way of not appearing, but it also indicated that he had not yet fully grasped the irresolvable tension between subject and object. His conclusion implies that the tension could be resolved in an admission of ignorance, but the line of his poetry writing pulled hard against that possibility. Only by compromising the position of the subject can the tension between subject and object be fully brought out and realized. One must grasp that thinking about that tension does not transcend it but is itself part of it and must fully enter into it. But could Browning do that, could he permit himself to do that, so long as Elizabeth was alive? He did not permit himself to attack publicly spiritualism and Napoleon III while she was alive. How could he permit himself to publish something which revealed what would be certain to be interpreted as an assertion that his love for her was self-created for his own purposes and therefore insincere, even though his position implied that insincerity is the only sincerity?

Could he thus wound a woman who had found her only happiness in him? Indeed, could he thus wound himself? Did he dare apply his insight to himself? That he was restless in the last years of her life is unquestionable. She says so in her letters, and is quick to find excuses for him. For a time he gave up poetry and dabbled in sculpture, possibly because he was discouraged at the failure of his poetry to find a public, possibly because he was jealous that hers was finding such a very large public, but also, and with equal possibility, because he could not take the next step in his development, could not perhaps permit himself to realize that it was the next step. At any rate, after her death he was free to return to London, to start raising Pen as a boy and not as a public spectacle, to attack spiritualism and Napoleon III, and to compromise his own powers to make true inventions.

In *The Ring and the Book* there are three novel factors in Browning's poetry. One is that instead of a single dramatic monologue he wrote a series, with one exception spoken by different people about the same situation. This dramatized as never before the different ways individuals interpret situations to maintain their self-definitions, and that this is so has already been pointed out in the above discussion of Guido, who tries two strikingly different self-definitions, only to have them both collapse into nothingness. Pompilia, Guido's wife, and Caponsacchi, her rescuer, are quite different. Looking back over their lives, they see themselves as engaged in a continuous discovery of themselves and their relations to situations. Yet this must not be imagined as the difference between good and bad individuals. Rather, Pompilia and Caponsacchi are at one end of a continuum, and Guido at the other. All the speakers are busy with the same fusing of the sincere and the insincere, since, of course, they have no real choice. But certainly Browning gives the impression that the individual who practices continuous redefinition of himself is the better individual. Even of Browning as speaker is this true, as his continuous redefinitions of the word "truth" imply and reveal. Even of the Pope is this true, for in deciding whether or not to permit Guido to be executed he redefines himself in historical terms; moreover, he is anachronistic about it. His position is that truth wears out, and that Christian truth has in fact worn out; but that his role as a Pope requires him to sustain it, even though he foresees the Enlightenment with uncanny accuracy.

Browning had for many years used historical material, but the use of it in this poem is novel. A particular intellectual development helped him to solve the problem of how to write the poem, but also stimulated him to deny the claims of that innovation. It was a new concept of historiography, documentary or scientific historiography, developed in Germany by Leopold von Ranke and introduced into England in the course of the 1840's and 1850's. It was the emergence of modern historiography, with its claims to be objective, though to be sure not all historians would make such claims. The difference between this and the older historiography was that instead of depending upon published accounts of events, other histories, the historian went to unpublished documents. One result was that the immense treasures of the European archives, hitherto closed, partly because nobody wanted to examine them, began to be examined, classified, indexed, published, and made available to scholars and historians. This was exactly what Browning needed to help him grasp how to handle the miscellaneous materials in the Old Yellow Book, which ranged from depositions of witnesses to legal briefs to contemporary pamphlets and private letters.

However, his use of the new historiography was peculiar. Instead of attempting to reconcile various accounts of the same event, he had each speaker present accounts which in part coincided and in part did not. The question he raised was whether or not the new historiographer was or could be correct in affirming that reconciliation of differing accounts meant that the past even had a real existence which could be recovered. Each of Browning's speakers distorts, but what does he distort? This has led to a common misapprehension of what Browning was up to in this poem. Critics who have discussed it have themselves been products of modern historiography; they have diligently compared the material in the Old Yellow Book, which has several times been translated, to find if Browning really did discover the truth of the matter. They assume that such was his claim. But that was not his claim at all.

The new historiography with its claim to scientific knowledge and objectivity was a direct challenge to Browning's position. If its claims could be substantiated, it would mean that his conception of the relation of individual to situation was in error. He saw the new historiography as an epistemological position which asserted that the individual could transcend his personality in his search for truth and which also asserted that historical truth could indeed be found. As one who had himself for many years been using historical material for his writing he was bound to react vigorously to the new historiography and its challenging epistemological claim. *The Ring and the Book* became a kind of casebook of what the historian does with historical documents. The work implied that the new historians were not doing what they thought they were doing, but were in fact doing something quite different. Furthermore, it was, I think, this challenge from professional history that precipitated his solution to his inadequate grasp of the tension between subject and object and gave him a way to compromise his position.

The major clue lies in the metaphor of the ring, with which he begins the poem. An elaborate and elaborately developed figure, it can be reduced to its essentials. A gold ring cannot be carved unless it is mixed with alloy to harden it into a shape-holding substance. Then it can be carved and a squirt of acid can restore *on the surface* of the ring pure gold; yet it continues to be held in shape by the alloy beneath that surface. An individual, then, the subject in any subject-object relationship— that is, all relationships—cannot structure the object, or the situation, without adding to it something which is not derived from it. Only that addition makes it possible for him to shape the situation into a meaningful and satisfactory pattern or structure.

Thus, after many years of concealment, Browning once again emerges on his own stage, but as an actor. There are in the poem two Robert Brownings. One is the speaker of the first book and the epilogue to the last. This Browning pretends that each of the monologists speaks for himself. But there is another Robert Browning, the author of the work; and his relation to Robert Browning the speaker is identical with his relation to the other monologists. Thus all the monologists, including Robert Browning the speaker, are creations of Browning the author. Consequently just as their interests, their self-definitions, the alloy they have furnished to their situation, controls the way they structure and make meaningful the interaction of themselves with their situation, so the alloy Browning the author was furnished controls his construction of the way his speakers control their constructions.

This is the way, he implies, the historian really proceeds, and his claims to scientific objectivity, to discovering the truth, are invalid. What Browning is saying is that historians are mistaken when they believe they have discovered the truth of a past event because they have created a coherent and consistent structure out of disparate accounts. It is their own interests, their own alloy, that makes that structure possible. The relation of Browning the author to his creatures, including Browning the speaker, is that of any historian to the figures and events out of the past he gives shape and meaning to. Thus he has shown himself defining himself, creating himself, has introduced himself, at last, on his own stage as an actor, as a wearer of a mask with nothing behind it except another mask, and has grasped the truly irresolvable nature of the tension between subject and object. There is no doubt that he believes he has found the truth of the story, the answer to the only real problem in it: Was Pompilia guilty of adultery with Caponsacchi? His answer is no, yet so well had he worked that Carlyle, for example, said that it was obvious she was guilty. The argument over whether Browning had found the "truth" of the matter, which has gone on for a hundred years, is quite beside the point, as so much of Browning criticism is beside the point. He does not assert that he has found what the truth really is, or even what it was, but only that he has found a "truth" which is satisfactory to *him.*

It is probably only the immense bulk of *The Ring and the Book* and its preternatural complexity and multiplicity of fact and incident that has prevented this implication of Browning's from being obvious. Certainly he did his best, within the limits of his cryptic ambiguous stance, to bring it out. "I have found the truth," he says in almost so many words, "but who am I?" Well, he tells us who he is. I have suggested that he was stuck with the legend of his own love affair and marriage. The sentimental public was enchanted with the notion of two *poets* loving one another and marrying; but it does both partners a great deal of credit, writers being what they are, that both were able to continue their independent courses in spite of their marriage. Very well, then, he was stuck with it; and in that case he might as well make use of it.

The parallel between Caponsacchi's rescue of Pompilia from familial oppression, and Browning's rescue of Elizabeth from the same kind of oppression can scarcely be missed, and few have ever missed it. And to underline it, he has Browning the speaker address Elizabeth in the famous conclusion to Book I, "O lyric love, half angel and half bird /And all a wonder and a wild desire," lines which he echoes at the very end of the poem. It would be difficult to imply more forcefully that his own interests were so deeply engaged in the story of Guido, Caponsacchi, and Pompilia that he *had* to judge Guido as guilty of tyranny and Caponsacchi amd Pompilia as innocent of any wrongdoing.

Long before he met Elizabeth, long before he eloped with

her, Browning had conceived an intense affection for the story of Perseus and Andromeda, and above his desk he kept a picture of Perseus's rescue of Andromeda from the sea monster. It seems fairly obvious that his interest in Elizabeth was that her position made it possible for him to assume the role of Perseus, to act a role and know that he was acting a role, and equally obvious that his having done so accounted for his fascination by the tragic story of Pompilia, whose rescue by Caponsacchi was pointless, since she was killed, just as Elizabeth died too. Furthermore, in the 1830's, as we have seen, the redemptive theme was paramount in more recently emerging levels of Romantic culture. *Sordello* is about the necessary failure of redemptive ambitions, and *The Ring and the Book* is the explanation of why that failure is necessary. To redeem a situation one must transcend one's personality, and that we cannot do, for personality is the foundation and the determinant of knowledge, of one's conception of truth. Objectivity is, then, impossible, but subjectivity is an illusion.

Henceforth Browning was free to return to his *Sordello* style, that style of such difficulty, irony, and perplexity that his later work has always been neglected. And now comes his great remark that his style was difficult in order to warn off his grounds people who did not belong there. The simplification of the *Sordello* style which he undertook beginning with *Pippa Passes* was not merely a matter of trying to find a wider audience, or to capture again and extend the audience which had responded enthusiastically to *Paracelsus.* Rather, his simplification was the consequence of still *wanting* to have an audience. Not yet having grasped in its full desolation the tension between subject and object, he had not yet achieved cultural transcendence in its full exalting deprivation. With *The Ring and the Book* he had.

With that work, between himself and the public he created the barrier of bulk. Beginning with *Prince Hohenstiel-Schwan-*

gau, published in 1871, three years after *The Ring and the Book,* he created the barrier of syntactical and intellectual difficulty, as well as the barrier of his Balzacian poems, stories peculiarly disagreeable and unpalatable, several of them based on fact. Henceforth also the extreme disparity between his public role and his private increased until Henry James could explain it only by proposing two Brownings, and after all in *The Ring and the Book* there are two Brownings. He created a body of work of immense difficulty and of an intellectual tenor that has striking resemblances both to his contemporary Nietzsche and a man whom Nietzsche had a deep effect upon, Wittgenstein.

The culminating monument of this final period of Browning's poetic life was *Parleyings with Certain People of Importance in Their Day,* published in 1887. This is his subtlest and most penetrating examination of the identity of personality and knowledge, of the irresolvable interpenetration of the mask and the truth. One of his four greatest works and intellectually certainly his greatest, this has been neglected as an incomprehensible puzzle, except for one completely mistaken effort. It still is neglected, and it will probably continue to be.

Yet as the modern world begins to comprehend what Browning grasped in the Victorian period, there will be more readers for the later work, especially the *Parleyings.* For what he seized upon was the conundrum of culture transcendence: to achieve culture transcendence is to abandon the foundation for action. To be sure, this is not entirely true. The ordinary habits generally remain, eating, sleeping, even making love, though that frequently suffers. One dresses, one behaves in public, according to the standards of one's culture, or in the Bohemian fashion, by inverting those standards. Between the two there is little difference, just as to assert that it is true that there is no God is very much the same kind of behavior as to assert that there is. What culture transcendence involves, at least at the beginning, is the explanatory end of the continuum of human behavior. As explanations of man's place in the world become increasingly untenable, as one position after another is surrendered, the individual can and often does suffer an attrition of behavioral resources, a kind of psychic suicide. The total disappearance of explanation means that there is no justification for decisions and no grounds for choosing between alternatives. Choice, as Browning showed many times, becomes possible only from what survives, an impulse, an instinct perhaps, to ascribe value to existence. This is what he meant by love. But even that can go.

Browning's solution for maintaining activity was to conceive the world as a theater and himself as an actor in it, but no more committed to its reality and its explanations for that invented reality than an actor is committed to believing that the stage he performs on is a real world. Browning accepted completely as the only possible metaphor for human behavior the metaphor of the role. He retained from his culture external habits, which he performed as one playing the role of actor, and the role of poet. But once he had grasped his problem thoroughly he played that in a way virtually incomprehensible to his culture; he had taken indirection almost to its vanishing point.

Browning, like Hegel, saw culture as a structure and a force that contains within itself inherent contradictions and confusions. The only way to escape those contradictions is to transcend them, that is, to transcend the culture. But unlike Hegel he conceived the real not as the rational but as the personal. There was no unquestioned assumption that new culture necessarily emerges from the old. Perhaps he did not go so far as Hegel, nor as Carlyle with his organic filaments weaving themselves toward a new culture. Yet perhaps he went farther. To detach oneself from one's culture can be to detach oneself from the notion of successive stages of culture transcendence, for that notion emerges from one's culture. If, as he implies at the end of *Parleyings*, the invention of printing may have been a disaster, it is because the facile dissemination of "truths" only means a delta-like spread in the interpretation of those "truths." Literacy means either cultural dissolution or an escape from that dissolution into the trivial. No one, it seems to me, has penetrated so deeply into the dilemma of culture transcendence as Robert Browning. It remains a dilemma.

4

The Uses of
the Unfashionable

I N THE mid-1950's abstract expressionism was at its apogee. It had survived ridicule and adulation and had become an established style. It had achieved worldwide acceptance and success; the prices of abstract expressionist canvases were staggering. Possibly it was so widely acclaimed because in that dull period there was nothing else of excitement going on. Its imperial reign was not, of course, to last more than a few more years, and terrible things began to happen to art in the early 1960's. In the meantime a few observers of the art scene predicted that there would shortly be a revival—another revival—of the later works of Turner. The prediction was verified—in 1966 the Museum of Modern Art held a magnificent show of late Turners. It marked the formal interment of abstract expressionism. A similar revival had occurred when impressionism in France had already been superseded and was about to be abandoned by the avant garde even in England.

More than anything else the history of taste exhibits how we use history for our own purposes. Taste in painting is a particularly admirable instance of T. S. Eliot's famous remark about how Milton influences Sophocles. A new style appears. It develops something that was always there but had not been noticed, or if noticed had not been valued. Suddenly those painters of the past who had been half forgotten, like El Greco, or who entered that Valhalla of monumental bores, like Poussin, are seen to have been doing something of great interest. When the art lover had learned to respond with some adequacy to the post-impressionists and the early expressionists, El Greco suddenly became a great painter, because he had done what new and revolutionary artists were doing. When the art lover had become used to cubism, he suddenly saw the cubistic character of Poussin, particularly those landscapes in which great fragments of architecture were mingled with the vegetation. Nevertheless his love of cubism and Cézanne and Poussin has not made him able to respond with anything but dislike to certain paintings of Burne-Jones such as "King Cophetua and the Beggar Maid" and "The Golden Stair," though this last may very well have been the inspiration for Duchamp's "Nude Descending a Staircase."

In all three paintings, as well as in the classic phase of cubism and in the mature paintings of Cézanne, is to be found a dense interlocking and shingle-like overlapping of small configurations, each implying a rectangle. In all three paintings the tall narrow shape is exploited, a device that emphasizes the formal excitement of these rectangles, which seem to be bursting out of the frame. The mocking title of Duchamp's masterpiece, "Explosion in a Shingle Factory," like so many attempts to denigrate, is a perfectly accurate and instructive response to what Duchamp had done, and the phrase could be applied to these works of Burne-Jones almost as well. Duchamp's work, like the classical phase of cubism, were comments on Cézanne's maturity, and after them it was easier to understand what Cézanne was up to. Yet there has been no revival of Burne-Jones.

The phenomenon of how a new source of visual gratification

restructures one's perceptual processes is itself an instance of the irresolvable tension between subject and object which Tennyson, Carlyle, and Browning so struggled to grasp. An experience of my own is a perfect instance. In 1957 I went to an exhibition in Holland Park in London, "Sculpture, 1857-1957." A cluster of recent works by British sculptors was displayed in the park, and in greenhouses were various Victorian pieces of the 1850's. As I came into the park I saw the trees in an impressionist manner, as masses of green light and shade. The recent sculptures I examined first, since they were on the way to the greenhouses. Many of them were the then novel welded sculptures, spiky and transparent. Instead of by solid sculptural mass the three-dimensional configuration was implied by the ends of spikes or stalks, generally radiating from a center or several centers. I was sufficiently familiar with the style to respond readily and with pleasure. I then turned back to the park itself. It now wore a wholly different aspect. The trees were no longer solid impressionist masses but transparent abstract expressionist sculpture, the mass defined by the ends of the limbs and branches radiating from a center, and the whole perceived as a half-confusing tangle of sticks going every which way, exactly like a number of the sculptures I had just seen. A more perfect instance of Wilde's aphorism that nature imitates art would be impossible to imagine.

My experience is a paradigm of the history of taste. An emergent style restructures one's perceptual process so that the values of that new style are now perceived in works of the past. Just as Browning used the material in the Old Yellow Book for his own novel purposes, so did I use the trees in Holland Park for my own novel purposes. In truth there is no past, at least no experienced past. Those artifacts and documents which are alleged to have been created in the past are after all actually encountered in the present. No matter when they originated, they are coeval with us; they move through time as we move through time; and they change. We pick them up, and then abandon them, as our adaptational strategies shift and as our modes of self-definition are redirected. And our critical pronouncements that purport to state which old works of art are good or bad are merely our justifications and explanations for our interests.

There is yet another reason why Romanticism was so interested in the possibilities of plunging into history as a strategy for achieving cultural transcendence. The revival of Turner, like the revival of El Greco, was but another instance of the numerous revivals in architecture, painting, furnishings, and costume, as well as literature, which began with the revival of Gothic architecture in the early nineteenth century, an event that was coincident with the revival of classic architecture, and of classicism in general, as in the poetry of Keats and later of Tennyson. It was not that the eighteenth and earlier centuries were ignorant of these artistic modes, nor even, by the mid-century, that advanced taste continued to denigrate the Gothic. Rather, the eighteenth-century Gothic revival was fused with the current rococo taste, just as Chinese decoration was, while the classicism was the continuation of the Renaissance tradition. The men of the eighteenth century used styles distant in time and space to confirm their perceptions, their sensibilities, their taste. The Romantics used the same styles to explode current taste, to mark their alienation, to get outside of and above their culture.

From the world around us we may for three purposes select artifacts and documents which originated in the past. One is to confirm our taste. Thus a great many people whose musical taste was formed in the Age of Eisenhower, which now seems almost blissfully, almost intoxicatingly dull, are devoted to the work of the lesser baroque masters, such as Vivaldi. To them the music of Schumann, for example, is schmaltzy, and is to be rejected. A second purpose is accomplished if we are among those whose artistic life finds its excitement in always being au courant with the latest emergent style. This is why one could predict in 1955 that there would shortly be a Turner revival. Both of these purposes reinforce one's taste, the only difference being whether one likes a stable taste or a fluid. Neither of these modes of taste, then, can be said to be anything but completely tied into the culture as it currently exists. One group finds its needed stability in Vivaldi; the other group finds its needed innovation in the latest electronic music. Both stability and innovation of this sort, however, fit firmly and neatly in the existing cultural pattern. From the point of view of the Romantic seeking to solve the problem of alienation by achieving some kind of culture transcendence both groups are victims of their culture.

There remains the third way of using the art that originated in the past. The first two groups simply respond to the approved taste of their times. The Romantic manages his taste. He uses it to escape the conditioned response to his culture. His anathema is fashion, and from his point of view the stable lover of Vivaldi and the novelty-seeking lover of the latest electronic music are as much fashion mongers as the adolescent who, five years ago, loved the Beatles. Burne-Jones is now unfashionable; it is impossible, therefore, for the people of either stable or novel tastes to see that in some of his paintings he was doing things with an extraordinary similarity to what Cézanne, classic cubism, and Duchamp did.

This is the kind of phenomenon the Romantic of the nineteenth century wanted to be able to observe and to respond to. His interest was not in art. To him art was redemptive, and such a man is not interested in art for its own sake. He has ulterior purposes. Even when he uttered his great battle cry of "Art for art's sake," he meant something quite different. He meant that art was important because it could do for the individual what nothing else could do; only unfashionable art, whether of the past or newly created, could help the Romantic break through the bonds of the conditioned response to the taste of his own time. The purpose was not to enjoy a new kind of art, but to break through the bonds, not because the fashionable art offered no artistic gratification, but because those bonds were woven of, to use Carlyle's phrase, the organic filaments of his culture. The effect on the culture has been that every school of art that has ever existed in the world's history is now accessible to the cultivated individual—except most of the art of the nineteenth century.

From that vast mass a single strand has been selected, that which led from Constable through Delacroix and the Barbizon school to the impressionists, the post-impressionists, and the moderns. The rest is for the most part literally invisible. It is not merely that it is difficult to respond to it. Most of it cannot be seen at all, for it is in storerooms, in cellars, packed away, neglected and forgotten. The Fogg Art Museum at Harvard has a splendid collection of Pre-Raphaelites, and if you want to see it, you can. But you have to know it is there, and when you do see it, you find that the paintings are hung from floor to ceiling on sliding racks that pull out from the wall. Unless things have changed since my last visit, nowhere else in the museum is there the faintest hint that it owns such a collection. However, the curators are kind; they are familiar with the art world, they know it is full of crazy people, and if you want to see their Pre-Raphaelites, you may, under circumstances abysmally unsatisfactory for looking at pictures.

Elsewhere in the world it is mostly only in provincial museums, or in dark out-of-the-way galleries of a few major institutions, that you can see unfashionable nineteenth-century paintings, and then only if a modern-minded museum director has not swept and garnished his museum to appeal to the taste-

135

ful young. Nineteenth-century art is an immense undiscovered continent; even the architecture is being destroyed faster than accurate records can be made.

The Pre-Raphaelites of the 1850's, the subject of this essay, are thus interesting for two reasons. On the one hand they present a fascinating instance of a deliberately planned effort to break the bonds of current fashionable taste, to use painting to achieve cultural transcendence; on the other, since even the kindest words said for them are grudging and patronizing, they offer the opportunity to transcend the fashions in painting of today. What were they trying to do, and why? And is the present state of culture such that they can once again be used? These are the questions to be explored.

To be sure, it is no longer quite true that the Pre-Raphaelites are entirely scorned. In the spring of 1968 a show of what was called Romantic Art was sent from England to the United States. Actually, a good part of it was not Romantic, but the highly emotional art of the late eighteenth-century, the equivalent of the Gothic novel; nevertheless it did include a number of Pre-Raphaelite paintings of the early 1850's. Auction prices for the Pre-Raphaelites are going up, and here and there a few people are beginning to collect them. This must not be construed as proof that the character of what they did is being recognized. One of the best hedges against inflation, of course, is paintings, and the crisis in the English pound has meant a flight of capital into paintings.

In the years after the war the prices for impressionist paintings rose extraordinarily. The problem for those who wished to buy paintings as an investment is that most of the great masterpieces are now in museums, and the financial future of twentieth-century art is a little uncertain, particularly since great stocks of paintings by Picasso and Matisse have been kept off the market by the painters themselves, as investments. Since there were few reliable old masters left, the best bet seemed to be impressionist paintings. The prices of these are now so high that less affluent collectors are turning to other nineteenth-century paintings, and indeed will buy almost anything in their desperation. Much of the interest in the Pre-Raphaelites derives from the highly speculative art market and has nothing at all to do with whether the investor has any comprehension or particular interest, even, in the paintings and the painters themselves.

Another source of interest in them comes from the general and increasing interest in anything Victorian, particularly anything that can be collected, from buttons to sculpture. Good eighteenth-century furniture, for example, is something only the wealthiest collectors can indulge in. For the less wealthy, Victoriana is the solution; and again almost anything is collected by somebody. Fifteen years ago late Victorian dishes were easy to find and cheap; now they are hard to find and expensive. Unless one is very wealthy, to collect anything before the nineteenth century is becoming almost impossible. At the same time vast new numbers of collectors, a class of people who never before collected anything old, are invading the market. The phenomenon is worth speculating on, for it can easily be mistaken for a genuine and serious interest in nineteenth-century culture.

It is said by Freudians that compulsive collecting is a mark of anality, but it is a little difficult to see how it could be that within the past couple of years there should have been such a striking increase in the anal population. It has also been proposed that collecting is a status-seeking activity, and no doubt there is some validity here. Collecting was the mark of the old aristocracy, and as a wealthy high bourgeoisie developed, in the seventeenth-century Netherlands, for instance, collecting paintings was for this class an imitation of the aristocracy. The

137

lesser aristocracy in Germany also started collecting at about the same time; and late in the eighteenth century Catherine the Great, an arriviste among the royalty of Europe, accumulated great numbers of paintings. Some of them, to be sure, were very fine, and among the very best of these are those now in the National Gallery of Art, purchased by Andrew Mellon when the Soviet government needed gold.

Nevertheless, a great many are the sort of thing collected by the minor German aristocracy, from which Catherine had, almost literally, sprung. They were seventeenth-century Dutch paintings. The spread of collecting in the Netherlands had inevitably led to an increase in the number of painters, and it was not long before this lesser industry had developed an exportable surplus. When one explores minor German galleries, now nationalized, but once the property of the German princelings, one discovers thousands of seventeenth-century Dutch paintings. It was an admirable school, but it is possible to get more than a little weary of it. In the late eighteenth century and well into the nineteenth, as late as Ruskin, English connoisseurs sneered at seventeenth-century Dutch paintings. Surely one of the reasons was that there were so many. What wealthy family in Europe did not have some?

The same phenomenon is now occurring in this country and in Europe. Victoriana is the vastest market for the collector there is, simply because the population of Europe quadrupled in the nineteenth century and because there was an even more rapid rise in the number of individuals who could afford good handmade furniture, dishes, silverware, and of course paintings. The Pre-Raphaelites at first achieved a moderate success, then met violent opposition. In a couple of art seasons this had been overcome, partly with the help of Ruskin, but mostly because there were more people who wanted to buy paintings. The situation in the early 1850's was a little like the situation today. About 1840 the increase in numbers of the well-to-do began to

138

have an important effect on the art market, and the numbers of young men who decided to become artists rapidly increased, just as a great many older artists who had spent their lives in difficult circumstances suddenly found themselves well off and able "to put something aside," that is, able to invest in an expanding economy. Today the only barrier for the young artist is the publicity barrier. If he can break that he can sell anything, including pieces of string tacked to the wall to make space sculptures. Contemporary mini-artists can raid the nursery with impunity and sell at handsome prices the spoils of their invasions.

The brief economic struggle of the Pre-Raphaelites was followed by a period of success for almost all of them who stayed with it. By the late 1850's Rossetti always had more commissions than he could, or at least wanted to bother, to execute. Consequently, like his seventeenth-century Dutch predecessors, he went in for replicas, copies painted by the man who painted the original—more or less. As Browning liked to point out, nothing fails like success, and if the later work of the Pre-Raphaelites is less interesting than their first and revolutionary efforts, it was because, like the Dutch of the seventeenth century, like the impressionists in their later period, and like almost all artists today, they were painting to be collected; they were supplying artifacts to meet a demand. If your style is such, as with Picasso and Matisse, that you can paint faster than the market can absorb your work without depressing your prices, you simply keep much of your output off the market, just as one famous art concern kept a great hoard of Renoirs off the market for years, for exactly the same purpose.

This is certainly one reason why the later work of the Pre-Raphaelites deteriorated, or at least why their aims changed. Their original aims required them to spend such a long time at a painting that even a successful artist could not make a living with such a low productivity. Several of Millais's canvases in the early 1850's show one way the problem could be met, if not solved; and one could predict from this that Millais would be both the first to take advantage of the rising market and the most successful of them all. "The Return of the Dove to the Ark" (1851) and the immensely popular "The Order of Release" (1853) are alike in that the scenes are set in virtual darkness in the interior of the ark and in the interior of a prison. This meant that large areas of the canvas could simply be covered in a more or less uniform blackness; the device cut down considerably the amount of time necessary for execution. Millais was particularly fond of scenes which provided an excuse for such relatively unworked areas, and it is not difficult to imagine why. He moved in fame and popularity faster than his fellow Pre-Raphaelites because he could usually offer two, three, or four paintings at each annual Academy show, while the others would have but one. He hedged his bets.

There is very little question that painting in the nineteenth century successfully shifted in England and France from commissions to entrepreneurism in a free market, and the Pre-Raphaelites' participation in this process was one of the important ingredients in their success. Rossetti discovered, for example, that there was a market for the highly finished and closely detailed watercolor, frequently of scenes from literature and legend. These did not require nearly the time to execute as a large canvas, finished to Royal Academy standards, which Millais could do so easily. Rossetti's discovery was fortunate, for his finest work is, generally speaking, in these watercolors. In later years he took to painting large canvases of extremely beautiful women, all of the voluptuous Pre-Raphaelite type which he made famous and which most people tend to identify with the school. This style has nothing to do with what he and the others were doing in the 1850's, and it is of these later paintings that he did not hesitate to make replicas. Some of his remarks suggest that he came to think of his artistic career as more of a business than anything else. At any rate he made quite a lot of money at it.

The general rise in wealth and the spread of wealth among large numbers of people meant that the achievement of status by collecting expensive works of art and thus imitating a very old tradition of the aristocracy was available to greater numbers than ever before, and this mania for collecting works of art— including Victorian buttons and Christmas cards—has spread steadily downward in the culture as affluence has increased. It is a sociological phenomeon of great interest, and it has much to do with the current art situation in which each season must see some radical new direction in art, some new ideas, some new style; nor is one sensation per season any longer enough to satisfy the market. Even the Museum of Modern Art, which for a while attempted to ride the storm and control it—to the ne-glect, according to some, of its proper role—has now been out-paced. The new styles now come so fast that the old days of pop art seem a stable period of the leisurely bloom of a classic style.

Browning, with his usual acuteness, caught the movement in its early phases, and in "My Last Duchess" gave the most per-fect portrait of the collector. He saw the link between the rejec-tion of a duchess who was too familiar for the duke's taste and the interests of the aristocratic sixteenth-century collector. The self-conception of the duke was not reinforced by the behavior of the duchess, though it was by the statue "which Claus of Innsbruck cast in bronze for me." So a modern collector will reject an art nouveau vase because it does not come up to his standards, or because it was not made by one of the manufactur-ers of the ware he specializes in.

The connection between such a man and the duke is subtle but decisive. Such matters as status are relatively superficial by comparison, nor is it merely a matter of connoisseurship, of knowing what is good, of being an expert. Rather—and here is the connection with buttons and Christmas cards—it is the sense of finding remote and hard-to-procure fragments of the environment and assembling them in one's own milieu. It is the sense of having mastered to the point of absolute control such representatives of a class of environmental fragments that the representation of that class is exemplary: one's collections can be said to stand for the whole class. There is an intellectual radiation from one's collection of exemplary representatives of a class to the entire class. Collecting is a very intellectual pleasure.

This gives us a further clue to the rise of collecting, which meant success for the Pre-Raphaelites, their exploitation of a market economy, and the rise and spread of affluence. To be a collector of Pre-Raphaelites before they became the rage, was to demonstrate that one had successfully mastered the direction in which art was going; one could spot the comers, advice often given by art dealers to nervous prospects, or "marks," as they are called in what is perhaps a more honest trade. Yet more was involved. It meant that one had sufficiently mastered the categorial field of one's collecting so that one could not only spot but also get representative control over an emergent sub-category of that field.

Too much collecting is private, even secretive, for a simple theory of acquiring status to be successful. The need is not status; that is only superficial; far deeper is the need for categorial completeness. That is why a collector does not have to own all the works of Rembrandt; one fine example is enough. Whatever value art may have, it scarcely seems that it arises from its service to the sense of categorial completeness and exemplary radiation. This is why collecting art, whether paintings, furniture, or buttons, can be carried on by people with very little aesthetic sensitivity. The class of fragments of the environment needs only be desired by others to be an acceptable field. That is, it need only have a recognized place, however small and insignificant, in the market.

142

Collecting emerges when a portion of one's income is disposable. In nineteenth-century England collecting among workers took the form of trading in pigeons and tulips, the more fantastically malformed the better. In this country in the lower-middle classes rock collecting has a tremendous popularity. That a serious interest in geology is involved is impossible to believe. Initially one had to collect one's own rocks, but this required leisure and money to travel, however simply, to remote areas, frequently very difficult of access. In the West, therefore, have sprung up shops on the fringes of such areas in which those with neither time nor money can purchase representative rock specimens. Thus the intellectual radiation of their collections can exemplify and cover great areas of desert and mountain which the collectors have never seen. To purchase rock specimens is felt somehow to be cheating a little, but the intellectual imperative overrides the moral, judging at least by the tremendous numbers of such rock shops that have sprung up throughout the West, especially along the principal tourist routes.

Adolescence is a time when almost everybody collects something. It is also, of course, the time of the greatest uncertainty, the time when the easy mastery of the environment of childhood has vanished and the difficult mastery of adulthood has not yet developed. On the whole the child's mastery of the environment is not representative: it is total. Hence the sense of desolation as that mastery is frustrated. With the coming of adolescence the child's sense of wholeness disintegrates. Facing away from the family and the mastered physical environment of its vicinity, the individual experiences the world as fragmented. To collect is to gain an exemplary and radiating mastery over a category of those fragments. The need to collect is an intellectual need; it arises from a deprivation, a loss of cognitive control. Collecting offers a *representative* wholeness.

When all is said and done, perhaps the most gigantic intellectual effort of the nineteenth century was in the field of economics, or, as it was called for much of the century, political economy. The dropping of "political" has been unfortunate, for it implies that the realm of economics is larger than the realm of politics, or at least different. The old term implied that there was an economic aspect to politics, and the change in terminology implied that, if anything, there was a political aspect to economics. Perhaps the old term was better, for it may be that one of the few terms that throws any light on human behavior is indeed the word "politics."

Politics is the management of the body politic, that is, society, and all human interaction can be reduced to management, or, to offer a neologism, intermanagement. Economics, sociology, anthropology, in that order, emerged in response to the tremendous forces which were completely restructuring European life in the nineteenth century, a restructuring by no means complete, perhaps hardly begun. These three disciplines, of which political economy was the first to emerge, were invented in response to the anxiety, the loss of control, which those shattering and restructuring forces, to which only Carlyle and Marx and a very few others responded with any emotional adequacy, inflicted upon the entire culture. Economics itself, the most sophisticated of these three, can as yet give us very little understanding, in spite of the intricate complexity of the models it is now capable of structuring, a complexity achieved first through the development of statistics and second through computer technology.

One of the most important events in England in the nineteenth century, perhaps in the long run the most important event, was the foundation in the 1820's of the Statistical Society of London and its imitation in the various growing cities of the provinces. Ultimately only statistics can help us understand anything, for though it cannot ask questions it is the only foundation for asking meaningful questions and the only way to arrive at meaningful answers. The importance of this to the question of why the Pre-Raphaelites were so very successful in such a short time is that statistics have to be collected. Like the great collections of art, or of buttons, statistics are samples; statistics have the representative radiation toward a category of fragments of the environment which is the intellectual appeal of all collecting, and they offer the relief from the anxiety of social dislocation, the problem of the adolescent and the need which all collecting tries to satisfy.

Economics was originally called "political economy" in response to the social dislocation of which the Industrial Revolution and the French Revolution and the Agricultural Revolution and the Communications Revolution were but the foam on the wave. The traditional principles of social management, which is the art of politics, were no longer applicable. The new model, "economic man," was developed in response to the resultant anxiety and sense of loss of intellectual control. So was collecting. Yet the need to collect emerges from a very odd kind of socioeconomic dislocation, the dislocation of affluence, of a disposable income of whatever size, whether it is just enough to collect buttons, old Christmas cards, and rocks, or whether it is on a scale to permit the collection of old masters. Affluence, the acquisition of a disposable income, permits, indeed demands choice. When Milton expels Adam and Eve from Paradise he ends *Paradise Lost* with these lines:

> The world was all before them, where to choose
> Their place of rest, and Providence their guide:
> They hand in hand with wandering steps and slow,
> Through *Eden* took their solitarie way.

They have an infinitude of choice, but their steps are wandering and slow. They are solitary. Yet Providence is their guide.

This last consoling qualification seems not much of a consolation when it is realized that the only guide Providence needed to give them was to labor in the sweat of their brows for the merest subsistence. And that conjunction of choice and place of rest is illuminating. To choose a place of rest is, of course, to end choice. Milton thought that the freedom of the will is man's glory, and it may be so, but the only consequence he talks about is sin, guilt, and exile from Paradise. The heavenly beings have freedom of will, and they exercise it in worshipping and obeying God. The one heavenly being who exercises his freedom by *choosing* to do something else is Satan, who, naturally, is cast out from Heaven.

Though Milton would be horrified, no doubt, by this interpretation, it is pretty obvious that he has identified the exercise of freedom of the will with sin; hence punishment by deprivation is the consequence of that exercise. Satan in Heaven and Adam and Eve in Paradise were members of an affluent society; they had a disposable income; and they got into trouble. In both cases they did so by an intellectual act; they questioned the belief-system of their culture. Satan wondered why the only proper way to exercise freedom of choice was to worship the grandeur of God; having the leisure of affluence and a disposable income it occurred to him to ask if there were not possibly something else to do. As soon as he had asked the question, the answer became obvious; there was, if only the negation of what was being done. Adam and Eve had only to collect and enjoy the products of Paradise; their only very trifling labor was to see to it that it did not run wild. Pruning was their only task. Thus they easily exercised control over their environment. Other than that they had only to obey the belief-system of their culture as established by God. Satan suggested to Eve that there were other possibilities—with the results that we are familiar with.

The problem that a disposable income presents is revealed in the very terminology with which it is identified. How shall one dispose of it? To exercise choice is to consider alternatives; to consider alternatives is to inquire into one's values, to ask what one really wants; to do that is to realize that the alternatives available arise from inconsistencies in one's belief-system. Such an incoherence is exactly what Milton wrestled so energetically with when he tried to justify God's ways to man, an effort foredoomed to failure. The attempt to reconcile freedom of the will with predestination is an attempt to make coherent a fundamental inconsistency in the belief-system of the culture. It cannot be done.

The emergence of affluence in an individual's life, therefore, is a serious dislocation. Threatened with choice he is threatened with cultural incoherence, that is, incoherence in the area of his life in which he experiences culture, his personality. Collecting is admirably adapted to relieving this dislocation and its concomitant threatening anxiety. In the nineteenth century, however, affluence entailed a relatively novel threat. It was not entirely novel, of course, since the bourgeois of the Netherlands had experienced something of the sort in the seventeenth century. But in that case, the source of the affluence could be understood. In the nineteenth century the intellectual dislocation was far more severe because the forces responsible for the affluence were so completely mysterious, and still are, for that matter. Hence on the one hand the enormous effort to understand those forces in the emergent sciences of economics, sociology, and anthropology, and on the other the equally enormous effort to dispose of the problem of affluent dislocation by collecting. As with the adolescent, collecting by the adult bourgeois in the nineteenth century and today serves the function of compensating for the loss of intellectual control over the environment.

In the 1840's collecting paintings began to be a significant economic and cultural force, and it was in that decade that Balzac, himself a passionate collector, wrote *Cousin Pons*, the story of a man who sacrifices everything, even comfort, to collecting. Balzac approved of this, because it was art that was being collected, and Balzac, as a Romantic, thought of art as socially redemptive. Nevertheless his gift was a marvelous sociological penetration; had a mature sociology existed—as it does not yet—his vast *Human Comedy* would have been intellectually and culturally unnecessary. Thus in *Cousin Pons* he sees the link between Pons's collecting, his self-deprivation, his happiness, and his keeping his collection a secret. Collecting always diverts the threat of affluence to one's culture and personality and at times of cultural crisis compensates for the loss of intellectual and categorial control over the environment by a diversion of resources into a representative and radiating sampling of some category of environmental fragments.

The key to the whole problem lies in the fact that the naked ultimate choice is between collecting and the attempt to understand the nature of one's dislocation and the cultural incoherences it reveals. Not to collect is necessarily to innovate, to move in the direction of alienation, and to encounter the problem of culture transcendence. The shattering effects of economics, sociology, and anthropology upon the culture of the nineteenth century and their continued and indeed increasing threat to the culture values of the twentieth is an instance of the sobering consequences of not collecting.

For example, suppose that all the resources now used for collecting were devoted to moving the poor out of poverty; it would be quite possible. There is, in fact, no longer much or any intellectual value to collecting, which merely moves fragile objects around. Registration of works of art and inexpensive reproduction of books and documents is all that is necessary. To move the poor out of poverty would be to conform to one value in our belief-system. Yet it is perfectly obvious that to do so would entail a sociocultural crisis of a character that could not possibly be predicted. Given a choice between doing our Christian duty by relieving the poor from poverty and giving up the intellectual though diversionary satisfactions of collecting, we choose the latter, perhaps wisely. To help the poor out of their abyss is to attack an equally strong factor in our belief-system, the conviction, statistically quite unjustified, that the affluence of even a very moderately affluent individual is a direct consequence of his own merit and—value.

Perhaps this is why every proper middle-class boy is as carefully trained in collecting as his sister is in clothes, cosmetics, and interior decoration, all of which may be profitably seen as forms of collecting, and certainly as ways of disposing of disposable income, the acquisition of which is so disturbing. Moreover, the culture is full not only of publicly owned collecting institutions but increasingly that most interesting phenomenon of the past twenty years, the privately owned commercial museum, operated as a business enterprise. Even amusement parks have taken on the character of museums. It would be indeed interesting to know what part collecting takes in the total economic activity of the country.

For any collector today who does not have virtually unlimited funds at his disposal and who wants to collect objects made in the past the output of the nineteenth century is the most obvious choice. The mighty river of industrialization has left its banks littered with manufactured objects for which collectors are competing with increasing savagery simply because there is so little else from the past to collect. The revival of interest in Victoriana, including hitherto neglected schools of nineteenth-century painting such as the Pre-Raphaelites, does not demonstrate any serious interest in the nineteenth century, in its arts, or in its problems, including those problems we have inherited from it and which if anything are even more pressing today. If collectors are beginning to turn to the Pre-Raphaelites, it is principally because there has been very little attempt to collect them for more than half a century. True, there is a limited supply of Pre-Raphaelite paintings available for collecting. Most of the famous examples are already in museums or other public collections and have been for a long time.

As we have seen, the success of the Pre-Raphaelites was precisely a consequence of the spread of collecting to a newly affluent upper-middle class. They were among the first artists to paint for collectors, many of whom left their collections to the public, while the establishment of museums for the collection of recent and contemporary art, rather than old masters, was another instance of the collecting phenomenon of the nineteenth century. The Tate Gallery, which holds so many of the finest Pre-Raphaelite paintings, is an instance. One can, after all, dispose of disposable income by turning collecting over to experts, by giving large sums to public institutions devoted to collecting. The ultimate function of collecting in the nineteenth and twentieth centuries is not so much to own things as to dispose of that affluence which threatens cognitive dislocation.

Nevertheless, a collector usually collects a category of fragments which has an appeal for him, nor is there any reason to doubt that some collectors of paintings, though very few, collect as the economist collects statistics, not to have a representative control over some category of fragments of the environment but to attempt some understanding of the environment from which those fragments have been torn and which can be conceived as having produced them. When with such a purpose one collects historically emergent objects, the aim is to facilitate creating a model of the environment from which they emerged, as Walter Scott built a nineteenth-century medieval castle and filled it with artifacts, particularly arms and weapons, as well as furniture, which had originated in the Middle Ages and the Renaissance. The purpose is that of serious historicism in the

150

nineteenth century; by studying a situation in which the variables can be controlled because they are limited by the accidents
of survival, it is possible to construct models of the relation of
personality to its social, political, cultural, and natural environment.

In the same way the serious collection of contemporary paintings has the same relation to historical collecting that the realistic novel had to the historical novel. The historicism of the early
part of the century, to which Scott made a contribution the
value of which can never be overestimated nor for which he can
never be praised too highly, was a kind of cultural rehearsal for
the comprehension of the contemporary world. John Ruskin is
a perfect exemplification of this supremely important cultural
development of the mid-nineteenth century. His study of architecture of the past led him directly to an examination of the
inadequacies of the present, particularly of political economy,
which he was convinced, on the basis of his study of architecture and society, was seriously distorting both the contemporary understanding of economics and society and
also the attempt to manage rationally the relation between
the two.

Thus the serious collector who started buying the Pre-
Raphaelites saw their paintings not as collectable fragments but
as clues to his own immediate sociocultural environment, and
for this purpose they were admirably suited. For in their principles and in their practice the Pre-Raphaelites were themselves
collectors, serious collectors, whose concern was precisely to
understand their environment and whose purpose was frankly
moral, to improve the social environment. This comes out more
clearly if we compare them with artists of the 1960's who seem
to be at first glance as different from the Pre-Raphaelities as
possible, the pop artists, for these artists too are collectors. Of
the two aspects of collecting—a strategy to escape crisis by
representative and radiant sampling, and a strategy to tran-

scend crisis by creating a model of a society and a culture—both appear to be at work in the activities of the pop artists. The juxtaposition of a goat and an automobile tire, or the construction of enormous artificial hamburgers, big enough for a bed, are instances of collection incorporated into works of art. On the other hand, a good many observers perceive pop art as a satirical commentary on the culture, that is, transcendence attempted by satire, something which, as suggested earlier, cannot work.

The artists themselves have advanced, in one form or another, both reasons for what they did. Certainly ours is a time of crisis, and one kind of pop artist clearly embraces soup cans and comic books into his art because he has an affection for them. Which is to say that in a world which from its complexity and its crisis has become progressively meaningless to him, objects of childhood affection, because objects of childish gratification, become the only objects toward which a current of positive and value-inducing feeling can flow. Thus for a pop artist to say that he paints soup cans because he likes soup cans is a devastating and indeed shattering comment. For him, only the trivial, the disregarded, the object of culturally low status, can be a stimulus for an affectionate and meaningful response. To make a cardboard box and paint it to look like a Brillo box is hardly different from simply exhibiting a real Brillo box in a gallery. For either, from this point of view, a high price is justifiable.

The artist, the implication is, has as his task to create objects of genuine value, and thus his task is to reveal value. That revelation of value is how he earns his living. In terms of culture crisis there are no publicly acceptable criteria for judging what reveals value and what does not. Therefore, the only criterion is what the artist finds valuable and revealing of value. He genuinely likes Brillo boxes; to him they are meaningful and redolent of value. Therefore, a price as high as the market will bear is entirely justifiable. It is obvious from this that pop art is in the center of the Romantic tradition, and I believe that it is equally obvious that Andy Warhol, whether he can explain his actions or not, is a genius, not because of what he has done, but because of his decision to do it. Either his penetration into the current state of culture is analytic or intuitive or both; it certainly is profound.

This kind of pop artist says, "This is what I like. Under the circumstances I think it quite an achievement to like anything. I reveal to you that affection for the world is still possible." The other kind of pop artist, the satirical kind, says, "This is what you like, the completely trivial. My art shows what a bad situation you and your culture and your society are in." Of such pop works one of the most interesting I have seen consisted of a small wooden panel. In the middle of the panel was a door, with tiny hinges and a tiny knob. One did the obvious and opened the door. Open, it revealed a photograph of a naked man, ungainly and fat. Between his legs hung a penis of staggering size, and on his face was a smile of equally transcendent fatuous self-complacency. To paraphrase Baudelaire, "You, hypocrite of an art lover, my fellow creature! *This* is what you really care about and would like to have, one way or another."

The art of assemblage, or of collecting, was originated by the precursors of the pop artists—the dadaists—at the time of the crisis of the last years of World War 1. It is an art which could originate only in a culture in which collecting is a strategy innovated to deal with a crisis situation, either to create an illusion of control over the environment or to create a construct for comprehending the structure of society and culture. It is therefore scarcely an accident that the Pre-Raphaelites emerged almost within the decade in which collecting began to be widespread, for their art is an art of assemblage. To be sure, unlike the dadaists and the pop artist, they did not assemble actual objects. They assembled visual signs of objects into individual paintings. Their aim was to produce by novel means the interaction of these signs with the situation in which they were presented. The pattern here was no different from that of the dadaists, whose aim was to assemble random objects in such a way that not only new meanings were avoided but old meanings were destroyed. Their ambition was to reveal the randomness of their culture and their society, and therefore its meaningless-ness, or, in other words, its lack of value. Such an artist as Kurt Schwitters was like the Pre-Raphaelites in that he succeeded in creating works of great formal beauty and even power, proba-bly because he had had traditional artistic training and very likely in spite of himself. The pop artists have been more suc-cessful, since they have not offered us any such works.

Furthermore, all three groups share alike in the high Roman-tic tradition of conceiving the artists as the source of cultural value, the pop artists by affection and satire, the dadaists by revealing metaphysical emptiness, and the Pre-Raphaelites by moral revelation. In the case of the last, the explanation is to be found in the fact that the whole movement took its origin from literature, particularly poetry, that is, literature in its redemp-tionist mood of the 1840's.

The first joint effort of this group of dedicated young men, some poets, some artists, one, at least Rossetti, both, was a maga-zine, *The Germ*. This was before Pasteur, and the Pre-Raphael-ites must not be suspected of a diabolical plan to infect society. Rather, one of Webster's definitions is appropriate: "Something from which development takes place or that serves or may serve as an origin." The title, then, served as a manifesto, and the manifesto has been the traditional way groups of Romantics have served notice that they have parted from received stand-ards and values, that they are in opposition to their culture, and that they seek to resolve their alienation by culture transcen-dence. The first manifesto in English literature was the Words-worth-Coleridge Preface to the *Lyrical Ballads* of 1798. Placing this title in the tradition of the manifesto makes it clear enough that these young men were out to change society. But not directly.

The year was 1850, and the events of the revolutionary years of 1848 and 1849 had led them, as so many others, to the conclusion that society could not be revolutionized directly, but only indirectly, by revolutionizing the culture. They deliberately decided to exclude discussions of politics and religion. The subtitle was "Thoughts Towards Nature in Poetry, Literature, and Art." "Nature" is a word of innumerable meanings, and to these young men the most appropriate substitute for it was "truth"—on the one hand, truth to the appearance of the natural world, truth to the phenomena, something very close to scientific truth, as a drawing in an anatomy textbook is "scientific truth"; and on the other hand, truth to what Keats had called "the holiness of the heart's affections," truth to one's most deeply experienced moral interpretation of the behavior of humanity, truth to the noumenon. Thus Rossetti in his poem in the first of the four issues of *The Germ*, "The Blessed Damozel," tells us the number of lilies in the damozel's hand and the number of stars in her hair, but he also affirms that it is morally defensible to wish that erotic desire have divine recognition and sanction in heaven.

After the revolutionary fervor of the 1840's and the failure of its sentimental socialism, the privatization of the moral life had begun. Redemption was to be found through art, privately experienced, for it was to be found by the individual alone, in the intense contemplation of the object, the purpose of which was to induce in the observing subject a grasp of his actual needs, not those needs which conventional religion and politics told him should be his. The choice of a title—*The Germ*—was thus both exceedingly modest, as for the most part the magazine's achievement was, and superbly arrogant. Sons of the bourgeoisie as they were, these youngsters did their best to make *The Germ* a self-supporting and even paying proposition. They failed, but its founding and its failure were the stimulus they needed to do something genuinely new in painting.

And something genuinely new was what they succeeded in doing. At the time there were three recognized types of painting in England. There was historical painting, in its effect something we would call literary painting or even illustration, but in its aims something different. Historical painting properly took some grand religious or political or social event and treated it in the grand manner, which meant the manner originated by Raphael and Michelangelo, integrated with Venetian painting by the Caracci, developed in the baroque styles of the seventeenth and eighteenth centuries, modified by the neoclassicism of the late eighteenth century, and spuriously revitalized by an infusion of Michelangelism in the nineteenth.

Then there was genre painting. This too was literary, as indeed was all painting, except portraits, until the late sixteenth century invented landscapes and still lifes. Genre painting was particularly a creation of the seventeenth century, and originally concerned itself with peasant and other lower forms of human life. In the eighteenth century it was picked up by the bourgeoisie and sentimentalized, and this is pretty much what it still was, taking its subjects more often than not from famous and widely known novels and plays. The English were very good at it, and the superb nineteenth-century English tradition of book illustration is descended from it.

The third great division was landscape. For reasons which must be for the moment postponed this was the kind of painting which means most to us today. It was of fairly recent origin, and had not the status of history painting. Yet to advanced critics, those who really understood it, it was the most important of all, and the only kind in which the modern spirit, Romanticism, could find its proper expression. After Constable and Turner, who was still active, it was fairly obvious that the future of painting lay here, and it was to reach its culmination with the abstract expressionism of the period after World War II. At the time, however, the accuracy of the depiction of nature was a central factor.

To these should be added picturesque painting, a landscape painting with buildings, preferably old and half ruined. Picturesque painting, mostly watercolors, fused landscape with social interest and is properly seen as part of the historicism of the nineteenth century. However, the future lay in pure landscape, for there the self was alone. In the painting of the future, that of the French impressionists, buildings were no more significant than anything else in the landscape, trees or cliffs or rivers; they did not imply a social world in which either artist or perceiver shared, as the picturesque clearly did.

The achievement of the Pre-Raphaelites was to fuse and synthesize all of these various types of painting. First they took from Constable and Turner and from the minor watercolorists and the picturesque painters a concern with scientific accuracy. In this they were inspired and led by Ruskin, whose *Modern Painters*, Volume I (1843), was devoted almost entirely to the principle of truth, that is, truth to nature. In Volume II (1848) Ruskin proposed an elaborate theological justification for this demand, which he later tended to repudiate. However, the effect of both volumes was a demand on the painter that he devote himself not merely to the truth of appearance but to the truth of structure, of the laws of organic growth, of a botanical accuracy. Thus the plants in Millais's "Ferdinand and Ariel" (1849) could be and were used in a lecture on botany. Likewise in "Ophelia" (1851-2) the plants were not only recognizable as particular kinds of plants, but each plant was studied from a living model, so that the specific form the laws of growth took in a particular, unique, individual, and unrepeatable plant or flower was unmistakably recorded. In Arthur Hughes's quite marvelous painting "Home from the Sea" (1856-63) every blade of grass, every leaf, every roof tile, every break in a Gothic window, every brick in the table tombs is portrayed with an intensity unparalleled in painting. The result is burnished, and the configurations seem cast in bronze. Yet the painting is not metallic, for the light is recorded as delicately as any French impressionist ever did, or Turner himself.

Never has truth to nature been carried in painting to such a high pitch. One result was a brilliance of color, a height of key that the French did not achieve until the 1880's. Those canvases of the Pre-Raphaelites which were executed in the open air have the intensity of color of nature itself, as well as, when appropriate, its softness. John Brett in "The Stone Breaker" (1857-8) and in "The Val D'Aosta" achieved an aerial perspective and depth which I have never seen equaled in painting, not even by Fragonard, the greatest of eighteenth-century painters. This last painting was only less fine than "The Stone Breaker," and it was the last good painting Brett did. Ruskin hammered at him (Ruskin's own term) while he was painting it. Thereafter his seascapes are said to be dry though scientifically accurate. Still there is no trusting anybody's statement about Pre-Raphaelite paintings, so out of fashion are they, even by people who try to sympathize; until I see some of his later work, I refuse to believe that a painter of such extraordinary talent should have experienced so complete a falling off.

Nevertheless it would be a great mistake to construe the Pre-Raphaelite efforts as similar to those of the French in the next or post-Barbizon generation. They did not paint impressions. None of them would have been capable of painting a series of the same haystack or the same cathedral in different lights. Their works are not impressions but constructions. The uniqueness of a place must, to them, be thought of in terms of the general rules applying to such places. A particular leaf had to be painted in its uniqueness, but at the same time sufficient information must be presented to show how that uniqueness is subordinated to the laws governing the structure and growth of that kind of leaf and of leaves in general. Consequently theirs is not a sensuous art but an intellectual art; the concrete uniqueness must also be a concrete universal. Rossetti's utterance that the first mark of a good poem is fundamental brain power applies also to Pre-Raphaelite painting. The attempted fusion of the individual and the universal is the Pre-Raphaelites' form of the Romantic tension between subject and object.

The French impressionists introduced that tension in their brushwork; a painting is, among other things, the unique calligraphy of the artist, which has an existence separate from and even in opposition to what is being painted, a tension which the first critics of impressionism felt and were disturbed by. For different reasons Pre-Raphaelite painting disturbs in the same way.

The ultimate source for this uncompromising recording of phenomenal appearance was Wordsworth's poetry, which offered the most exact verbal description possible of natural appearance and at the same time the subjective interpretation of that appearance. But the Pre-Raphaelites added something to the Wordsworthian appearance. The plant must be both unique and universal; that is, it must be a categorial sign of that category or species of plant. One must not only be able to recognize the plant painted, but any plant of the species; one must, from studying the painting, have learned something about the attributes that define it as a species. And so with everything else in the painting. This is why their paintings are constructions, not impressions. They are, in fact, categorial constructions, or, as we have seen, collections. Just as Kurt Schwitters organized scraps from a trash basket or a junk heap into a work of art of great beauty, so, for diametrically opposed reasons, the Pre-Raphaelites assembled the various objects in their paintings to illustrate the laws of nature, or, if it was appropriate, the laws of society.

Ruskin has a famous passage about William Holman Hunt's "The Awakening Conscience" (1852-54). It is worth quoting to illustrate the principle of collection or assemblage in Pre-Raphaelite painting, but to understand his remarks some account of the painting is necessary. The subject is that of a girl who has become the mistress of a wealthy young man about town. No doubt the setting is St. John's Wood, the area of London where kept women were kept. She has been sitting on her lover's lap; he plays a cottage piano. They have been singing some new music. Something in the song has suddenly roused in her the sense of what she has come to and what she has lost; and she has leapt to her feet, hands clasped and with an anguished face. In a letter to the *Times* (May 25,1854) Ruskin wrote:

> ... There is not a single object in all that room—common, modern, vulgar (in the vulgar sense, as it may be), but it becomes tragical, if rightly read. That furniture so carefully painted, even to the last vein of the rosewood—is there nothing to learn from that terrible lustre of it, from its fatal newness; nothing there that has the old thoughts of home upon it, or that is ever to become a part of home? Those embossed books, vain and useless—they also new—marked with no happy wearing of beloved leaves; the torn and dying bird upon the floor; the gilded tapestry, with the fowls of the air feeding upon the ripened corn; the picture above the fireplace, with its single drooping figure—the Woman taken in adultery. ...

It is insufficient to dismiss either Ruskin's comment or the painting itself as mere Victorian sentimental morality. It is not, it seems to me, particularly sentimental to realize that one's life is ruined. Unless she manages to marry a lord, as a few such girls did, her future was exactly as Ruskin said it would be, prostitution on the streets. No, such dismissal would be superficial. The important thing is the cognitive process involved, the assembling of objects meaningless in themselves into a construction or collection which will give categorial grasp of the sociocultural situation. It is instructive that the purchaser of the painting persuaded Hunt to repaint the girl's face, for in its original form it expressed such anguish that he found he could not live with it.

This highly intellectualized approach to painting appears in the way the Pre-Raphaelites fused historical painting and genre. "The Awakening Conscience" certainly belongs to the tradition of genre painting; it is of an intimate, domestic scene, and the objects in it are thoroughly familiar, down to the cat and the embroidery frame. However, the crisis is the sort of thing that rarely appeared in genre painting as it was currently practiced, though Greuze, the originator of this tradition of genre, had certainly used something of the sort. Hunt bent every effort to infuse the painting with the emotional power of a religious or historical scene of great and legendary and mythical significance. An even finer example of this fusion of the historical and the genre traditions is Millais's "Christ in the House of His Parents" (1849-50), which created a terrible scandal when it was first exhibited. We see a carpenter's shop as it might have been in Palestine in the first century A.D. The child Christ has wounded himself in the hand. His mother is consoling him, and Joseph is reaching out to examine the wound. On the right, the young John the Baptist is bringing a basin of water to wash the wound. On the wall at the back are hung carpenter's tools; shavings litter the floor, and the nail which has hurt the boy is prominently displayed.

The fury the painting aroused came from its utter violations of the traditional expectations for a religious painting. There is nothing, it would seem, grand, or noble, or awe-inspiring; everything is homely, ordinary, even poverty-stricken, in short, as historically accurate as Millais could make it. Here the art of assemblage or collection has a new function, one that illustrates very well the principle of collecting as an effort to understand the sociocultural structure of some period in the past. What Millais has tried to do is to create a new Christian iconography. The wound in the hand foreshadows the crucifixion; the kneeling and comforting and sympathetic and careworn mother foreshadows the pietà. The water brought by the boy Baptist foreshadows his baptism of Christ. The sheep in the background are a sign of the future Christians and of the pastoral care of the future church. The planks on the other side, especially a very tall one, foreshadow the cross. On a ladder at the back, which foreshadows the ladder which was raised to remove Christ from the cross, sits a dove; the Holy Spirit is present here also. But it is not the traditional dove of religious paintings, splendid, with outspread wings, centered in a burst or halo of light. It is just an ordinary domestic dove. On the workbench are the pincers with which the boy Jesus had been attempting to extract the offending nail, an emblem of the nails which were to nail him to the cross and of the pincers which were to remove those nails. And Anne, Mary's mother, is leaning forward to remove them from harm's way.

The critics and the public complained because the bare feet were so ugly! What did they think a Palestinian peasant's feet looked like? But of course they had not thought of that at all, nor did they intend to. They only expected everything about sacred persons to be beautiful. Nor did they notice that the organization of the painting was highly traditional, one that Watteau might have used, and in fact did, a great implied oval upon which is superimposed a great implied triangle. The organization of the work is in fact baroque, another instance of the turning of the Romantics to the baroque for the sake of formal interest, but here obliterated for most observers by the explicitness of the homely details.

Two other paintings, both by Rossetti, are organized in a quite different manner. The subject of each is the Virgin Mary. One, "The Girlhood of Mary Virgin" (1848-51, though dated

162

1849), shows Mary with her mother at an embroidery frame; at
the left on a pile of vast folios, labeled with various virtues—
Charity, Temperance, and so on—stands a vase holding a tall
lily stem. A small angel contemplates it. Mary is copying the lily
in embroidery. At the back St. Joachim is tending vines. On a
branch of the trellis sits a dove; on the floor are palm branches
and a briar, bound together. The scene is vaguely medieval,
rather than an historically correct Palestine, as in the Millais
painting. The other (1849-53, though dated 1850) is an annun-
ciation scene, "Ecce Ancilla Domini." At the left is an angel, a
beautiful young man, not winged, with fiery feet, floating above
the floor and offering Mary a lily branch. Above the branch
floats a dove. In the foreground is once again the embroidery
frame with the completed lily. Mary is crouching on the bed,
huddling against the wall, gazing with wonder and terror at the
angel's lily stalk.

Millais, like Hunt, created new symbols by assembling common objects the symbolic function of which is implied by the
situation. Rossetti, however, used traditional symbols; in both
Mary paintings the figures of sacred legend have halos, and the
dove is surrounded with a glory in one and wears a halo in the
other. His traditional iconography is freshly observed, literalisti-
cally rendered, and used in completely novel ways. No one
before had presented Mary copying a lily in embroidery,
though any number of paintings show the lily standing in a vase
between Gabriel and Mary, and in the second picture the device of having the angel offer the lily to Mary is equally novel.
Once again the painting is highly intellectualized; it requires to
be "read," to be interpreted. Ruskin praised the Pre-Raphaelites for exactly this quality, for to him, quite correctly, painting
was "language," that is, a semiotic system of visual signs. Subsequently, to be sure, especially in this century, "literary" applied
to painting became a term of opprobrium. Yet all historical or
religious painting in the past has been literary. What is the

difference? What is the novelty, the strangeness?

It lies precisely in the fact that the iconography of traditional painting was well established. Though forgotten now, and the subject of scholarly research, traditional iconography was well understood by most people of some education, and the elaborate allegories of the seventeenth century used a system conventionalized by Cesare Ripa's *Iconologia* (1593). In any case, the system was so standard that one responded to the iconographic symbols without analysis. The modern viewer, interested in what he considers purely aesthetic qualities, for the most part ignores them, thus missing, incidentally, both instruction and amusement. But in the Pre-Raphaelite paintings one can do neither. One is forced to ask questions, since the iconography is neither conventionalized nor, if so, used in a conventional way; it is not something one can easily ignore.

But this is not the whole matter of the modern observer's difficulty with these paintings and his temptation to dismiss them. Most of them have a curiously old-fashioned look. They "date," as, let us say, a Raphael or a Fragonard does not, nor a Constable nor a Turner. The exceptions are Rossetti, not the paintings of the 1860's and the 1870's, which do look old-fashioned, but those of his first years. The two paintings of Mary, especially the first, are unquestionably technically very deficient, yet as William Bell Scott, another painter closely associated with the group, realized, they are curiously impressive. They do not look old-fashioned; they do not date. They have a freshness about them and a modern feeling. This suggests that the difficulty with the other artists is not merely that they are not yet remote enough in time to lose their old-fashionedness. That is not true of Rossetti.

Nor is it the realism that is troubling, the explicit, though categorial, copying of phenomenalistic appearance. That literalism is to be found in all the painters of the nineteenth century whom the modern observer finds still acceptable, including the

French impressionists. Cézanne is the first notable departure from that literalism, whether of configuration or of light.

The difference of Rossetti from his companions has a quite different source. It is the composition, the devices for organizing the painting into a visual field. The oddity, the strangeness, and the modernity of the two Mary paintings are at first glance negative. They are not put together from the implicit forms of the Renaissance of the baroque, as are those of Hunt, of Millais, of Brown, and the others. Nor are they medieval, literally Pre-Raphael, or better, Pre-Leonardo. They do not imply large dominating configurations—triangles, circles, ovals, x's, and so on. Rather the formal aspect of the paintings consists of implied overlapping rectangles. Even the figures can be contained within such rectangles, and the draperies imply such rectangles. Taking our cue from "Nude Descending a Staircase" we may call this the shingle style, and it was the style of the future. One can see it reemerge in Puvis de Chavannes, in Burne-Jones, and most significantly for the future in Cézanne, who probably got it from Puvis de Chavannes. If we forget the term cubism and the perplexingly inappropriate attributes the term might be expected to carry with it, it is obvious that the period of classical or analytic cubism, when Picasso and Braque were working in so virtually identical a manner, consists precisely of this shingle style of overlapping and interlocking implied rectangles.

Rossetti had trouble with perspective, and he cursed and swore over his failure to master it. It is no wonder. His compositional style is antithetical to a perspectival style; it implies not depth but a flat surface. As later artists of the twentieth century concluded, the first thing to note about a painting is that it is a painting, a flat surface covered with configurations. To maintain the integrity of that flat surface while still making it interesting with variegated shapes and implied configurations became their ambition and goal. Rossetti worked on "Found" from 1853 to his death in 1882, but never completed it. From this point of view it is not difficult to see why. He was attempting a more traditionally organized picture, one the subject of which required a deep background, probably a vista down a street. The figures he completed, but the background he could not manage to his satisfaction, even after many trials. To master the principles of perspective is not, after all, very difficult, and Rossetti was a very intelligent man and a gifted and accomplished artist. Rather, perspectival depth worked utterly against the grain of what he was trying to do. The shingle style, as it was finally worked out in the twentieth century, is contrary to perspectival depth; its feeling is utterly different, antithetical. In creating the shingle style Rossetti revealed his genius by a leap to a genuine culture transcendence. He made an important initial step toward abstract art.

In creating what came to be known as cubism (surely a misleading and wrongheaded term) Picasso fused two nineteenth-century traditions, the gradually emerging shingle style, which insists upon the painting as an object rather than as a representation, and the landscape, in which as the century wore on representation or imitation of nature gradually gave way to something else, to expressiveness. It is by no means an accident that painting as a system of signs of feeling-states and painting as object were fused in the landscape tradition, for in the nineteenth century landscape painting had the same relation to other kinds that music had to the arts as a whole.

In the discussion of Tennyson in the first essay in this book I suggested that music consists of signs of feeling-states, and that it is peculiarly important to a cultural situation in which alienation and cultural transcendence are the central problem, since it concentrates on a flow of feeling-states, divorced from any action, any attempt to manipulate the environment. The experience of music is isolating and incommunicable, and thus it separates experientially the self from the role. Not only does the listener concentrate on his own feeling-states, but the formal aspect of music forces him to abstract the sense of identity, or selfhood, from the matrix of sensory and cognitive experience, and to experience its ebb and flow, its instability as a felt continuum. Music does this by setting up and then violating certain expectancies, as in a theme and its variations, in which the important factor is not the similarity of the variation to the theme but its dissimilarity, its configurational discontinuity. Such devices, however, are not strictly speaking signs, for they are not conventionalized into meaning functions. The signs of music consist of the directionality of pitch motion, of major and minor (in the diatonic tradition), of fixed or wave pitches, of loud and soft volume, of fast and slow speed, and of several kinds of rhythm, phrasal and ictus. These, I have proposed in my remarks on Tennyson, are signs of feeling-states. I would suggest that painting consists of signs besides phenomenalistic signs—verticality, horizontality, light and shadow, chiaroscuro, color, depth, shallowness, and configurational sequence and line.

If this position can be accepted it is possible to comprehend why the fruitful direction for the future in nineteenth-century painting was the landscape, and why the landscapes of the century are today its most acceptable product in painting. In fact, in the first decades of this century the principle was recognized, for more than one abstract painter since 1910 has said that abstract painting is a kind of visual music. "Expressionism" was not a bad term for the early developments of modern painting, nor in the 1950's was abstract expressionism a bad term for what was happening then. Kandinsky was one of the first to work out in some detail a theory of the abstract element in painting, which has always been present, which cannot help being present, as a set of signs of feeling-states. Early in the nineteenth century Goethe worked out a similar notion in his *Farbenlehre* and developed a theory which deeply influenced Turner, who after the 1830's increasingly was interested in

167

landscape as an occasion for presenting signs of feeling-states, rather than as an occasion for imitating in configurational scenes the appearances of the phenomenal world. In his last years he occasionally achieved a nearly full-blown abstract expressionism.

For such purposes landscape was peculiarly suitable. Insofar as the intellectual or assemblage interests of the Pre-Raphaelites were important, to that degree the social world was important. It is therefore significant that Rossetti, who alone plunged into the shingle style, tended to paint scenes of very private experience, particularly of an erotic character, the most private of feelings and experiences. The rest, attempting to achieve cultural transcendence in intellectual and moral terms necessarily concerned themselves with much more public situations, and their paintings tend to be crowded with figures. Even in such paintings as Hunt's "The Scapegoat," which consists simply of a goat abandoned in a most desolate region of Palestine, the social implications of the casting out of the goat require an intellectual and moral consideration of social relationships. The casting out of the scapegoat is a public, not a private act. In landscape, however, the social world could be excluded, and it was excluded with increasing frequency. The paintings of the French Barbizon school of the 1840's and the 1850's are here very much to the point.

The Barbizon subject was the forest and rivers and marshes of the Fontainebleau region, near the center of which was the little town of Barbizon. Generally, the paintings of this school show no human beings at all, frequently enough not even houses or boats. The nearest things to humans are cattle, but they are presented as visual parts of the landscape, not intellectual and moral counters or signs of social existence. They are plunged into nature and separated from man; they might as well be wild creatures. The artist and the observer of the painting as well confront a nonsocial world, and that is the important factor. It is not that nature is present but that man is absent.

A first clue to what was happening can be found in the paintings of Casper David Friedrich, beginning in 1808. He does present a figure in the foreground, sometimes two or more, but they always have their backs to the observer. They too are contemplating the landscape. Ultimately this observer within the painting is often enough reduced to a little pool in the foreground; man has become merely an eye. The Barbizon school tended to have a dominating tree, frequently outlined against the sky, often enough against a sunset. Here the observer, and the painter, have been abstracted to a simple assertion of pure being, stripped of all social dimension. More magniloquently Cézanne was to do the same thing with Mont St. Victoire. Pure selfhood in a desocialized landscape—this became the dominant theme of landscape painting in the middle of the century. An exception within the Barbizon school was Millet, and his intellectualized and moralized paintings have, in spite of their many virtues, the same old-fashioned look as those of his contemporaries, the Pre-Raphaelites. Even so, Millet tended to concentrate on the single figure, as in the famous "The Sower," man isolated in nature, and socialized man almost crushed by the weight of political, economic, and cultural oppression.

The lonely tree against the sky is a significant clue to what was happening. To the degree society is eliminated, to that degree, for the Romantic, selfhood emerges; but the only way to symbolize selfhood in painting is through signs of feeling-states. It was easy enough in music; once that had been divorced from situational control—the achievement of Beethoven—the problem had been solved. In painting, however, which consists of signs of the phenomenalistic world, the problem was more puzzling. It took a hundred years to arrive at the answer, the separation of the phenomenalistic sign function of painting from the function of visual signs as signs of feeling-states, signs of demand or masculinity, of acceptance of femininity, of adequacy and inadequacy, of fixity or rejection and flexibility or openness, of expression of emotional loading and inhibition of it, of energy release and conservation, of the smoothness and roughness of emotive flow.

This is the true meaning of abstraction, the abstraction from configurational signs of feeling signs, the desocialization of the personality as the expression of alienation, and the transcendence of society into states of pure feeling, with the aim of experiencing and symbolizing in painting the feeling of pure being, pure because it transcends the social matrix. In landscape everything is at the same level of meaning, and for this reason the phenomenalistic signs can be manipulated in the service of feeling signs. It was only a matter of time and the desire for complete cultural transcendence for the phenomenal function of landscape signs to vanish, leaving only feeling signs.

From this position it is possible to arrive at an interpretation of the development of what I have called the shingle style. It had in fact already begun to appear in landscape, even as early as Constable, and had gone a long way in the work of the Barbizon school and some of the English watercolorists. The problem was to fulfill the requirements of representation by the perspectival presentation of depth, but at the same time to emphasize the painting as painting, that is, pure surface, without depth. To present depth, but to deny it, was the direction in which Romantic landscape painting moved until the twentieth century abstracted feeling signs from phenomenal signs. The reason for this impulse is in the function of depth as a feeling sign.

Recognizably modern landscape originated early in the seventeenth century, the century in which European culture turned away from theological explanations of man toward scientific explanations of nature and of man-in-nature. That plunge or release of energy into the natural world appeared in painting as the adaptation of deep Renaissance perspective to landscape painting. It is not surprising that it was first achieved in the empirical, Protestant, and commercial culture of the Netherlands. Dutch painting became popular and widely collected all over Europe, and the new style was so congruent with the feeling-tone of advanced cultural interests that landscape painting which directed the eye to the remotest horizon became the emergent style. Even backgrounds of religious paintings used it. Deep and prominent and irresistible landscape perspective, then, became conventionalized as a sign of feeling-states characterized by a heavily laden emotional involvement with the phenomenal world. It was a way of presenting the epistemological position that the categories of the object subsume the attributes of the subject. The observer became part of the natural phenomenalistic world.

But the aim of Romanticism was to separate self from nature, noumenon from phenomenon, subject from object, and to establish between them an irresolvable tension. In the nineteenth century, we observe in landscape painting a steady abandonment of straightforward perspectival depth in favor of a return to signifying depth by successive planes, as in the sixteenth century, though for quite different reasons. Simultaneously the painting began to be organized by implying large rectangular areas overlapping and interlocking. It was the first manifestation of the shingle style. Thus the continuously more effective assertion of the painting as an integral plane served to place the surface of the picture in tension with the represented depth. The picture as plane rather than as illusionary depth assumes the function of signifying the self, the subject, as opposed to the object, the nonself, the fragment of the environment signified by the empirical signs of the painting, of opposing the noumenon to the phenomenon.

This, then, is the reason for Rossetti's failure to master so highly conventionalized a system as perspective, one which any art student of very modest talent could master with relative ease long before Rossetti was born. The shingle style is part of the same process which was responsible for the abstraction of feeling signs from phenomenal signs. They are parallel and related developments, devices whereby the conventionalized and highly public signs of painting were gradually converted into signs of alienation and cultural transcendence. Even the other Pre-Raphaelites' intellectualization of their art of assemblage or collection was part of the same process, the deconventionalization of conventionalized signs, whether inventing new signs for old concepts or using old signs for new concepts.

The difference, however, between Rossetti and the other Pre-Raphaelites was profound. Their aim in the intellectualization and moralization of their art was to redeem society. As his rejection of political and religious material for *The Germ* indicates, his interest was to redefine himself as one for whom the redemption of society is an illusion. At best the individual could redeem but himself. In this he is with Tennyson and Browning and Carlyle in *Frederick*, and he is modern. The program of Pre-Raphaelitism was, for advanced thinkers, already out of date when it was formulated. Only Rossetti knew it. Half of him was with the others, but the important half of him was pulling away from them almost as soon as the group got started. When he organized his pictures not as they did but by overlapping and interlocking implied rectangles, thus establishing the surface and the picture as a picture, he had already, though he scarcely knew it, withdrawn from the movement.

I have proposed an answer to one of my questions, What were the Pre-Raphaelites trying to do, and why? To the other—Is the present state of culture such that they can once again be used? —the immediate answer is, No. But that is the Establishment answer. Most people today who are interested in art at all, and almost all critics and art historians, reject the Pre-Raphaelites utterly. Yet here and there there are signs of interest. Perhaps that interest should not be taken too seriously. Two factors for that interest can be recognized. One is collection as a strategy of escape, though collection as a strategy of investment should not be minimized. The other is scholarly and professional. Professional scholars have to write and publish. To do so, they must do research. An area of art history, therefore, which has been neglected, on which little that is modern and professional has been written, is a godsend. The increasing professional interest in all neglected aspects of nineteenth-century culture has its primary motivation in the simple fact that they have been neglected. No pressing internal reason of self-comprehension or of sociocultural comprehension, no deeply felt cognitive demand, is responsible for the increasing flow of articles and books about the Victorians, only the professional necessity to find something to study which has not yet been studied.

For the serious student of art and culture, a type rarely found in academic and professional and art-establishment circles, there is perhaps a valid reason for learning not to study the Pre-Raphaelites but to respond to them as one responds to any currently acceptable style of painting. Since it is the current state of culture to deny the artistic validity of the Pre-Raphaelites, they present an opportunity to do exactly what they did themselves, to deny the values of one's culture, no matter how high-level it may be nor how thoroughly validated, and to transcend its limitations. The tradition of Romanticism, in which even now we are still living, requires that it must alienate itself from its own established values, must transcend itself. What Romanticism recognizes is that the most valuable, informative, and complete clue to the character of human culture is fashion.

Fashion amounts to this: Once a behavioral pattern has been established it is continued by others simply because it offers something to do and thus restricts and almost eliminates the necessity for choice. Whether it is the fashion of mini-art, or the fashion of rioting in the ghettos, or the fashion of student rebellions, once the fashion has been established it becomes an establishment, a rival establishment perhaps, but still an establishment. It is institutionalized, and the primary interest comes to be the maintenance of the institution, because the institution provides a fashion of behavior. There is, then, one sound reason for learning to like the Pre-Raphaelites—and it is not easy. To develop a taste for their paintings offers at least a temporary mode of denying the currently established principles for determining artistic value.

5

The Romantic Birth of Anthropology

I T IS our happiness to live in one of those eventful periods of intellectual and moral history, when the oft-closed gates of discovery and reform stand open at their widest. How long these good days may last, we cannot tell. It may be that the increasing power and range of the scientific method, with its stringency of argument and constant check of fact, may start the world on a more steady and continuous course of progress than it has moved on heretofore. But if history is to repeat itself according to precedent, we must look forward to stiffer duller ages of traditionalists and commentators, when the great thinkers of our time will be appealed to as authorities by men who slavishly accept their tenets, yet cannot or dare not follow their methods through better evidence to higher ends. In either case, it is for those among us whose minds are set on the advancement of civilization, to make the most of present opportunities, that even when in future years progress is arrested, it may be arrested at the higher level. To the promoters of what is sound and reformers of what is faulty in modern culture, ethnography has double help to give. To impress men's minds with a doctrine of development, will lead them in all honour to their ancestors to continue the progressive work of past ages, to continue it the more vigorously because light increased in the world, and where barbaric hordes groped blindly, cultured men can often move onward with clear view. It is a harsher, and at times even painful, office of ethnography to expose the remains of crude old cultures which have passed into harmful superstition, and to mark these out for destruction. Yet this work, if less genial, is not less urgently needful for the good of mankind. Thus, active at once in aiding progress and removing hindrance, the science of culture is essentially a reformer's science.

With those sentiments Edward Tylor concluded *Primitive Culture: Researches into the Development of Mythology, Philosophy, Religion, Language, Art, and Custom.* In this massive work, first published in 1871, he founded modern anthropology, though it was not until 1896 that Oxford fully recognized the new science, established a professorship of anthropology, and gave it to Tylor. In England anthropology, or at least one branch of it, social anthropology, has remained a reformer's science, in a very special sense. As Sir John Lubbock, another of the founders, realized, anthropology, or that branch of it called ethnography, i.e., cultural anthology, promised immense practical value in administering that huge worldwide empire which the English created in the nineteenth century and the dismantling of which has been one of the most interesting—and threatening—spectacles of the twentieth. To understand contemporary primitives and to raise them to a higher cultural level—this was the white man's burden. To be sure, those primitives have concluded that the true intention was to exploit them and the resources of their native lands, to subject them to the domination of the insatiable demands of European capitalism. Since to manipulate others successfully one must understand them, and since to understand others is almost necessarily to manipulate them, these once primitive peoples are probably right.

Tylor would have been unthinkable without Darwin, who saw that adaptation to a continuously changing environment, no matter how slowly, by continuously changing species was the dynamics of evolution. Culture, as Tylor saw it, is the mental adaptation of man to environment, but environment necessarily includes other men, whether the individual thinks of himself as the instrument of adaptation, or his tribe, or his nation, or his race.

The bear that catches fish is adapting himself to his environment, but he is also manipulating that environment and exploiting it. Thus each individual is in competition with all other individuals, since to every individual, whatever its species, vegetable or animal, all other individuals are rivals. But at the same time, as Darwin was fully aware, cooperation between and among individuals within and between species was equally important, though the Social Darwinists, believing that in Darwin they had found a natural justification for capitalist ethics, tended to ignore this point. Nevertheless, whether it involves individuals or species or all animals or the entire living world, adaptation means exploitation and manipulation. By their own principles the social anthropologists of England were concerned with the native primitives of the British Empire, were an important instrument of the adaptation of England to the rest of the world, and thus, whether they admitted it to themselves or not, were necessarily manipulating and exploiting the peoples of whom, often enough, they considered themselves guardians. Even the most innocent anthropologist in the world is, after all, adapting himself to the tribe he is studying, and manipulating them and exploiting them for his purposes. Possibly this is why natives, sensing this, so often take a mischievous pleasure in giving wrong information, or sometimes when the investigator asks questions they cannot answer, in offering obscenities which the anthropologist cannot understand and solemnly records. Only later and more thoroughgoing workers discover the joke.

In the United States, on the other hand, anthropology has been less concerned with utilitarian, imperial, and exploitative possibilities. In the Indians, American anthropologists had an immediately and easily available field, and the Rochesterian, H. P. Schoolcraft, was the first great American investigator into the indigenous peoples of this country. Because of this situation the American anthropologist has been more scientific, more professionally intellectual than the British, for he was not concerned either with social management or exploitation. American social policy was not to make use of the Indian but rather to destroy him and segregate him on reservations. There was no political reason to understand Indian culture, since the Indian could not be directly exploited by slavery and since integration into the white labor force was unthinkable. Thus the United States made no effort to create any kind of economical or adaptive bridge between the civilized and the savage worlds. The American anthropologist could be singularly disinterested, and could be a very pure scientist. Or at the most he has been interested only in preserving Indian cultures as living museums and to create in the reservations living habitat groups, modeled on the most advanced zoo and museum techniques. What Tylor was aware of, that anthropology is a subversive science, seems to have been grasped by relatively few American anthropologists, or if grasped, scarcely publicized or put to use.

If the anthropological point of view is applied to American anthropologists themselves, the general pattern emerges clearly enough; it is the pattern of extreme intellectual professionalization to be found throughout the American academic world. In the nineteenth century Englishmen who were members of the two universities, that is, graduates as well as fellows and dons, had immediate access to the power centers. No wonder. Oxford and Cambridge were the training ground, not for a life of pure science and scholarship but for entry into the governmental world, the world of social management. That is why the debates in the universities' debating societies, the Unions, were reported in the *Times*. The great task of Oxford and Cambridge was not so much to educate but rather, in the process of a pretty casual and cursory education, one which left almost everything to the ambition and drive of the individual student, to sift, to select, and to transmit to the places of power those sons of the power class who promised to be able to maintain that establishment. As the establishment became larger, as population grew, as the Empire was extended, more recruits were necessary. The history of Oxford and Cambridge in the nineteenth century is one of progressive reaching down into the middle classes to recruit and select replacements and, especially, subordinates for those who really ran things. And thus, as the value of anthropology for imperial management became manifest, a chair of anthropology was founded at Oxford.

Since this was the case, it is to be expected that the English should consider it right that the study of man should properly be utilized in the management of man, and the sooner the better. American professional intellectuals, however, have no such access to power, nor are the universities selective instruments for transmitting the promising young to the power centers, with the possible exception of the Harvard School of Law. It is to be expected, therefore, that American anthropologists should emphasize the purity of their scientific discipline: the study of man should properly be used to further the study of man. It is one of the curiosities of American academic intellectuals, a special minority of academics, that they should complain bitterly about the way they are neglected by power and at the same time preen themselves for the moral purity of their intellectual enterprise.

The resulting anxiety appears in the American anthropologist's eager and self-searching inquiry into whether he is really and truly engaged in a genuinely scientific enterprise. At the present moment one of the problems in the development of all the sciences in this country is that the pure, or theoretical, scientist enjoys so much higher status in his profession than the practical scientist. As with the saved, so with the pure scientists; many are called but few are chosen. And the consequence is that we seem to have reached a limit on how many are called. Indeed, the proportion of college students selecting science as their life's work is declining.

The English notion of the relation of scientific knowledge to power emerges in Lubbock's major work, *The Origin of Civilization and the Primitive Condition of Man*, published in 1870. Lubbock, Baron Avebury, was completely committed to a doctrine of progress, and for this reason makes an interesting contrast with his friend Tylor, who, as the opening quotation shows, had his doubts. Without hesitation Lubbock plunged into the development of character and morals, of religion and law. To him primitive men, judging by contemporary primitives, had no morals at all. He did not deny that their behavior was governed by rules, indeed frequently enough by very binding rules. But this, he maintained, could not be called morality, which is an understanding of the distinction between right and wrong. It is evident that Sir John knew perfectly well what civilized religion is: Christianity purged of its superstition. A more ethnocentric position would be hard to think up, but that is not the point, which is considerably more subtle.

Sir John was firmly convinced that primitive man had no morality because the sanction for his rules was force, naked power, armed authority. Thus he was convinced that marriage by capture was probably to be found in the history of every culture; he found it, for example, still surviving in symbolic and attenuated form in the folklore and customs of the European peasant of his own times. Here was a clear case of force as the

180

ultimate foundation for morality. By a true morality, then, he meant rules not maintained by externally imposed force and violence. The test of whether a culture is moral, and hence civilized, is whether or not the rules governing behavior are internalized. But "internalized" was not his term, nor would it have been possible in 1870 for him to have thought of it. It comes from a later stage of cultural history. Instead, he used the term "duty." And in doing so he unwittingly revealed much of his own culture, very possibly something about all culture.

It is fairly clear that Lubbock thought of morality, of right and wrong, as transcendental, something, that is, which could not be thought of as imposed on man from a superhuman source but as something that by the laws of progress must necessarily be arrived at. Perhaps there is something of Kant here and the categorical imperative, the notion that if a moral position is arrived at by a rational process, it must be obeyed as equally binding on all men. In any case, it is clear that Lubbock did not turn the light of anthropology on himself, for he did not question the absolute validity of his concepts of right and wrong and of his concept of duty. What it comes down to is that the sense that one's duty is to follow rational principles of right and wrong, which makes social management by force and violence unnecessary. Duty takes over the function of force.

It is interesting that Lubbock, for all his concern with primitive man, ancient and surviving, as representing the childhood of the race, paid no attention to the use of force in inculcating the sense of duty in the child of his own time and class, force exerted by superiors, parents and teachers, and force exerted by peers, and student superiors. Even though he had gone to Eton, where he must have experienced personally and by observation the use of force for conditioning the youth to a sense of duty, he seems to have made no connection between force in the child culture of his own society and force in primitive societies. When we put all this together, it is obvious that Sir

John should have said that civilization is moral because force as a sanction and validation of moral rules has been pushed within society from adult behavior onto childhood behavior. It is odd that he did not say this, since it would be so coherent with his analogy between primitives and children. Yet the reason he did not is, it would seem, precisely his connection between power and duty *in his own society.* That he did not question; and his failure to do so makes it abundantly clear that the English interest in using anthropology for social management was not such a matter as philosophical utilitarianism. Rather the professionalized intellectual felt it his duty, his moral duty, his awareness of the distinction between right and wrong, to put his knowledge at the service of power and social management.

This comes out with fascinating clarity in the conclusion of his book.

> ... if the past has been one of progress, we may fairly hope that the future will be so too; that the blessings of civilization will not only be extended to other countries and to other nations, but that even in our own land they will be rendered more general and more equable; so that we shall not see before us always, as now, countrymen of our own living, in our very midst, a life worse than that of a savage; neither enjoying the rough advantages and real, though rude, pleasure of savage life, nor yet availing themselves of the far higher and more noble opportunities which lie within the reach of civilized Man.

This is the theme of the barbarian or savage within, that vast mass of human beings brought into existence by the industrial revolution who, most of the English ruling class was convinced, would destroy English civilization if admitted in any way to political power. Since they now have been admitted to political power, and since English civilization is in a very bad way indeed, perhaps the Victorian fear of the masses was justified.

Be that as it may, it is instructive to compare Tylor's conclusion with Lubbock's. Sir John was incapable of turning anthropology upon himself and his own class; Sir Edward, as he came to be, thought first of his own intellectual class and turned anthropology upon that: "But if history is to repeat itself according to precedent, we must look forward to stiffer duller ages of traditionalists and commentators." Baron John's attitude was that of the editors of the English *Book of Knowledge*, published before World War I. The frontispiece showed a typical upper-class English girl holding a lighted lamp, and the caption read, "The Heir of All the Ages." To the Baron, the England of Victoria was the point to which aeons of human progress had led, and the task of its minority of civilized human beings was "to extend the blessings of civilization ... to other countries and to other nations," and even "to our own land." Kipling's theme of "the white man's burden" had its source not merely in jingoistic imperialism, as is commonly asserted, and very possibly not in imperialism at all, but rather in the English conception of scientifically sound anthropology.

Edward Tylor, however, had a subtler mind, and a less ethnocentric one. He saw no law of progress, though he saw progress, or rather, as he usually preferred to say, cultural evolution. And there is a subtle but important difference. To the blunt mind of Lubbock progress was a law, and laws of nature were immanent in nature, to be discovered by civilized man. To Sir Edward, a scientific law was a proposition that subsumed a set of sufficiently similar instances. It was, in Darwin's great phrase, "a mental convenience." Sir Edward interpreted Victorian England as an exceptional, even an historically abnormal cultural situation, "When the oft-closed gates of discovery and reform stand open at their widest." He saw no absolute assurance of future progress immanent in the present, but rather in the present a rare opportunity which required rapid exploitation before it was too late.

Ortega Y Gasset saw the death of the cultural openness of the nineteenth century in the revolt of the masses; today Philip Rieff, the great sociologist, sees that same death in "the triumph of the therapeutic"; and our youthful rebels of the campus seem to be disengaging themselves from the cultural norms of the innovating middle classes in favor of a timeless, static, lubberland. Lubbock, a bad Darwinian, saw in Darwin a confirmation of himself; Tyler, a good Darwinian, understanding that adaptation of organism to environment is never perfect or final, could turn anthropology on his own class and even on himself and perceive cultural evolution as a never-ending process. At one point, indeed, he envisions the end of the human race with its adaptational problems still unsolved.

Lubbock was the perfect Victorian of popular conception, the man supremely self-confident in his own values and his own civilizing mission. Tylor, however, had been touched by a cultural relativism. His "natural" ethnocentricity had been shaken, and he was on the way to that cultural relativism without which no American anthropologist can be self-respecting. It is the foundation of his scientific purity. The English are still studying and applying the lessons of social anthropology in the management of lesser breeds without the law in the interest of extending European culture, no matter how humanitarian they are nor how much they respect the natives they are working with. While the Empire existed they were government anthropologists; and now that it has virtually ended, they work for the new native governments. The joke is that enough of those very natives have gone to European schools and universities, or their local imitations, to have learned cultural anthropology themselves, as well as the concept of cultural relativism. Frantz Fanon was such a man. Thus, at a time when the Lubbocks have triumphed, when there is but one viable culture left, European culture, the new non-European societies are torn between the assertion of native traditions and the Europeanization of those same cultures. If, as Mary McCarthy has asserted with such noble self-abnegation, the white race is the cancer of mankind, then galloping metathesis has set in and all of mankind is at its mercy. It may be so.

If English anthropology emerged from a group of men whose parents were members of the power class and who were rigorously trained and selected for access to power, even in a subordinate position, then it is scarcely surprising that English anthropologists have seen their duty in placing their science at the service of social management. If American anthropologists emerged from no such class and by their academic lives and profession have been denied access to social power, then it is scarcely surprising that they have seen their duty in maintaining the theoretical purity of their science and in taking cultural relativism as the foundation and touchstone of their self-respect. By this contrast Lubbock was the perfect Englishman, but Tylor was more American.

Lubbock was the son of a banker. He went to Eton but at the age of fourteen began to work in his father's banking house. In 1856, when he was twenty-two, he became a partner. As the son of a banker he had access to the intellectual world—and it was very impressive—of the high London bourgeoisie. Like Darwin himself, and by modern standards almost all scientists of his time, he was an amateur, dividing his life between his bank, his interest in bees and ants, and his quite remarkable achievements in the study of prehistory. He originated, for example, the distinction between paleolithic and neolithic. But he also was a Member of Parliament and succeeded in passing more than a dozen important measures—including the Bank Holidays Act, the Shop Hours Act, as well as the more predictable Ancient Monuments Act. In short, he was a social manager, and he took seriously his task of raising the British workingman from "a life worse than that of a savage."

Tylor was more like an American. His father was a brass founder, a manufacturer. His family were Quakers; he was educated at a Quaker school, a very different education, in all possible ways, from Eton. When he was sixteen he entered his father's business, but threatening consumption drove him to travel. By an accident, to be discussed later, he became interested in anthropology. Though by origin an amateur, again by modern standards, he made himself into the first truly professional anthropologist, at least in England, and was rewarded as we have seen, by being appointed first professor of anthropology at Oxford, having been for some years the Keeper of the Oxford Museum, already an appointment in anthropology. It is interesting that his elder brother was a geologist, a member of a profession that was already emerging from the amateur to the professional state. The point is that, unlike Lubbock, Tylor was not born into, or for, or spent his life in roles of social management and access to power, except for the nearly fifteen years he spent as a professor, and part, therefore, of the selective process of the English university. As a Quaker, he was already an outsider; he was one who had no such fund of unquestioned self-confidence as was given to Lubbock. He was, then, more American, and more amenable to strict scientificity, to a more sophisticated conception of scientific law, and to cultural relativism.

In reading American anthropology I have encountered a thousand sneers at cultural ethnocentricity, but never have I seen questioned the absolute validity of cultural relativism as a scientific principle.

Since it is not questioned, it is as much a received truth as Baron Avebury's ethnocentric self-confidence; since it is a received truth, its force is by now a moral force. And since its force is moral, is its intellectual origin—by the very principles of anthropology—suspect? By those very principles, must it not itself be a cultural product, one relative to the cultural situation

186

from which it emerged? Is it not reasonable to suppose, since the Baron's ethnocentricity is so easily traceable to the self-confidence of a class, that cultural relativism is as easily traceable to some classes' lack of self-confidence? And is it not obvious that that unconfident class is that of the professional academic intellectual?

The air of American university campuses has always been rent with cries of grief and outrage that our society does not grant the academic intellectual the validation he so obviously deserves. The university professor loves to travel in Europe, because there the professor is given the deference, he firmly believes, which is his due. The anti-intellectualism of the United States is the source of an endless lamentation in the groves of academe, and there never seems to be an effort on the part of these intellectuals to see that there is another side to the story. The anti-intellectual sees the professor as the source of a continuous threat to his own moral stability and to the stability of his society. The intellectual, in his objectivity, questions all things, including all values, and he does so in the name of rationality. But he fails to grasp the fact that the belief-system of any society is incoherent, and that to urge a culture to be rational is to urge it to tear itself apart. Thus his commitment to rationality is itself irrational, and thus he fails to grasp what the anti-intellectual feels at his nerve ends, the threat of rational objectivity. Nor does the intellectual perceive that his rational objectivity, his cultural relativism, is a function of his lack of access to power.

An instance of this and a splendid example of the resulting confusion is the hatred linguists have for departments of speech. The modern linguist proceeds from an anthropological background, and he loathes the speech people because they teach their students correct speech habits. Dominated by his cultural relativism, the linguist insists that there is no such thing as correct speech, and that the student has a *right* to his own speech habits and those of his cultural community. Aside from the fact that in this society the standardization of speech habits in patterns acceptable throughout the country on the upper cultural, social, and status levels is the principal key to access to those levels, to the transcendence of one's own speech and cultural community into a wider life, it is obvious that the linguist as a scientist committed to cultural relativism and objectivity is utterly irrational and subjective in doing anything but studying the interesting cultural phenomenon of the function in American education of training in nationally validated speech habits.

As a cultural relativist, he has no rational justification for telling someone else that he *ought* to be a cultural relativist. Indeed, the moral irrationalism of cultural relativism is an endlessly fascinating phenomenon of modern American culture. Perhaps the real reason is that, deprived of access to power and to the channels of social management, the unfortunate academic intellectual is reduced to exerting power over his colleagues. Hence, perhaps, the savage infighting between colleagues and departments and schools within a university. Whatever the university of today is, it is not an intellectual community, a notion which is but a myth to sustain self-confidence in a sociocultural situation devoted to undermining it.

An example will illustrate the failure of American anthropologists to turn their anthropology upon themselves, and will lead us more directly into the difficult problem of how and why anthropology emerged in England when it did.

In 1964 Paul Bohanaan edited and abridged Tylor's first attempt to create a science of anthropology, *Researches into the Early History of Mankind and the Development of Civilization*, originally published in 1865. One paragraph of Bohanaan's introduction is of great interest.

It is difficult, in the years after Whitehead and his followers have made the subject-object confusion a part of the armory of every analytical mind, to appreciate how far along the path Tylor had proceeded in his discussion of "this confusion of objective with subjective connexion." . . . [Tylor] lived in an age . . . before it was possible to turn the full glare of analysis on the self. . . . But in his time he did not have the tools to sustain the self-examination necessary to bring the scientist's viewpoints into the data, thereby creating a real theory of social, psychic and cultural analysis. We still may not have that capacity, but we are much closer to it than was Tylor—and we know that this capacity is what a real theory in the social sciences demands.

It is an astonishing paragraph. When Tylor was writing his *Primitive Culture*, Browning was writing *The Ring and the Book*, and we have seen how far along the path he had proceeded "in his discussion of this confusion of objective with subjective connexion." Indeed, the subject-object problem was anything but novel in Tylor's time. The Romantics, poets and philosophers and historians, had been discussing it for decades. *Not* to have been aware of it at the time would have been astonishing for anyone of intellectual sophistication. Even Lubbock shows traces of awareness, though, to be sure, not very many, nor very strong. Bohanaan himself does not show very much or very sophisticated awareness of what the problem involves. To turn the full glare of analysis onto the self is, of course, to discover that the self's perceptions and cognitions are dictated by its interests, its adaptational interests, if we are using an organism-environment mode of explanation. But, equally, it is to discover that the full glare of analysis is also dictated by interests, and so on, into an infinite regress. And the regress continues until it is realized that one can only erect a towering superstructure of interest upon interest, of explanation upon explanation, until the whole thing topples over into the awareness that interests are in fact inaccessible, and that even if one achieves a cultural transcendence, cultural interests are still at work, and the strategy of the transcendence and the interests at work in that strategy are also inaccessible. Turning the full glare of analysis on the self is but an exercise in rationality, and ultimately rationality, traced to its sources, disappears into a mist whence can come only paralysis or an action without justification.

And thus it will be with a "real theory of social, psychic, and cultural analysis." The cultural relativist will discover that his position is itself culturally relative. He will discover what Browning already knew, that "to turn the full glare of analysis onto the self " is but to create still another mask, and that from behind that ultimate mask emerge oracles as ambiguous as those of Delphi. He will be forced to abandon his objectivity, his rationality, to realize that his cultural relativism is in the interests of his own culture, and that the study of man must be in the interests of what we want to do with man, in the interests, then, of social management and of social power. The good Sir John knew this in his bones, and so, with less certainty and self-confidence, did Tylor. Anthropology is a reformer's science. From Tylor's frank recognition of the subjectivity of his own investigations, American anthropology shyly and modestly averts its gaze.

The reason is its eagerness to be a science, and so it sees its origins as emerging from a scientific problem. But it was not so. Anthropology emerged from a cultural crisis, and it was, particularly in Tylor's hands, polemical to the highest degree. It emerged from a furious battle, one that embroiled all intellectual England. It emerged from the crisis of Darwinism, but that crisis was only part of a still more inclusive crisis, in which Darwinism, though a notable storm, was but a single storm center in a multitude of storms.

190

One aspect of that crisis was a conflict with which both Tylor and Lubbock were directly concerned. Is the history of man one of progressive development or of degeneration? Bohanaan, as might be expected, given his cultural circumstances, treats it as a scientific problem and thus gives no inkling of what the issues really were. The two principal proponents of the degeneration theory were Whately, Anglican Archbishop of Dublin, and the Duke of Argyll. Their biological theory was biblical. If God created man in his own image, then man was not related to the primates. He had a soul and reason, and these were given him by God. Fresh from the hands of his Maker, his reason, it is rationally incontrovertible, was at its most perfect and his soul strongest in his affirmation of Deity. Since nowadays reason is uncertain, morality is unreliable, and religious doubt is rampant, it must follow that man has degenerated since his making. The primitive tribes currently existing in the nineteenth century were, therefore, not survivals of an earlier state of man, but degenerative tribes which had been pushed to the edges of civilization by those peoples who had not degenerated so far, or who had, in the arts of civilization at least, even improved. That is, in the effort to counter the developmentalists, the Duke of Argyll admitted that there had been improvement since the Middle Ages, and suggested that in his original form man was a kind of medieval man.

Now the developmentalists admitted that degeneration was possible, though rare. Even so staunch a developmentalist as John Lubbock was ready to admit that the industrial population of England had degenerated from the primitive state. Nevertheless, they insisted, the degenerative theory could not possibly explain "survivals." By this term they meant those superstitions and practices found in both primitive cultures and high cultures, magic for example. Were the degeneration theory correct there must be countersurvivals of high culture in primitive cultures. And there were no such survivals. They were willing to grant that monotheism of the Christian variety is the highest possible form of religious belief, but it must have evolved through cultural development. Otherwise, there would be traces of it in primitive cultures, and there are none. (Since then they have been discovered.)

The issues involved were grave. Obviously the religious issue was important. But what was at stake was not merely revelation and the Bible, not merely original sin, from which degeneration is a biological-cultural deduction, but also the whole sociocultural structure which was seen as validated by God and revelation, and particularly the European technique of social management which was seen as validated by the explanatory proposition of original sin. To assert that it was a problem of the warfare between science and religion is to simplify the situation and to conceal the intellectual and cultural struggle that was going on, as well as to weigh and resolve the problem one way or another, according to one's tastes.

There was a deeper issue, and that issue was central to English culture, as it is central to any culture, the relation of the mode of validation to a mode of explanation, or theory construction. To attack the mode of explanation is to attack the mode of validation, and the reverse is also true. We have already seen several instances of this. Romanticism emerged because the Enlightenment mode of explanation developed irreconcilable incoherences; it collapsed, for a few men at least, from its own internal contradictions. Initially, until they had developed a new mode of explanation, the Romantics could perceive no way to validate their social values or social roles. Consequently they turned to the self, or more precisely, they invented the self, originally on a quasi-Christian foundation, as a new mode of validation.

The intimate connection between validation and explanation can also be seen in the preceding account of cultural relativism. Whatever its sources, it was first seen as a solution to the intellectual problem of studying primitive societies in their own terms. But it has become, *because* it is an ultimate explanatory mode, a mode of validation. That is why the culturally relativistic linguists attack the speech professors. The speech people explain dialectical differentia by appealing to sociocultural hierarchy. The linguists attack because cultural relativism has become for them a mode of validating themselves, their status, and the intellectual worthiness of their scientific enterprise.

It is against this background of the identity of explanation and validation that much of Lubbock's and Tylor's efforts must be seen, particularly their discussions of religion and morals. The 1870's were of crucial importance in English culture, because it was during this decade that in the intellectual world theology became centrifugal. Up to this time theology had been centripetal. The ultimate questions were asked in theological terms. Or to put it another way, the infinite regress of explanatory superstructure was terminated by theological propositions, validated by an historical revelation. Agnosticism, which received its name in this decade, and atheism were however becoming increasingly conspicuous, and the association of the latter with radical politics threatened the identity of explanation, validation, and social management, which was central to the stability of English society, or so, at any rate, a good many people thought. Consequently, there were innumerable books and magazine articles proving beyond the shadow of a doubt that a nonbeliever could not be moral, that religious belief was absolutely essential for morality. The authors of these works—and they included some of the most conspicuous names in England—insisted that to question religion was to undermine morals and therefore to destroy society. The identification of explanation, validation, and social management could not be plainer, nor the importance of the degeneration theory to that identification.

Against this background it is of the highest significance and interest that Tylor and Lubbock went to enormous trouble to demonstrate that religion and morals were not connected, and to trace religion to the primitive belief in spirits. To dissolve the connection between religion and morality was to assert that social structure was inherent in the developmental process, that, as Tylor put it, "the primitive condition of man was one of utter barbarism," and that "from this condition various races have independently raised themselves," and that, furthermore, "these views follow from strictly scientific considerations." This was to undo part of the knot that tied together explanation, validation, and social management. To untie the rest of it Tylor turned to mythology.

Although he politely sidestepped the issue of whether or not Christianity is a mythology, it was perfectly clear from his discussion that the conclusion was unavoidable. He saw myth as a form of explanation, but explanation free of any principle of verification. Thus myth became a causal explanation acceptable not because it is true but because it is satisfying to the imagination. He was strongly influenced both by Hume's *Natural History of Religion*, and by Comte, both of whom proposed personification, the ascription of human attributes to nonhuman objects, as the fundamental mode of primitive perception and causal explanation. From this he developed his famous doctrine of animism, which he identified with Comte's notion of fetishism, and established his minimum definition of religion, the belief in spiritual beings.

This was to attack the knot of identification on two fronts. On the one hand it implied that the degeneration theory was itself a derivation from animism, a development of primitive modes of thinking. And on the other hand it was to attack the dominating mode of explanation, causality. Thus the attack on the degeneration theory uncovered not only its origins in primitive thought but also its mode of explanation, pseudo-causality. In quoting Hume he underscores the phrase "unknown causes."

He seems to have come extraordinarily close to the notion that causal explanations do not link events in the real world; they only link statements about those events. To be sure, he would have said that causal links are to be found in the mind, as Hume did, and the use of that word is the source of inextricable confusion. Nevertheless, it is of the utmost interest that he scarcely uses the word "cause" at all.

To be sure it appears on the first page of *Primitive Culture.* "The uniformity which so largely pervades civilization may be ascribed, in great measure, to the uniform action of uniform causes," just as on the next page he talks about "the unity of nature, the fixity of its laws, the definite sequence of cause and effect through which every fact depends on what has gone before it, and acts upon what is to come after it." Nevertheless, just as later he asserts that a scientific law is a subsumption of similar events, so his method of procedure, his thinking, is not causal at all. These opening statements look like a promise to provide laws and causes, but it is a question as to how seriously they are to be taken. Certainly the promise is never fulfilled, except the conclusion that man has developed from primitivism to civilization. Moreover, he scarcely ever discusses causality, or proposes a causal explanation. Rather, his whole method is organized around the notions of recurrence and regularity. - Whatever he may assert, his method is not causal but analogical.

Regarded as rhetoric, these opening paragraphs, as their stately and ponderous style suggests, so different from the rest of his writing, merely claim that a scientific approach to man, no matter how repugnant it may seem, is justified. He is using the strategy of identifying his enterprise as a scientific one. Thus his language seems to imply a philosophical determinism, but elsewhere he disclaims any concern with either determinism or free will. In actual practice his explanations are not causal. Rather, he is concerned with patterns of cultural data, "knowledge, belief, art, morals, law, custom, and many other capabilities and habits acquired by man as a member of society," and his explanations amount to little more than the assertion that there are patterns, and that there are what one might call meta-patterns, that is, patterns of patterns. Thus the whole idea of development is that there is one grand pattern subsuming all patterns.

The importance of this is that the knot of identity of explanation, validation, and social management was a causal knot. In showing the basic pattern of myth-making to be a causal explanation and in demonstrating that human behavior is to be understood not in terms of causality but in terms of analogically similar patterns of behavior, he implied not only the inadequacy of the degenerative theory but equally the inadequacy of the mode of explanation from which it had emerged. He defeated it by making the conclusion irresistible that it was but another causal myth, satisfying to the imagination, but that was all; and he made his attack the more effective by not offering an alternative causal explanation.

This is worth exploring in a little more detail, because Tylor's rhetorical appeal to the principle of causality contrasted with his noncausal and subsumptive explanatory mode places him on the frontier of modern science. His very inconsistency in appealing to the order of the universe and to natural laws and by contrast asserting elsewhere that a natural law is something like a mental [i.e., a verbal] convenience is an indication that we have here a neat example of innovation and culture transcendence.

Like all terms, "cause" has a number of meaning functions, but for our purposes two may easily be distinguished. Consider these two sentences: [1] "Letting go a stone causes it to fall to the ground." [2] "When one lets go a stone, gravity causes it to fall to the ground." The first may be easily and correctly rewritten as, "If one lets go a stone, it will fall to the ground." That is, it is a simple predictive sentence and can easily be tested. Now the second sentence can be rewritten in precisely the same way, except that when one does so "gravity" and "cause" are eliminated. The only way to keep them is to write two sentences. "If one lets go a stone, it will fall to the ground. Gravity causes it to fall." Obviously the second of these two sentences is not predictive at all and cannot be tested as the first one can be. For example, if one asks, "Why does gravity cause the stone to fall?" the answer is, "If there is nothing to hold them up, all objects fall to the ground." "Gravity," then, is a word that subsumes all cases of objects without support falling to the ground. In the first sentence, "cause" is predictive of the consequences of nonverbal behavior performed according to the instructions which emerge if the sentence is rewritten. In the second sentence, "cause" is not predictive in function but subsumptive. Thus, if a literary historian writes, "Romanticism caused Tennyson to write as he did," it would be an error—one that is universally made—if "Romanticism" is conceived of as having predictive causal power. On the contrary, the sentence merely asserts that Tennyson properly belongs in the category of writers already determined as Romantic. Romanticism did not cause Tennyson to do anything, though it would be a *little* more correct—a *little* more predictive—to say that the notion of Romanticism held by that literary historian caused him to subsume Tennyson under "Romanticism."

More than a third of *Primitive Culture* is devoted to Tylor's discussion of animism, and his intense concern with language made him aware of the fact that language embodies and transmits animistic conceptions. However, he tended to think of language as a symbolization of a mental concept, of something in the mind. Had he lived at a time when it was intellectually possible to abandon the word "mind" he could have made the next step. He could have seen that in our two original sentences, the attributes of a human being have been transferred from the human being who causes the falling of the stone to the word "gravity." And he would have seen that scientific language tends to be as mythological as primitive myth itself. Whether we say that Zeus causes the stone to fall or gravity causes the stone to fall, in either case we are using "Zeus" and "gravity" for the same explanatory and subsumptive purpose, and we are using "causes" in precisely the same way. It would be no great step, therefore, to build a temple to Gravity and sacrifice at an altar. And indeed in the eighteenth century that sort of thing was very commonly done.

Now actually Tylor came very close to realizing this, because he saw with great clarity that abstract conceptions emerged from mythology by the gradual stripping away of human attributes from divine beings, leaving only their subsumptive explanatory function. Anyone, for example, as familiar as he was with the history of metaphysics in the seventeenth and eighteenth centuries can see this happening to the term "God." Milton's God is already perilously close to demythologization, and after Newton "God" gradually was reduced to, "Whatever it is that makes a unitary explanation of physical phenomena possible." And in fact, what happened was that even that attenuated conception of God became further attenuated into "natural law." Thus Laplace could make his famous remark that in creating his theory of the stability of the solar system "God" was a hypothesis he did not find it necessary to use. The next step was "scientific law," a further attenuation, since the attributes of "nature" were now stripped away, leaving only the attributes of "science," a human activity.

In the twentieth century this has meant the gradual realization that "science" is a common human behavior which a man specializes in when he is playing the social role of scientist, and the currently emerging notion, as yet barely perceived, except by a few, that all the sciences are, ultimately, behavioral sciences. Thus when Tylor uses the rhetoric of law and causality, he is paying pious and no doubt perfectly sincere tribute to the mythology of science of his day, but actually in practice has advanced from the mythological conception to the verbal conception of causality.

Thus he effectively challenged the current mode of explanation in two ways. By his rhetorical appeal to the physical sciences, he allied himself with those cultural forces which had already been responsible for the attenuation of religion and theology as explanatory systems; and by creating a novel model of explanation he went beyond that attenuation by implicitly denying the validity of causality in scientific explanation. In effect he showed that the predictive function of "cause" is completely different from its subsumptive or explanatory function. But baldly, the predictive function is a verbal instruction to do something with the nonverbal world, while the explanatory function is an instruction to do something with language.

The results of manipulating language and manipulating the world are obviously very different, but as Tylor's studies clearly showed, the tendency to confuse the two kinds of instructions is a human universal. It is easy to see why. If you give me detailed instructions for finding the red croquet ball, and if I follow the instructions, then I can say with some adequacy that "red croquet ball" in your instructions referred to the red croquet ball I found. Therefore, when you say, "Education is the solution to our social problems" I have an irresistible tendency to assume that "education," "solution," and "social problems" refer to something that I can, by investigating the nonverbal world, actually find. But these are subsumptive, not predictive words; they are the names of categories of human behavior. If they "refer" to anything they refer at best only to classes of predictive sentences.

Now to say that Tylor would have described his analysis of human culture in these terms would, of course, be absurd. It is quite possible that he had no notion that he did not do what he proposed to do in his introductory rhetoric but rather did something vastly more interesting and fruitful. He made ethnography, or cultural anthropology, into a science. How he proceeded is of some interest.

There existed a vast body of miscellaneous information about primitive and barbarian peoples, about non-European civilized peoples, and about European religion and folklore. So far ethnography was a mere "science of observation," not yet a constructive science. What had been published, much of it by Germans, consisted of descriptions of primitives which did not do much more than supplement and carry on the tradition of travel literature as it was to be found in those vast and fascinating compilations of the late sixteenth and early seventeenth centuries, Hakluyt's *Voyages* and *Purchas His Pilgrime*. To these could be added reports of missionaries, to be used, of course with great caution, particularly in matters of religion, on which they had a tendency to be biased. What Tylor did was to go through this material, selecting passages having to do, for example, with ways of making fire. His chapter on that in his first attempt, the *Researches*, is still one of the best summaries of the subject. Thus he began with certain categories, selecting them as everyone does by a combination of cultural tradition, innovation, verbal deduction, and personality interests. His peculiar sensitivity emerges in the *Researches*, which begins with language and is mostly about language, including mythology and certain nonverbal signs, such as gesture. The same sensitivity displays itself in *Primitive Culture*. Language and the structure of meaning was his primary interest, and this is why he was able to attack the validated modes of explanation in his own culture. Strictly, what he did was to classify statements about human culture into various categories, and the technique of his classificatory procedure, his categorization, was analogy. He laid the foundation for the very modern realization that the terms "culture" and "meaning" are interchangeable; this was the long-term consequence of his sensitivity in beginning with the problem of language. Working with extreme care and great analogical subtlety, he then organized his categorized data by means of another analogy, evolution. Darwin's *On the Origin of Species* had been published in 1859, and there is not the slightest doubt that it was Tylor's model.

Since Tylor had by no means fully entered the world of modern thinking but was only beginning to detach himself from the old way, it is not surprising that he himself should have been the victim of his own animism, of his own magical notion of reference, and should have assumed that the word "mind" referred to a discoverable entity. Consequently, he thought he was talking about the mind of primitive man. In this "mind" are "ideas" and these are expressed in various forms of language and non-verbal behavior. After all, even the current Webster still preserves this usage. Tylor and other early anthropologists have been properly castigated by the anthropologists of today for so naïve a way of constructing anthropological discourse; but it is no matter. All "mind" does in Tylor is to categorize "those capabilities and habits acquired by man as a member of society," that is, those capabilities and habits which cannot be categorized by biology and physiology, or as we say, learned behavior. When he says that an idea can be expressed in different cultures, he is merely asserting that two apparently different myths, for example, or rituals, such as initiation, can be usefully subsumed under the same categorial term. The word "mind" is harmless enough, for the most part, at least in scientific discussion, so long as it is remembered that it is not a predictive term but a subsumptional or explanatory term.

"Culture," then, is what has been produced by the human mind. Does it show any regularity? This is where Darwin came in, for the *Origin* showed biological succession as moving from the simple organism to the complex organism through time, ultimately to man, the most complex of organisms. Now Tylor was too subtle to take over such a paradigm just as it stood. Rather, he depended on Darwin's explanation, which was the novel idea of the *Origin*, not the movement from the simple organism to the complex organism which had, in fact, long since been established. What Darwin showed was that the emergence of new species could be explained by adaptation of organism to environment. Tylor, therefore, basing his work on the fact of man's larger brain, saw mind, the manifestation of brain activity, as an instrument of adaptation. The dynamics of culture, then, could be explained on the assumption of an increasingly fine-grained adaptation. Thus techniques of fire-making could be organized in a sequence from the less efficient to the more efficient. And so with all tools. And so with "thinking" itself, that is, explanation. The example given above of the attenuation of "God" into a verbal convenience is exactly to the point. In various cultures, independent of each other, the same sequences of adaptationally effective cultural patterns emerge. To put the whole scheme in briefest form, Tylor categorized cultural patterns on the basis of analogy, and then organized those patterns into meta-patterns on the basis of analogically similar historical sequence and emergence.

This was the structure of his thinking, and it was explosive. It exploded the degeneration theory, not by offering an alternative causal theory but by offering a kind of theory construction, absolutely novel in discourse, about man and one of overwhelming power and conviction. It undid the causal knot of explanation, validation, and social management. It is no wonder that he called anthropology "the reformer's science." Now it is worth observing that with one exception Tylor's method was the method of the physical sciences. That exception, of course, was that he was classifying statements. Closer to the physical sciences is classifying observed configurations. When Malinowski in the 1920's made it clear that the anthropologist cannot depend on reports of what people do but must observe what they do in the full context of their ordinary lives, he was making anthropology more of a science. It has not gone on to the final step, manipulating the world, that is, experimentation. Yet in calling anthropology the reformer's science, that is exactly what Tylor was calling for.

This can be made a little clearer if we observe what the physical scientist does and why experimentation, ever since the early seventeenth century, has been the foundation of science. The fact is that the physical scientist also works analogically. He asserts that a scientific proposition is not acceptable as a scientific truth unless it is based upon experiments which can be repeated by another scientist. If we break this down, we can see that it amounts to an assertion that scientific law must be capable of generating specific instructions for nonverbal behavior. If those instructions are correctly carried out, the result will be a manipulation of the phenomenal world which will lead to the consequences predicted by the law and the instructional statements. The results of the manipulation, then, must be sufficently similar to the original experiment so that, by analogy, they may be placed in the same category as the original experiment. But even the physical scientist depends upon language, upon reports of experiments, exact accounts of which come first in scientific papers. The full scientific enterprise depends upon experiments, observations, and reports. Working analogically, the scientist moves backward, to use a spatial metaphor, from the empirical world into the timeless world of theory construction. But he also moves forward from theory construction to the world again.

Science is so successful because it exploits the irresolvable tension between subject and object, between theory and experiment, although it was not until the twentieth century that scientists began to be fully aware of what they are doing. Tylor's achievement was to establish anthropology on a scientific model and to found it in such a way that his own theory construction could be corrected. What Tylor was proposing is that to be a complete science the science of culture must do what the physical sciences do; it must manipulate the material which is its subject matter. That subject matter is human behavior. Having shattered the religious mode of validation, having abandoned the dominating mode of explanation, he proposed that anthropologists should be responsible for social management. It seems to me reasonably clear that such a daring proposal could only come from a situation in which the professional and academic intellectual is accustomed to access to power, the source of social management. From this point of view the cultural relativism of American anthropologists is a refusal to complete their science. The source of that refusal is a timid rationalization of the fact that the social structure denies them access to power. It also seems to me reasonably clear that in Tylor we have a remarkable, even a thrilling example of cultural transcendence. And it seems equally clear that it could have emerged only at a time of cultural crisis.

It is worth asking how such a cultural leap came about, but to do that with some hope of success it is necessary to have a general and theoretical notion of what the anthropologist Anthony Wallace in his recent book, *Religion: An Anthropological Approach*, has called cognitive resynthesis. Several recent studies of individuals responsible for important scientific breakthroughs are useful guides into the problem. One demonstrates that scientific revolutions occur when someone notices a fact or some experimental effect which had previously been neglected. The reason for the neglect is that the datum in question can be exploited neither by the experimental behavior of current science nor by the current theories prevailing in that area of scientific investigation. To put it in subject-object language, the subject is so committed to the establishment and reinforcement of the subjective ways of explaining the world that he cannot do anything with the data his metaphysic cannot absorb. It does not occur him to question his theory; he simply ignores the data. It is the common, the standard, nearly the universal form of behavior. The man capable of refusing to ignore the recalcitrant data, is one who can experience the tension between subject and object. In this case, as it were, he resolves that tension in favor of the object. The theory, the metaphysic, the mode of explanation collapses. A period usually of great cognitive disturbance ensues, and the new theory emerges.

The other study fits into this one very well. It is an examination in some detail of the great scientific breakthroughs, principally of the nineteenth century. Its conclusion is that such breakthroughs, such cognitive resyntheses, do not happen the way they are supposed to happen according to the current mythology of science. That mythology asserts that scientific discovery is the consequence of painstaking examination of all the evidence, careful experimentation, and cautious and logical construction of a new theory. Everything we know about the emergence of new visions of reality, of new subjective constructs, denies the validity of this theory. It is a successful technique of scientific discovery only for adding some new bit of knowledge or new theoretical extension to an already existing theory. It is supplemental, not radically innovative. On the contrary, the really revolutionary breakthroughs happen all at once. They are ideas that flash into existence, either full-blown theories, or theories that though initially rudimentary rapidly become fully structured, though of course at first, until investigation and testing and gathering of information take place, skeletal, not yet fleshed out.

Further recent investigation into the operation of brain cells is of additional help in understanding this conundrum of the cultural leap. "The central concept of the new model is that of the stochastic or indeterminate behavior of nerve cells, requiring statistical analysis in terms of probabilities of firing, and thus making any meaningful statement of the relation between an individual response and a particular single stimulus impossible." [*Mind*, April, 1969, p. 313] This provides us with some understanding as to why behavior is both predictable and unpredictable. Free Will and Determinism are not alternative and antithetical theories of what human beings can do but merely two poles between which lies the continuum of what people actually do. Information, it would seem, is patterned somehow in the brain cells, and it looks as if the indeterminacy of cell firing both reinforces those patterns and alters them. This would certainly fit in quite well with recent theories of dreaming, which suggest that dreams integrate new information into old patterns and at the same time necessarily restructure those patterns.

At any rate, speculative as this new information is, it provides some understanding of why the norm of human behavior is innovation. That is, we learn behavioral patterns, but in using them we always change them. Everybody innovates; and another way of saying this is that nobody ever gets anything right. Early in this book I proposed that creativity is socially validated innovation. To this it is now reasonable to add that error is socially invalidated innovation. The scholar who studied great creative breakthroughs in scientific discovery and found that they happen all at once should also have studied those revolutionary breakthroughs in scientific thought which turned out to be quite useless. Admittedly, great creative failures would be harder to find information about than great creative successes; not only do they frequently not get to the point of being recorded, but they are usually buried. However, there are plenty of discarded scientific theories which were considered very important at one time—degeneration, for example, though of course that is a minor instance, since it was simply a logical development of an existing metaphysic, not, as in Tylor's case, an entirely novel way of organizing data. I know of one great anthropologist who spends an afternoon each week thinking up as wild and as far-out theories as he possibly can. He writes them down, and then in the course of the week discards those he thinks useless and saves those he thinks worth developing.

His behavior is an excellent model of "creativity." To put it as paradoxically as possible, creativity is socially validated error, and error is socially invalidated creativity. My friend acts as society and either validates or invalidates his innovations, naming them either errors or creative ideas. Vast efforts have been made, both theoretically and by investigation and study, to determine the attitudes of the "creative mind" or the "creative personality." From this point of view, such efforts are doomed to failure, as so far they have been. What should be studied is not the process of "creativity" but the process of social validation, including how the individual, acting as a representative of society, validates and invalidates his own errors.

The creative personality then, is one who does not discard his errors but preserves them and develops them. If his society validates them as well, then he is labeled a "creative personality." In kindergarten today and in the early grades children are encouraged to be creative. Given directions, for example, to paint a picture, those who depart most widely from the norms of the semiotic behavior of children are given the greatest praise. Their errors are validated and become creative acts. Similarly, studies both here and in England show that college students who have majored in the humanities are more creative than those who major in the sciences. This has the leaders of the scientific establishment gravely concerned, and perhaps they should be. From the present point of view, however, the explanation for this is that the culturally established patterns of invalidating innovation are much more firmly established in the sciences than they are in the humanities, by which is meant principally literature and the arts and history. Certainly in art the means of deciding whether or not a work of art is good are as various and uncertain and as full of disagreement as anything could well be. For the past one hundred and seventy years, since the coming of Romanticism, the social process of validating works of art has become increasingly uncertain, so that now almost anything that shows sufficient error is validated by somebody, and usually sold at a high price. In the humanities generally, including history and philosophy, validation is extremely confusing, and the social processes by which it is arrived at are exceedingly incoherent and uncertain.

Another instructive tendency in our universities is that students have swung in increasing numbers from majoring in the sciences to majoring in the humanities, so that the sciences are now actually threatened by recruitment insufficient to maintain the vast scientific enterprise. At the same time student unrest has grown, erupting in riots and constantly producing demands that the whole educational system be restructured. Perhaps it should be, but that is not the point here. The point is that these outcries are filled with terms like "creativity" and "innovation" and "revolution" and so on. Is the reason that from kindergarten these students have been trained to validate error as creativity? And to judge anything insufficiently innovative as invalid?

In short, when Coleridge and the other Romantics, alienated from their society and their culture by the breakdown of the Enlightenment, generated the theory of the Creative Imagination, they started a cultural process the consequences of which we are seeing today. It would be idle to say that it is not a process of the greatest possible interest. The least one can say is that it has finally produced a generation with an unusually large number of individuals who are highly tolerant of innovation and who have a culturally built-in tendency to validate almost any innovation as creativity.

The point of all this is to understand a little better what Tylor did. To begin with, it is evident that he himself was the original validator of his own extraordinary innovation, the full nature of which, I have suggested, he did not necessarily entirely understand. It is not necessary that a man be able to respond to what he has done with full verbal explanation in order to have done something extraordinarily novel. Wagner himself admitted that he could not really explain *The Ring*; he simply knew that somehow it all hung together, as indeed it does, though it is so profound and subtle that it takes a lot of study and thought to see how. Shaw, later in the nineteenth century, pointed out that a genius makes but one creative leap, as Ibsen did in *Brand*, and then spends the rest of his life explaining it. Indeed, Shaw himself implied everything he had to say in *Man and Superman*; the rest of his plays are footnotes to that masterpiece.

Now we do not ordinarily tend to think of science in the nineteenth century as being a part of Romanticism and the Romantic tradition. As I pointed out above, Bohanaan saw Tylor's work only in the light of a scientific problem and seems to have had no inkling that Tylor was responding to a problem general within the culture, at least at its higher levels. Nevertheless, everything we know about the principal scientists of the Victorian world is, first, that by modern professional standards they were amateurs, including Tylor and his great predecessor and model, Darwin, and second, that their educational background, their adult interests, and their supportive culture gave great weight and significance to what we call today the humanities. Because they were not professionals, but amateurs, they were very much aware of what was going on in the nonscientific worlds of literature, poetry, music, philosophy, and the various visual arts. They all read Carlyle, as well as Tennyson and John Stuart Mill. Furthermore, the world of the educated, the cultivated, the artistic, the scientific, was small and highly interactive, partly because of the phenomenon of English life discussed above—the training and selection of individuals for roles in power and social management. London social life was intense and it included Oxford and Cambridge. The probability, therefore, of a scientist knowing the new ideas in the humanities was far higher than it is in America at the present time.

But there is not only this general probability to indicate that Tylor was aware of Romantic thinking. There is the evidence in *Primitive Culture* itself. Not only is it liberally sprinkled with quotations from the poets of England, including such a Romantic poet as Shelley; there are quotations from Greek and Latin poets in the original and without translation, thus indicating that he himself was a humanistically educated man and writing for a public of his peers, who could be expected to read Greek and Latin. There are also frequent references to the imagination, and it is evident that it is the Romantic doctrine of the Creative Imagination to which he was referring. Tylor seems, for example, to have had a sufficiently wide acquaintance with the poetry of the nineteenth century to assert that it was, in many ways, a "survival" of primitive myth-making, though watered down and not intended to be taken seriously. It is curious that one school of twentieth-century poets and critics, strongly inspired by James Frazer in his *Golden Bough*, himself working in the tradition of Tylor, should have insisted that literature is essentially myth-making, and that the task of the modern poet is to create myths for the modern world, myths that would give meaning and value to modern man. Hart Crane tried to create out of Brooklyn Bridge a myth for modern America, a myth that would gather together all that was positive in American life. Indeed in his great poem Brooklyn Bridge becomes a symbol for the process I have called culture transcendence; and he concludes the magnificent, an ode to Brooklyn Bridge, with, "And of thy curveship lend a myth to God."

Furthermore, Tylor found in animism the beginning of religion and mythology and the commencement of that process which in the course of endless centuries led to science and to himself. "For example," he writes, "one of the greatest metaphysical doctrines is a transfer to the field of philosophy from the field of religion, made when philosophers familiar with the conception of object-phantoms used this to provide a doctrine of thought, thus giving rise to the theory of ideas." He also says, "it is proved that among the lower races all over the world the operation of outward events on the inward mind leads not only to statement of fact, but to formation of myth." Here again is an instance of his not grasping fully what he himself had accomplished, and an indication that, like all innovators who make a cognitive resynthesis, he put his together from the new and the old. Had he fully grasped the implications of his awareness that a law of nature is rather a law of science, a mental convenience, he would have been able to overcome the internal incoherence of his book. He would have been able to see what at least a few people see today, though by no means everyone, that between the Creative Imagination of the poet, the artist, and the Creative Imagination of the scientist there is no difference whatever. The sources of all innovation are identical. It is a matter of cultural support as to whether any of these validates his own innovation strongly enough to classify it as creativity rather than error and to submit to the public processes of social validation.

The literature of the nineteenth century, throughout Europe and America, is filled with discussions of the imagination and of creativity. In the preface to the 1800 edition of the *Lyrical Ballads* Wordsworth already presents not only the Romantic doctrine of the imagination but also associates the scientist and the poet as essentially engaged in the same enterprise. "Poetry is the breath and the finer spirit of all knowledge; it is the impassioned expression which is in the countenance of all Science." And Wordsworth clearly meant the natural scientist. This is something that Tylor almost certainly would have known. More than anything else, the Romantic doctrine of the

Imagination was responsible for the great sensitivity, understanding, and respect with which Tylor treated primitive and civilized mythology. Myth and scientific theory are alike; both are imaginative constructs of the same data. Tylor dimly saw this. What he did not grasp is the difference. Science is corrected myth. Myth reinforces and stabilizes interpretations of experience. Myth, then, resolves the subject-object tension in favor of the subject. Science exploits the tension by linking verbal to nonverbal behavior. Since he did not grasp the difference between science and myth, Tylor did not fully grasp the similarity.

His difficulty lay in his belief that primitive man cannot tell the difference between subject and object, but that civilized man can. Yet over and over again he shows that "among the lower races ... the operation of outward events on the inward mind leads ... to statement of fact." That Tylor himself used the subject–object terminology indicates that he was aware of and responding to the currents of nineteenth-century culture, for it was a terminology and a distinction connected with the German philosophers. His notion that civilized man can tell the difference between subject and object indicates that he had not grasped what German philosophy was really saying. He had taken terms without fully understanding their place in the systems from which they had come. It is quite possible that he derived the notion of the mythical or heuristic conception of scientific law from Dugald Stewart, who wrote early in the century, and Stewart is probably where Darwin learned it. However, Stewart's epistemology was not complete, as Carlyle realized. With the aid of the Germans Carlyle went on to grasp that cognition is always in service of human interests, that modern man can tell subject from object no more than primitive man could. To Carlyle—whom Tylor no doubt read but probably like most of his contemporaries did not fully understand—who was writing *Sartor Resartus* when Tylor was born, clothes wear out, the metaphors or myths which sustain us fray and tear under the grinding of reality, and have to be renewed. To Carlyle, the source of cultural dynamics is the tension between subject and object. From this point of view, it is clear that for Tylor the cultural support for his innovation came from Romanticism, and from his case it is possible to generalize that it was the cultural atmosphere created by Romanticism that was responsible for the extraordinary nineteenth-century increase in scientific enterprise, including the founding of new sciences, particularly the sciences of man, anthropology and sociology. Wordsworth the Romantic grasped the intimate relation between science and poetry. Romantic philosophy and literature and art created the model for the scientific enterprise.

There was, moreover, another factor in Tylor's cultural situation which was a force, and a force of the highest importance, in his cultural leap. That factor was the historicization of European culture accomplished by the Romantics. To approach its importance to Tylor, however, it will be useful to take another suggestion from Wallace on religion—the separation, as he calls it, that is, the preparation for cognitive resynthesis. Separation makes use of "what might be called the law of dissociation." This is the principle that any given set of cognitive and affective elements can be restructured more rapidly and more extensively the more the perceptual cues from the environment associated with miscellaneous previous learning of other matters are excluded from conscious awareness, and the more those new cues which are immediately relevant to the elements to be reorganized are presented. "How permanent such a new cognitive synthesis will prove to be depends, presumably, in part on the maintenance of the dissociation ... and in part on reinforcement in the conventional learning sense."

This point, reinforcement, is what I have been talking about as validation. As Wallace later points out, cultural support for the new cognitive synthesis is of the highest importance. Thus, for a strikingly new and culturally transcendent theoretical synthesis, such as we find in science, philosophy, literature of high cultural value, and even literary criticism, matters are certainly greatly helped if the culture includes a theoretical justification of cultural transcendence, originality, radical innovation. And, as we have seen, Romantic culture did contain just such a theoretical justification in its notion of the Creative Imagination.

Before we can make use of Wallace's notion of separation to understand Tylor, however, it needs certain corrections and extensions. Wallace distinguishes five stages in what he calls the ritual process; prelearning (the prior knowledge of at least some elements of the new cognitive synthesis), separation, suggestion (from one's self or others), execution, and maintenance. Now if we examine the life history of every Romantic figure who went through the experience of leaving the old Enlightenment culture and entering upon the new one, we find every one of Wallace's stages represented. In *Sartor Resartus* in the Everlasting No, the Center of Indifference, and the Everlasting Yea it is possible to find the most penetrating and thorough analysis of Wallace's scheme in English literature.

Emerson's journals and letters record the same process, and his essays make constant use of it. In his case, the separation involved resignation from his pulpit and departure for Europe. Indeed, for the American Romantic, the trip to Europe is of decisive importance, and has been culturally established as a ritual separation. Furthermore, if we examine the internal development of any great scientist we find the same pattern. Darwin's trip around the world in H.M.S. *Beagle* accomplished the same end, for he returned with the skeleton of his theory complete. Yet in the 1840's the culture support of the Creative Imagination had not yet penetrated widely and deeply enough in the culture for Darwin to profit by it. Consequently he spent years postponing publication, postponing what Wallace calls execution, that is, what I have called exposure to social validation. Only the crisis brought by Alfred Wallace's arrival at the same conclusions precipitated Darwin into publication.

This suggests that Anthony Wallace's definition of religion is either too wide or too narrow. Like Tylor he has not been quite able to make the connection between science, religion, and philosophy. (In "philosophy" I include the working out of a cognitive resynthesis in literary discourse, as in *Sartor Resartus* and *In Memoriam* and *The Ring and the Book*.) Thus he thinks of science (and government) as historically competing with religion and gradually displacing it. It is worth glancing for a moment at his definition of religion: "Religion is a set of rituals, rationalized by myth, which mobilizes supernatural powers for the purpose of achieving or preventing transformations of state in man and nature." Surely "transformations of state in nature" is applicable to science, and Tylor, as we have seen, wanted to make it applicable to man. "Myth" surely is also applicable to science. As we have seen, there is no structural difference between myth and scientific theory though there is a semantic difference. Myth, as Tylor plainly saw, uses metaphors; scientific theory uses dead metaphors, called abstractions. The difference is how they are used, myth to stabilize the subject, scientific theory to exploit the tension between subject and object.

"Supernatural powers" seems harder to fit to science, but it is not really much harder. The "mind" transcends nature, or is supernatural, other than nature, in two ways. First "mind" is a word that bridges the abyss of absolute ignorance between stimulus and response; and the way nerve cells fire accounts for this, as we have seen. Second, insofar as "mind" means covert verbal behavior, its other principal semantic function, the structure of language is not identical with the structure of nature, or rather the structure of language is such that we cannot say what the structure of nature really is. Hence the Kantian unknowable *ding-an-sich*. To say that this abyss between stimulus and response, between language and the world, between subject and object, is filled with a supernatural force is, of course, to say one cannot account for it but can provide an explanation which will satisfy but need not be verified except by further unaccountable experiences.

Since scientific resyntheses occur in the same manner as religious resyntheses, by suspending the normal patterns of behavior and exploiting the possibilities of resynthesis, "supernatural powers" seems a term perfectly applicable to science. In other words, there is no problem if we shift from the constitutive function of "supernatural," which posits beings unknown to men, to its categorial function, which recognizes the similarity of instances of arriving at unanticipated cognitive resyntheses.

Thus when Wallace says that science is displacing religion, he should say that correcting a theoretical construct is displacing the mere reinforcing of it. But, of course, to correct such constructs, or myths, is part of the history of religion also, and the first great overhauling of Christianity, the Reformation, coincided with the emergence of modern science. Speaking very broadly, religious beliefs validate the explanatory and social management systems of a culture. When the culture is faced with a challenge which those two systems cannot manage, religion is necessarily affected and requires a radical overhauling, a resynthesis. But Wallace's failure to see all this is but another instance of the anthropologist's failure to turn his anthropology upon himself, and particularly American anthropologists' narrow notion that their science emerged from the recognition of a scientific problem when actually it was from a culture crisis.

The most important event in Tylor's life was in fact a separation, interestingly enough precipitated by an illness. He was tubercular, not very badly off yet, but enough to send him on foreign travel to warmer climates, a common prescription in the nineteenth century. This illness is interesting because Wallace points out that a common factor in the strategy of separation as occasioning the opportunity for cognitive resynthesis is in fact illness. It would be of great interest to have a study of the illnesses of nineteenth-century Romantics. Over and over again, it appears as an incident that began the process ending in a fully developed Romantic position. Indeed, in the later nineteenth century it became a literary theme. Walter Pater used it several times, and the masterpiece of the late nineteenth-century Romantic, Thomas Mann, *The Magic Mountain*, is about a very ordinary young man whose illness, discovered during a separation, led him to a total revaluation of his and human existence.

Tylor, then, was sick and went on his travels. From the United States he went to Cuba, where in 1856 he met Edwin Christy, an early ethnographer. Christy was one of those eager and miscellaneous ethnographical collectors who went all over the world to every primitive culture they could get access to, procuring everything interesting and revealing about primitive life they could lay their hands on. Christy was one of the greatest of these men, and his superb collections ended up in the British Museum. He was about to set out for Mexico and persuaded Tylor to go with him. Tylor was already intensely interested in history, and the long journey through Mexico was the making of him. A few years later he wrote a book, *Anahuac; or Mexico and the Mexicans, Ancient and Modern*. There were already two fascinating books in existence on the subject, both by Americans, Prescott's *History of the Conquest of Mexico* and John Lloyd Stephens' *Incidents of Travel in the Yucatan*, the first widely known account of Mayan ruins.

In Mexico Tylor for the first time entered fully into a completely alien and extraordinarily revealing cultural situation. There were the ruins and the memories of an early civilization, there was the colonial life which had swept it away and su-

217

perseded it, there was urban Mexico, which was just beginning to feel the impact of the nineteenth century, and everywhere there were the peons, the eternal peasant population, in some ways hardly changed from the times of the Aztecs, in others profoundly changed, but everywhere showing the fusion of two cultures. The past that in Europe could only be guessed at was here in Mexico and he could see it. A central notion in his doctrine, survivals of primitive culture into modern culture, was proven on every corner. The worship at the shrine of the Virgin of Guadaloupe was obviously a continuation of preconquest religion.

Tylor has been criticized by modern anthropologists, particularly Americans, for his doctrine of survivals. It is not that anyone denies that there are survivals. Rather, what is objected to is the interpretation he gave them and his subsequent recommendations for applying anthropology. His interpretation was evolutionary. Possibly he was influenced by Darwin's proposal that certain physiological features—the appendix is the most famous instance—are survivals from biological history and no longer have a function. The modern notion is that if cultural patterns have survived they have a function. The difficulty with the functional theory is that it cannot make discriminations. That is, it is extremely difficult to maintain that any mode of behavior is dysfunctional to the culture. If one analyses on an a priori theory that a culture is coherent, then whatever happens in that culture is functionally coherent. If one goes on a theory that a culture is incoherent, then if some pattern of behavior is dysfunctional to the culture as a whole, it will be found on investigation to be functional within some small corner of that culture, itself incoherent with the culture as a whole. For if a culture is incoherent, then there must be some parts of the culture discontinuous from other parts.

The functional theory properly used, of course, is a different matter. It directs that the anthropologist look for behavior variables which vary together. It is predictive rather than historical or genetic. It asserts that if a particular event occurs in one manifestation of the culture, a change will occur in some other manifestation. Thus Anthony Wallace asserts that if an individual goes through all five stages of the cognitive resynthesis ritual there will be in that individual a permanent personality change. Since it is impossible to tell whether there is personality change in anyone unless he begins to behave differently in the kinds of situations he acted in before his ritual experience, the term "personality" seems somewhat unnecessary. What Wallace means is that there are behavioral changes in any or all of three categories of situation: in one category, the kind previously acted in, there is observable behavior change; another is a category which he now seeks out but which he previously avoided; and the third is a category of situation which he now avoids, although previously he sought it out. Thus Tylor himself turned from his manifest destiny in a brass foundry to an entirely new destiny in the scholar's study.

Now it is by no means evident that Tylor was not a functionalist. On the contrary he was deeply interested in providing explanations as to why some patterns survive from an earlier stage of the culture into a later one, though it is true that he apparently took great pleasure in pointing out that an awful lot in the popular and in the sophisticated religion of his day consisted of survivals, and unfortunate survivals at that. And to generate explanations of why something is done in relation to what is being done around it at the same time is, of course, to be a functionalist. On the other hand, he was an educated Englishman of the nineteenth century, and it would have been virtually impossible for him not to be familiar with the ideas of utilitarianism.

Wallace proposes that the source of functionalism is utilitarianism. Since functionalism originated in England, he is probably right. But it would be an error to assert that functionalism and utilitarianism are identical, as Wallace certainly seems to. Functionalism is an anthropological technique for describing interrelated behaviors in such a way that predictive statements may be generated. The aim is that these statements will then be verified by observation, though, as we have seen, in the most stringent sense, an observation without manipulation can never verify anything. Utilitarianism is quite a different matter. It is an ethical, economic, and political technique for generating judgments as to the desirability of behavior, granted a certain goal for a society, a minimum physical well-being for all of such quality that all can share in the cultural superstructure, to the degree that they are interested in doing so, and capable of doing so. There is a world of difference between asking, "Why do people do as they do?" and "Should people do as they do?"

Tylor was interested in asking both questions. And he was a geneticist, interested in how and why certain behavioral patterns—such as myths—got started. He went on the assumption that if one knew that, one was in a better position to understand what a pattern's current function was, and above all, in a better position to judge whether social management should be directed at eliminating certain behaviors, including the lasting deposits of those behaviors, certain cultural objects. He assumed that the goal of any society is to raise its standard of living, intellectually and what he would call spiritually as well as economically; it is reasonably clear that he saw all of these spheres as functionally interconnected. A society, he appears to have believed, cannot raise its behavior to a higher adaptational level in any one sphere without doing so in all three. A dysfunctional survival, therefore, was one that prevented or hindered that adaptational improvement.

For example, it is painfully evident that throughout Latin America the insistence upon not controlling the birth rate is clearly dysfunctional. It is also clear that not controlling the birth rate throughout the world has very possibly become dysfunctional for human survival. But it is not dysfunctional if one believes that the proper aim of a society is to create souls to be tested and saved or damned by God. And it is not dysfunctional if one does not believe that the survival of the human race should be a proper goal of that race, and of all the cultures and societies that compose that race.

It is no doubt true that Tylor thought improvement in the quality of human life was a proper goal for a society, and for all societies, the human race itself. Even today there are probably very few people who publicly assert that it is of no importance whatsoever whether the human race survives or not, though it is equally probable that a great many, probably most, do not govern their behavior by that goal. Tylor's point was that the improvement of the quality of life for all its members is the proper goal for a society, but that a great many things human beings do which were once useful and functional in improving the quality of life no longer are. Who could possibly deny that he was right?

Certainly in Mexico wherever he could turn he saw living proof of his interpretation of survivals. It is easy enough today, and it may have been even easier then, hard as it may be to imagine it. To be sure, he could have had such an experience in England, but it took Mexico to do it. It took separation. In Mexico he saw a splendid example of colonial degeneration and of survival in the efforts of the Mexican reformists to bring the all-dominating Church under the control of a nonclerical social management. The outcome was not yet decided when he was there, nor was it to be decided for a long time; in many ways it is not yet decided. One significant thing about his Mexican experience was that though he was an evolutionist he was not one of those who interpreted Darwin, mistakenly, as proof that cultural progress is inevitable. On the contrary, as his concluding remarks to *Primitive Culture* show, he felt that his own time was one which could validate radical innovation designed to improve the quality of human life on the basis of scientifically organized knowledge.

He could say this with confidence because he had experienced it in his own life. He had himself generated a radical innovation, and he had himself experienced the cultural support of the idea of the Creative Imagination to a degree that made it possible for him to offer it for public validation. But at the same time he was also aware that such times as his, as he had experienced them, were rare in human history, and could not be counted on either to last or to recur. He foresaw a time when cognitive resynthesis would again function principally by stabilizing the subject, not by exposing the subject to the withering recalcitrance of the object. In this he is considerably more pessimistic than Anthony Wallace, who sees the disappearance of what he calls religion in favor of science and government; but then Wallace does not see that science and government also have their rituals of cognitive resynthesis, possibly because he is a scientist. Tylor, however, was not primarily a scientist, nor primarily an ethnographer, nor cultural anthropologist. He was primarily an historian.

History was a factor in his original cognitive synthesis, a factor that remained and came to the fore during his time of separation, and it was the central and organizing factor in his new vision of mankind and man's development. Thus the title of his great book, *Primitive Culture*, is misleading. As he says in his opening paragraph, culture's "various grades may be regarded as stages of development or evolution, each the outcome of previous history, and about to do its proper part in shaping the history of the future." In speaking of Tylor's response to Mexico, Bohanaan most acutely says, "the potential of self-realization (always dormant in fascination with strange peoples) caught the imagination of this cultured but uncommitted man ... *Anahuac* was only a little more than a travel book about Mexico. Yet that 'little more' contained the seed of what was to become modern anthropology." Behind this remark, I suppose, lay many years of experience with anthropologists—and also with himself.

Now "self-realization" is a Romantic concept, closely related to the Creative Imagination, for that doctrine was generated to solve the problem of self-realization for those who had separated themselves, become alienated from, the explanatory and validational modes of their culture, and of course of its mode of social management as well. When Tylor implicitly undermined the beliefs and values, particularly the religious values—his primary interest—of his own culture, he was revealing the inadequacies of his own former self, before the separation of the Mexican adventure and the ensuing cognitive resynthesis. As an educated man, he had an overwhelming chance of knowing *Sartor Resartus*, and also *In Memoriam*. Very possibly he knew Goethe's *Faust*, either in the original or in translation, and it is very likely that he had read Wordsworth's *Prelude* when it was posthumously published in 1850. These are the works that any well-educated young Englishman would know if he was only twenty in 1852. They were the works the young intellectuals were concentrating on. And each of them is concerned with self-realization. Today there is probably no discipline or body of knowledge so immensely serviceable for self-realization in the Romantic manner as cultural anthropology itself. To encounter that discipline is immensely liberating. It is liberating from one's own culture and therefore from one's self.

The individual for whom a factor of self-realization is already present, no matter how obscurely, is one who is experiencing as incoherent what is normally cognitively grasped as coherent—his own culture. And that means, if he takes the path of alienation, himself. To make a distinction, what is commonly called alienation today, particularly by our "alienated" youth and their slaves, the reporters and columnists and article writers of the public press, and far too often educators as well, is not alienation at all, but polarization. The polarized individual has cognitively grasped his culture as incoherent, but his response is not self-ironic. His attempt to become coherent is merely one of fastening on to one set of values already in the culture.

The alienated individual sees himself as part of his culture, sees, though he may not spell this out overtly or even covertly, "personality" and "culture" as two different names for two different perspectives on the same data. To him culture transcendence is the only solution to alienation. The polarized individual has really no self to realize. For the alienated individual, as Kierkegaard in the 1840's so exhaustively analyzed, a self-ironic perspective has already created the mode of a self, at least in the Romantic sense. Such a self is one for whom none of the roles of his culture is adequate, since each reflects that culture's incoherence. The polarized individual, however, readily accepts a well-established role, that of rebel, outcast, or social discard, as the case may be. The alienated individual plays his roles self-consciously and ironically, since to exist he must play a role; the polarized individual identifies self and role. That is why, for all one's sympathy with them, the rebellious students of today are so wearisome and so repellent.

Furthermore, the alienated individual, if a genius, may accomplish his culture transcendence by creating a new role. From this point of view, Tylor's doctrine of survivals takes on a new interest and a new meaning. By this mode of explanation he was insisting that his culture was not coherent but incoherent, and he was urging those responsible for explanation, validation, and social management to become aware of this fact. And that meant—to become alienated themselves. Again the Mexican experience was of the highest importance for him, for it was there that he saw with a glaring intensity an incredibly rich cultural incoherence. Given that vision, he could turn back to European man, in whom he was primarily interested—he makes little use of Mexico in his professional writings—and see the incoherence not only in the European past but also in the England of his own day. The result was that Tylor achieved not only a remarkable transcendence, but he also created a new science in order to create a new role.

Nevertheless, he conceived of his enterprise as an historical undertaking. He saw cultural anthropology as an historical subject. It is true that his followers went too far with this, and in their attempts, as Frazer's, for example, to reconstruct the mental history of man discredited the whole historical dimension of cultural anthropology. This was the main reason for the rise of functionalism, utilitarianism stripped of its aim to provide a foundation for moral judgments. Moreover, since the scientific status of history has never been satisfactorily resolved in the intellectual world, the eagerness of the American anthropologist, with his lack of access to power, to gain status by identifying himself successfully as a true scientist was very great. For a long time it was absolute anathema to say that modern primitives were a good guide to what prehistoric man actually was like. Nowadays, however, that is changing, and anthropology, almost in spite of itself, is becoming willing once again to consider historical matters. In the last chapter of his *Religion* Anthony Wallace even has sections on "The History of Religions," "The Evolution of Religion" (greatly daring), and "The Future of Religion." After wild swings of the pendulum, anthropology is coming back to its point of origin—history.

Working backward, the importance of history to Tylor can be briefly stated. We can take Bohanaan's phrase "the potential of self-realization (always dormant in fascination with strange peoples)" and rewrite it to do service for the cultural situation in the nineteenth century: "The potential of self-realization (always dormant in fascination with history)." The historicization of European culture was one of the most interesting accomplishments of Romanticism. We have already seen Carlyle's concern with it, and Browning's with the whole problem of historiography. To grasp its importance to Tylor and its place in the crisis of his time and its central place in his and ensuing anthropology, it will be useful to trace it rapidly from the beginning of the century.

The first step was the historicization of the personality, the cognition of oneself as a series of historical events. As we have seen, the genuinely alienated becomes aware of his own incoherence. This is a common occurrence, and happens at all times. In relatively noncritical times, what Carlyle called the organic periods of history, the perception of this incoherence is resolved by using the validation available in the culture to reject part of the personality. Ordinarily the explanatory system is capable of doing the job. But at times of culture crisis, such as at the end of the eighteenth century, the explanatory modes and the validational modes are grasped by a few individuals as themselves incoherent, just as later Tylor so grasped the religious validation and explanation of his contemporary culture.

There was, however, one factor in Enlightenment culture which could be used, and that was historiography. The rationalistic efforts of the seventeenth and eighteenth centuries had changed history writing from chronicle to what we can recognize, though dimly, as history, that is, chronicle with an explanatory dimension. Already in the eighteenth century the Renaissance repulsion against the medieval world had diminished, and there were even the faint stirrings of what was to become cultural anthropology. It was not what we would recognize as history today, that is, historiography as Romanticism has made it. But the historical consciousness was there. Even in biology and geology historicism was beginning faintly to appear. The problem was emerging.

Wordsworth, as a first generation Romantic, and as he recorded in *The Prelude*, took this historical consciousness and applied it to himself. Something of immense value in his childhood he had had; he had lost it, and he had recovered it. He rightfully believed himself a paradigm or model of the future consciousness. The difference between the historical consciousness of the Enlightenment and his was that in the eighteenth century history was used as exemplary material for the current explanatory and validational systems either in service or in simple polar opposition to the current systems of social management. Wordsworth took the historical consciousness, so to speak, stripped it of the explanation and validation which were useless to him and applied it to himself. It comes out clearly in his famous statement that poetry "takes its *origin* from emotion *recollected* in tranquillity: the emotion is contemplated till, by a species of *re-action*, the tranquillity gradually disappears, and an emotion, *kindred* to that which was before the subject of contemplation, is gradually produced, and does itself actually exist in the mind."

I have italicized the key words. He sees the whole process historically, and furthermore, he sees the perception of one's self as discontinuous. And this is the pattern of the *Prelude.* One's self-comprehension is not all of a piece through life and continuous, as it was for Alexander Pope, for example; on the contrary it was discontinuous, emergent, innovative, and also recovering and reintegrating. One's own past as the material for an innovative self-definition—that is the importance of personal history.

Carlyle was to write the story all over again, and even more clearly, in *Sartor Resartus.* Or rather, since the *Prelude* was not published until nearly two decades after *Sartor,* Carlyle was the first to make it available in English. It had already been written several times in German, but Carlyle was to take the next step. The notion of organic and inorganic periods of history he took from the French Saint-Simonians, but he gave it a new twist. He made it clear that it was an historical explanation of history based upon the already established historical explanation of the personality. This may sound far-fetched on his part, but it is nothing of the sort. As far as human life is concerned, there is no such entity as history. There are, after all, only human beings going through certain "moral and intellectual" processes. History consists of men interpreting the world. Since the resultant actions are recorded, in fragments to be sure, and unreliably, historiography is concerned with explaining those fragments. But ultimately, all historiography is an attempt to provide explanations for the *decisions* responsible for those actions. Ultimately, all historiography, as opposed to chronicle, is moral and intellectual history.

Consider, for example, such a brilliant piece of modern historiography as A. J. P. Taylor's *The Habsburg Monarchy*. Every source has been explored, every skill of research has been employed to find out what really happened, yet ultimately the explanations are moral and intellectual. It is the great achievement of the Romantic poets and novelists, such as Scott, that they established the internal history of the alienated individual, that is, the discontinuous history of self-cognition, as the foundation for modern historiography. Taylor's frequently very acid work is the history of the consequences of the ways the Habsburgs and their subordinates and enemies understood themselves and their roles, and the consequences that had for Europe. To be sure, he is at great pains to reconstruct the circumstances to which they were responding, economic and racial and all the rest, but so did the Romantic poets and novelists. It is the source of their unquenchable drive toward reality, the source of their deliberate self-exposure to the unresolvable tension between subject and object.

It is instructive to compare Tylor's with something of Hegel's philosophy of history. Hegel's notion of cultural dynamics, or historical change, was that the reason (or the consciousness) is self-developing. It discovers its own internal contradictions, and transcends them, moving always in the direction of increased freedom, mastery over itself and over the world and recognition of that mastery by others (or validation). Thus his model is that of an early stage of Romanticism, for it is clearly based on his own self-cognition in abandoning the Enlightenment and committing himself to a resynthesis. Hegel's explanation for his dynamics is to be found in the notion that every concept implicitly contains its negation. This is very mysterious indeed, but the fact that it is really incomprehensible is no reason to reject it. Hegel was talking about something of great significance, but in the wrong way. To bring his insight out into the open from the confusing and mysterious depths of the implicit, it is necessary only to observe that to a proposition in response to which the answer "yes" has been culturally conventionalized, it is possible, after all, to say, "no." Such a revalidation takes place when the proposition, considered as a set of directions governing behavior, ceases to be applicable with any success to the kind of situation it is supposed to enable its responder to handle successfully.

Consider a woman who has been brought up to believe unquestioningly that divorce is a mortal sin, and is an impossibility for a decent religious woman. However, her husband is an alcoholic, a bad provider, and too lazy even to be a successful criminal. He has also fathered on her a large batch of children, too numerous to feed and clothe and house except at a level of well-being below what she can accept. She is now faced with an internal contradiction, an incoherence in culturally validated propositions. Something has to give, and she concludes that her convictions about the wrongfulness of divorce were in error. She may solve the problem by concluding that the morality of her church is deficient, or that she has been badly instructed in that morality, or that there is no validity to religion. In any event, it is the situation in which the initial moral statement was used which has led her to invalidate the proposition that divorce is sinful.

Thus though Hegel was clearly on the right track when he grasped that the source of cultural dynamics is incoherence, he limited his vision—as is to be expected from so early a Romantic thinker—by conceiving of incoherence as self-generated within the consciousness. Although he was certainly aware of the tension between subject and object, a little more awareness would have made him realize that it is the situation in which the idea is interpreted that leads to revalidation. Had he talked about language instead of mind, reason, and consciousness, he would have been better off, for in fact he was talking about language. His examples of consciousness are covert and overt verbal behavior, as of course they had to be, since nobody can talk about what happens between the stimulus that leads to the generation of an utterance and the utterance itself.

A glance at Marx will show the insufficiency and incompleteness of Hegel's system. Marx said he turned Hegel right side up: it is not consciousness that controls human behavior but human behavior that controls consciousness. At the lowest and most primitive level of behavior Marx's notion is useful. When the first primate grasped the first stone and used it as a tool, man, one may hazard, was already on the way. Grasping stones and using tools changed, eventually, the brain. But Marx was not talking at this level, about which, after all, he knew absolutely nothing since nothing was to be known. He was talking about modern history, particularly the Middle Ages, and his point was that the means of production changed the consciousness. One result was a change in the means of ownership, and the result of that was the alienation of the worker from the means of production.

Now it may be wondered why it is necessary for the worker to own the means of production so long as he benefits from that production, and in fact it has turned out that way. As a society becomes increasingly industrialized, as the productivity per man hour goes up, the productivity is increasingly spread throughout the society. The worker does benefit, and the twentieth-century political result is that as production increases workers lose their interest in Communism. They don't care any longer whether the means of production is alienated, so long as it is providing them with a steadily improving standard of living and increased access to the resources of the culture. It is evident that the assumption that the worker cannot stand alienation from the means of production goes back to Hegel's notion of mastery over the world, goes back therefore to consciousness and freedom. Had Hegel been sufficiently aware of the importance of the situation for revalidation, it is doubtful if Marx could have created *his* cognitive resynthesis, which has caused us all so much trouble.

Tylor's notion of cultural dynamics as history is both Hegelian and Marxian; it presents both an earlier and a later stage of Romantic thinking. When he discusses mythology, he sees it as following the laws of the development of the human mind, as a process primarily of consciousness. The heart of the process is the attrition of the attributes of mythological figures until they have become metaphysical abstractions. His procedure is remarkably similar to Hegel's. On the other hand, when he discusses his favorite theme, animism, then he is more like Marx, because he sees science, the awareness of the conditions and situations of the real world, as instrumental in gradually undermining animism and creating in its place materialism, just as Marx substituted materialism for Hegelian idealism. Both Tylor and Marx saw history as dialectic, that is, as the consequence of the dialectic or tension between subject and object. Neither were quite able to transcend that position and grasp the notion that both idealism and materialism are idealisms, that both are explanatory constructs, and that both are products of their own historical condition.

Yet there was a profound difference between Tylor and Marx. Both attacked the current modes of explanation, validation, and social management. Both wished to put science in control of social management, though Tylor's was a true science while Marx's was a "science" in the older sense of the term, as in the "science of theology." Both, also, saw their sciences as redemptive, but again with a considerable difference. Marx saw his science, if applied to social management, as leading to a finally redeemed social system. In that, his "science" was a reversion to the Enlightenment. His difficulty was that though he was writing about society he knew very little about it, so little was then to be known. Hence the only way he could imagine the consequences of a new kind of social management was in pretty pictures of everybody doing his own thing.

Tylor was born in 1832, the year after Hegel died. Marx was then fourteen. He received his education and grew up in the 1830's and 1840's. By 1850 his system was complete, and it has the prime attribute of that period of cultural history—redemptionism. Innumerable schemes in those two decades were proposed that would redeem man and redeem the world, so that man would enter into a condition of absolute, final, and unchanging value. It was the last time any advanced thinker could imagine that the tension between subject and object might some day be resolved. Marx's system was but one of many, though admittedly far better than most.

From that period Tylor retained something of the redemptionist dream, in that he hoped that his new science of anthropology could be brought to bear upon social management. Yet his cognitive resynthesis came after that period, and it did not occur in response to the European situation, but to the Mexican. To Hegel the primary material for the history of consciousness, of the Geist, was a handful of philosophical documents, the oldest of which dated only to the sixth or seventh centuries B.C. For Marx, the primary material for dialectical materialism was a primitive knowledge of European economic development during a few centuries preceding his own. For Tylor the material for the history of man's mind in his actual situation was worldwide and dated back hundreds and hundreds of thousands of years. Though there was a touch of redemptionism in him, he saw human history as unpredictable, intermittently open and free, and his own period as unusual in its readiness to validate the radically innovative.

Hegel saw the stabilization of the subject in the infinitely distant future; Marx saw it as the consequence of the revolution of the proletariat and the establishment of socialism; Tylor, the scientist who emerged from Romantic thinking, saw it as constantly and vainly sought for in the past and the lust for it as probably recurring in the future. In the meantime, a better adaptation of man to environment might be achieved if his culture transcended itself, as he had transcended his culture, and arrived at a new grasp of explanation, validation, and social management.

From the historicization of the self, through the historicization of the European consciousness and the historicization of the relation of that consciousness to the economic aspects of the human situation, to the historicization of man and the dialectic between consciousness and environment—so runs the line of thinking to Tylor. The key to his extraordinary achievement is history.

History did for Tylor what cultural anthropology can do today, if the individual who encounters it is already sufficiently alienated, not merely polarized, and has already arrived at the stage of self-irony which is the mode of the emergence of an opposition of self to role and of the ironic playing of roles. And this irony is in Tylor's playing of the innovated role his innovated science demanded of him. He pretends to say nothing about the religion and the religiously validated morality of his own culture; he pretends modesty and a turning away from that spectacle. But his book is a devastating comment on the religion of Victorian England and on the intellectual morality of those religious leaders who devoted their religion and their morality and their intellect to sustaining the current mode of social management. That anthropology is the "reformer's science" is ironic. It is not reformist; it is revolutionary.

6

Eroticism=Politics:
Politics=Eroticism

WHEN KANT said that the mind cannot know what the world really is, but can only know the world in terms of its own self-created categories, he broke with the Enlightenment; for the Enlightenment position was that the mind is naturally perfectly adapted to the world and congruent with it. Its reformist ideal was that social management founded on this notion could eventually lead to creating a perfect match of personality, society, and nature. The most radical form of this belief was that such perfectibility was almost within human grasp. A little goodwill, and we could make it. On the other hand, a number of late Enlightenment figures were increasingly troubled, and well before the end of the century, here and there, a discouraging pessimism was beginning to appear and to be cautiously suggested, though sometimes in a most veiled manner. But this pessimism was not based on a Kantian epistemology or anything like it. It was simply that the more they studied human behavior, and the more they learned about human history, the more they began, against their own reason, to suspect that the necessary fund of goodwill is simply not to be had. Besides, a third group

235

developed the notion that personality, society, and nature were already in perfect congruence.

In these same last years of the eighteenth century a strange figure entered upon the stage of cultural history, and he has never left it—the Marquis de Sade. As the problem of social power has become increasingly acute, insistent, and perplexing, so the Marquis has come from the back streets of cultural history to the town square. For up to that time no one had peered so deeply into man's biological nature as an organism living vis-à-vis an environment and what, therefore, his deepest necessity is. That necessity, according to de Sade, is mastery over the environment. What are called the Sadian philosophical ideas, which have received far too much serious attention and the point of which is almost universally missed, are actually an ironic parody of Christian explanation and validation, and of Enlightenment equivalents. God is said to be all love and justice, but if we look at the way things are, it is obvious, according to de Sade, that this conception of Deity is a mask which men have placed over the intolerable truth. The truth about God is that his active pleasure and the purpose of his creativity is the infliction of suffering.

God's ways to man cannot be justified on the grounds that He is interested for their own sake in creatures that can suffer. Quite the contrary. He is interested in them *because* they can suffer, and that is why He created them. Since He is all-powerful, He could easily have created a world without suffering. Were He interested in justice He would not have devised an eternal hell of suffering for those who are not responsible for their behavior since they are not responsible for their existence.

Though he did not, to my knowledge, make the point, yet de Sade could have cited the medieval notion that only a fraction of mankind would be saved, and their eternal pleasure would be gazing from the ramparts of Heaven at their fellow creatures suffering in Hell. Here, he could have pointed out, the mask of

Christianity is stripped away and its true insight revealed: those who are saved because they identify themselves with God are rewarded by participating in His eternal pleasure, the spectacle of suffering. Or he could have cited the eighteenth-century English sect, the Sandemanians, who believed that only a tiny fraction of what the Middle Ages would have saved are in fact to be redeemed to Heaven and the eternally joyous and inexhaustibly delightful prospect of watching the suffering of others. By the same argument, God, by a delightfully ingenious ironic trick on man, sent his Son to earth to seduce men into believing that suffering, not the infliction of suffering, was the true way, thus increasing His harvest of pain. Or de Sade could have used the Albigensians of the Middle Ages, that anti-Christian sect with an ancient tradition behind it, extending back to the anti-Christianism that emerged when Christianity began to spread into Mesopotamia and Iran. They asserted that Christianity was in fact a religion of the worship of evil, invented by the true Satan to ensnare men into hatred and pain, and that Satan was the power the Christians worshipped as God.

As for the Enlightenment concept of nature as beneficent, the most advanced thinkers had already arrived at an inverse Darwinism. The different species had been created by the power of the God of Nature, not directly, as in the Bible, but indirectly through natural forces. They did not emerge through variation, as Darwin was to claim, but rather were created as different species. Nevertheless, there was variation, and natural forces acted as a kind of pruning process, trimming away those plants and animals which were not true to the species. This, they claimed, amounted to an explanation and validation of the suffering in natural processes.

Contemporary with de Sade, Malthus created the greatest possible stir and controversy, greater by far than de Sade's, who was scarcely known; Malthus asserted that for man the population outgrows the growth of the means of subsistence. Thus there is a radical defect in the natural world. The notion, therefore, that man could ever adapt himself perfectly to the natural world was an illusion. The nineteenth century was haunted for a long time by the Malthusian nightmare and the vision of nature red in tooth and claw; and those ghosts are haunting us again.

Like de Sade, Malthus saw the course of man's problem in the sexual impulse, and insisted that the only way to control the excessive population growth was by a combination of sexual restraint and sufficient suffering to control the numbers of the poor by early death. As was pointed out at the time and has been pointed out innumerable times since, he would deprive the poor of their only pleasure as the price for longevity. Unwittingly he underlined de Sade's position, for Malthus was a clergyman, and his argument was designed to justify God's ways to man by justifying the suffering of the poor on natural grounds, and by explaining and validating the New Testament proposition that the poor are always with us. It was almost as much a parody of Christian apologetics as de Sade's, and like that recognized the sexual drive as the source of all our trouble.

De Sade insisted that the sexual drive was not the source of our trouble but the source of our salvation, if we understood it properly. Christianity's suspicion of sexuality was part of the religious mask it placed over the real character of the human condition. De Sade's "philosophy" was an ironic use of Christian and Enlightenment rationalizations designed to reveal their internal incoherence and absurdity, and their incoherence with each other. He reduced to intellectual rubble Christian apologetics, Enlightenment rationalization of nature, and any attempt to fuse the two. By encouraging Christianity and the Enlightenment to cancel themselves and each other out, de Sade found room and living space for his own insight. Man's deepest psychological necessity is mastery of the environment; man's deepest physiological necessity is sexual activity; therefore, he concluded, man's deepest satisfaction is finding his psychological satisfaction in the realm of sexual activity; the deepest sexual pleasure is combining sexual activity with the infliction of pain. That is, only if that over which you have mastery registers pain can you know that you have actually exerted mastery.

Freedom is the exertion of mastery; the greatest freedom is to cause both physical suffering and psychological humiliation in the course of sexual activity. Thus, and thus only, can man be in harmony with nature and in a condition of the fulfillment of the will of God by identifying our will with His. As Dante said, with, to be sure, a somewhat different intent and emphasis, "In His will is our peace." Dante wrote in his greatest line of "the love that moves the sun and the other stars," but de Sade would have written, "The hatred and pain that moves the sun and other stars and everything else in the created universe."

De Sade knotted together explanation of man's place in nature, validation of the infliction of suffering, and politics, or social management, the proper aim of which is freedom. Certain modern commentators have taken de Sade's morality as ironically as his parody of Christianity and Enlightenment naturalistic philosophy, and have selected from his schema only freedom. They interpret de Sade's notion of freedom as the infliction of suffering upon others as an ironic parody of *l'ancien régime*, the traditional form of social management. Thus they emphasize the validity of what the Judaeo-Christian-bourgeois moral tradition names sexual deviancy and proclaim the importance of sexual deviancy in asserting and acting out human freedom. The humiliation and the suffering they tend to forget.

The recent off-Broadway play, *Futz*, insists that it is better to love a pig, both emotionally and physically, than to use flame-throwers on the peasant children of Vietnam. No doubt. But the true Sadian position would be that it is still better to make the pig squeal with pain and to combine flame-throwing with sexual

239

pleasure. It seems likely, in spite of the Army's effort to elimi-
nate from its personnel certain kinds of sexual deviancy, that
some soldiers who use flame-throwers do indeed get sexual
pleasure in doing so. If this is indeed the case, it is, according
to the true Sadian position, authentic existence.

No, de Sade cannot be saved for a contemporary version of
Enlightenment politics, which is all that *Futz* and similar efforts,
politically, amount to. An interesting comment on de Sade, one
that reveals his weakness from the Romantic point of view, is
Hegel's, though it is scarcely likely that he ever heard of de
Sade, or took him seriously if he did. At the time, if de Sade was
recognized at all, he was merely classed as a pornographer. It
has taken the twentieth century to make him, at least in public,
a figure to be taken seriously. Nevertheless Hegel speaks directly to de Sade's position, for he begins with a kind of Sadian
situation, the master-slave nexus. This he takes as the historically basic or primitive situation. We can say with certainty now
that he was wrong, or at least with as much certainty as any
historical construct permits. On the other hand, there is good
reason to believe that large-scale polity was in fact made possible by the institutionalization of slavery.

To repeat Sir John Lubbock's point, before there was morality
there was violence, violence being internalized morality, or as
he sweetly called it, in proper middle-class Victorian fashion,
duty. We can put it another way. Morality—or duty—or social
management by violence functions by inducing in oneself and
others predictable behavior. Slavery, then, was the first large-
scale attempt at inducing predictable behavior, the first large-
scale effort in social management. Who could deny that in some
areas of European culture it was economically successful until
well into the nineteenth century, and that in some culture areas
of the world it still is, still the only known mode of large-scale
hierarchical social management?

240

In the master-slave situation, Hegel finds the first significant transition from nature to civilization. The master treats the slave as part of nature, thus creating the man-environment, mind-nature, subject-object tension. Consequently the basic human drive is mastery over nature, but since that first emerged in the master-slave relationship, equally important is the recognition of mastery, or validation. Thus at this point his position is remarkably like de Sade's, with, however, an important exception. De Sade still thinks in the Enlightenment fashion; he still sees the attributes of the subject, man, exhausted by the categories of the object, nature. But Hegel sees that man begins at the point at which he separates from nature and begins the process by which mind transcends nature, the transcendence of nature being freedom. However, there is a difficulty lying in wait for the master. His success is due to his daring in facing the risk of death in order to subdue others and achieve their recognition of his success, that recognition being the slave's awareness that the master can at will impose death on him. Thus the first act that separates man from nature is the transcendence over death. But the penalty for this transcendence is the confidence in the reality of the abstract. The master lives in freedom and luxury on the products of the activity of the slave, but the slave, in the long run, develops the separation of man and environment by continuing to struggle with the recalcitrance of nature. Thus he penetrates nature with mind. The path of further transcendence lies in the activity of the slave, while the master is entrapped by the seductions of the abstract, by hypostatization or reification, the belief that an abstract word, such as "freedom," corresponds to something in nature. In fact, however, it does nothing of the sort.

Hegel's point may be understood better if we return to the distinction between religion and science, proposed in the discussion of Tylor. The aim of the first is the stabilization of cognitive syntheses; the aim of the second is the testing of cognitive syntheses and their correction or, if need be, destruction. Religion and its descendant, philosophy, at least up to Kant and Hegel, are the illusions of mastery. Only by entering into the eternal dialectic, into the tension-filled struggle between mind and nature, between subject and object, and also only by becoming aware of the internal contradictions of thought itself, can such abstractions as freedom be made concrete. Hegel carefully distinguished between absolute or abstract freedom and concrete freedom. True to his tension between subject and object, he perceives that concrete freedom cannot exist without an opposing restraint. Concrete freedom is incomplete unless it is in a dialectic with restraint. Politics, social management, is the union of freedom with restraint. When, however, abstract freedom is acted upon without regard to restraint, without regard to the dialectic, it becomes negative freedom and its use is characterized by violence and destruction. Such, according to Hegel, was the freedom manifested in the French Revolution, a negative freedom. Only the philosopher can experience absolute or abstract freedom successfully, for he deals only with concepts, with ideas. His task is to exercise freedom by discovering the internal contradictions in an historical culture's concepts and by preparing concepts for use. This absolute freedom, or abstract freedom, is only an incident in the development of concrete freedom, which is human history.

What the individual does who reifies or hypostatizes abstract freedom, is to attempt to resolve the attributes of the object into the category of the subject, while he imagines that he is resolving the attributes of the subject into the categories of the object. And this, as we have seen, is actually what de Sade was doing. His freedom was an abstract freedom. Its assumption was that the tension between subject and object can be resolved. And this is very possibly why he chose the sexual sphere for the demonstration of his abstract freedom. His thinking was important and truly philosophical, even by Hegelian terms, because he revealed the incoherence in Christian and Enlightenment thinking and their various fusions. On the other hand he had not transcended his culture to grasp the irresolvability of mind and nature. He and the French Revolutionary Terror would represent exactly the same cultural stages, except that he goes farther and exposes the contradiction and sentimentality at the intellectual root of the Terror. His interest was not really in seeing into the nature of sexuality but rather in choosing a sphere of activity which for fictional and exemplary purposes would be the best for working out the implications of his position and illustrating them.

For such purposes the field of sexual behavior is certainly the best. No other field is under such little social control, for it is private, secretive, and as concealed as possible. It is the field in which in fact there is the greatest spread of deviancy from the publicly professed and validated norms. Consequently it is the best of all fields in which to transgress those norms and get away with it. To put it differently, it is the best possible field for working out the implications of abstract freedom. The reason is that, except for pregnancy, which can always be avoided or terminated by the firm and the imaginative, it has less economic importance than virtually any other kind of human behavior. That is why it has always been the special pleasure of the poor. It is also, therefore, particularly well-suited for those who wish to acquire an addiction without running the risk of drugs, for addiction may be called the illusion of those who take abstract freedom to be reality. The very physical activity of intercourse steadily reduces the awareness of the objective world, acts as a kind of psychic insulation; at the moment of orgasm there is the illusion of absolute freedom, the kind of illusion any kind of climax always gives, whether it be that of fornication, music, tragedy, or reaching the top of an Alp.

For these reasons it is the source for a very subtle intellectual error, one which in fact de Sade made. Possibly it was the error which made it impossible for him to transcend the Enlightenment, instead of merely transcending its sentimentality. That error is to identify the genitals and genital sensation with the subject. At this point Hegel's notion of the concrete universal is helpful. That extremely interesting concept can be exemplified by considering a rock. Insofar as it can be felt and seen, the rock is part of the concrete world; it is objective. But it has no meaning as part of that world, as object, for meaning is a purely human phenomenon. It is human interests that give it meaning. It can be given meaning by weighing it in the hand, by throwing it at a bird, by cracking an oyster with it, by categorizing it as a lump of granite, by collecting it and putting it into a geological museum, by building it into a wall, and so on. Thus it is the occasion for employing the universals of weighing, weaponry, tool-using, classification, collecting, building. Its universal aspect is its meaning, and its meaning is how it is used according to our interests, of which, according to Hegel, the highest is absolute freedom, experienced in philosophical activity, less so in religion, still less in art, but only in these three.

Now one's own body is a concrete universal. And so are one's sensations, which are meaningless in themselves, but are universalized as pleasant, unpleasant, pleasurable, painful, and so on. This is why a sensation that provides pleasure can so easily be converted into pain, and vice versa. The genitals and genital sensation are concrete universals. To regard them as manifestations of the pure subject, free from the recalcitrance of the object, is to be in a condition of cognitive error. Yet because of the peculiar nature of sexual activity, it is almost uniquely adapted for tricking the consciousness into that error and for tempting one into the illusion of experiencing in the objective world the nonobjective experience of absolute freedom.

This Hegelian point of view provides an explanation as to why in the master–slave condition of society, the master, entering into the world of abstract freedom and rapidly gaining the illusion that absolute freedom may be concretized, traditionally devotes so much of his wealth to accumulating sexual objects, including slaves, and so much of his leisure to sexual activity. Sexual addiction is the traditional addiction of slave-holding aristocracies, including the wage-slave-holding of the industrial entrepreneurs of England in the nineteenth century, together with their subordinates, the factory managers and foremen. The Hegelian criticism of the Sadian position is that it merely perpetuates the illusion of abstract freedom which is the mark of the primitive master and his descendants, the eighteenth-century aristocracy, of which de Sade was a member.

And he was a proud member, for his family was of the very old nobility. He never could quite understand why, as an aristocrat, he could not do exactly as he wished, and he felt that his incarcerations were most unjust. Again, from the Hegelian point of view, his position, though intellectually more advanced than that of the Terror, actually was of far less service in the movement toward freedom, which according to Hegel is the dynamics of history. For the Terror, by revealing the distinction between abstract freedom—which acted upon is negative freedom—and concrete freedom, made it possible to grasp the nature of the latter. From the point of view of Romanticism, de Sade's failure was that his consciousness was not historicized; while Hegel's, for all his shortcomings and failures—and they were many, including, as even his admirers admit, his prose style—must always be listened to with attention, because his consciousness was historicized.

However, there was a subtle factor in de Sade's position of which Hegel seems not to have been aware, and even de Sade himself seems not to have grasped it with any power or certainty. Both begin with mastery as the basic human drive, both are interested in freedom as the manifestation of that mastery, but both neglect the enticements of submission. It was not until the second half of the nineteenth century that these were at all adequately explored, by, of course, Sacher-Masoch. Strictly speaking, the masochist submits to humiliation and physical suffering in a sexual context, but for the reasons which make sexual behavior such an appropriate field of endeavor for working out the implications of absolute or negative freedom. Thus the implications worked out in sexual masochism are those of absolute or negative submission. If the primary need of man is mastery over the environment, of mind over nature, of subject over object, then presumably masochism is a secondary formation that emerges from the social form of the tension-laden struggle between subject and object. The masochist is the slave in the master–slave relationship who substitutes for the struggle with the environment the submission to the master. One of the most interesting things about a great deal of sado-masochist pornography is that the sufferer is so frequently presented as in a state of blissful happiness. Often enough the inflicter of torture is not even present, so that one suspects there is such a thing as very pure masochistic pornography.

This should not be surprising, for the masochist has a dual source of gratification. One source is obviously absolute or negative submission. The recent work, the *Story of O,* is to the point. In that novel the protagonist, a woman, gradually learns to find her whole meaning of life in submission to punishment in a sexual context. Most instructive, there is a preface to the book, purportedly by another writer—and it may be—which retails an incident of French colonialism; certain slaves, having been freed, return to their masters and beg to be made slaves again. The charm of absolute submission is the charm of letting go, of giving up the struggle to master the environment. Perhaps that is why people who get lost in the woods die so readily. This charm is presented so powerfully in the *Story of O* that many readers have been profoundly disturbed by the book. In all of this, it seems, there is the drive to submit, to surrender, to abandon the responsibility, as Hegel would have it, of creating freedom, of participating in the history of man.

246

If concrete freedom is unthinkable without restraint, there is that in us which willingly accepts restraint. Historically from the most primitive times this internal incoherence in our needs has been resolved by assigning to men the role of mastery and to women the role of submission, while women in turn have their share of mastery vis-à-vis children, in the role of mothers. Clearly the boy, in becoming a man, must switch from submission to mastery, and as Anthony Wallace points out in his *Religion*, a ritual of cognitive resynthesis appears to be essential in this process. Certain primitive societies have socialized such failure in the institution of the berdash, a man who dresses in women's clothes and does women's tasks, or in some societies becomes a shaman, a bearer of messages from the spirit world, a validator. The boy who fails to make this cognitive resynthesis will have a profound interest in seeking situations of submission, and for the reasons already given, it is possible that he may seek them in the sphere of sexual endeavor, as well as in the realm of spirits.

However, there is an indication in the *Story of O* that submission is really a secondary formation. O's reward is the experience of absolute freedom at the moment of sexual intoxication and orgasm. All her suffering is justified by that. This can be understood in terms of the relation, often made, between sexual masochism and extreme religious asceticism, though, to be sure, the error is usually indulged in that the sexual masochism is the cause of religious asceticism. Not so. Both are means of working out the implications of absolute freedom, but the mastery is the mastery over one's own body. This puts the masochist and the religious ascetic in a very interesting and very small human category. Since the normal temptation, one which de Sade surrendered to, is to perceive the body as the manifestation of the subject, the one who submits to torture is escaping that error and perceiving the body as object. And yet more subtly, the submission to humiliation is the perception of the personality as

247

object, for the personality is the internal, the inside-the-skin, environment of the subject, and is truly object.

The surrender to humiliation and suffering, the attempt to experience absolute or negative submission is but a mask for the primary drive, mastery over the environment. The masochist is engaged in the most intimate possible struggle between subject and object, but his ultimate aim is that of the sadist, absolute freedom, that is, negative freedom. His aim too is the absorption of subject into object, though he imagines, like the Enlightenment, that he is resolving the subject-object tension by resolving that tension into the object, with which he identifies himself. But masochism is a secondary formation, not a primary one, for the subject cannot become the object. So the sadist and the masochist are silent conspirators, because both wish to realize absolute freedom in the concrete world, and both choose the sexual sphere, since it is the safest sphere, the sphere with the fewest social consequences.

When negative freedom is sought in spheres of great social consequences, the result, according to Hegel, is the sort of thing that the Terror was. It is instructive that a recent commentator on Hegel, H. B. Acton, has suggested that "the links between egalitarianism, antinomianism, violence, and contempt for human life are not wholly accidental." Sadism and masochism in the sexual sphere seem, then, to be more exercises of the Geist, to use a Hegelian term, than efforts to concretize absolute freedom as negative freedom. Researchers of the Institute for Sex Research know of but one unquestionable sadist in Chicago, and he insists that he is the only real article in the entire city. There is good reason to believe that the amount of sado-masochist pornography circulated is out of all proportion to the actual number of practicing sadists and masochists. This state of affairs is a further suggestion that the interests at work in sadism and masochism are not sexual—indeed they cannot be—but political in the fundamental sense of social management. They

248

are metaphors of social management, of the organism-environment, mind-nature, subject-object relationship in the sphere of
social behavior. And both are deeply involved, therefore, with
the problem of freedom, for both are explorations of the master-
slave relationship.

Yet even more can be said. Every ongoing relationship between people involves a constant interchange of domination
and submission, of masterhood and slavery. One of the interesting things, for example, about the history of slavery is the frequency with which the pet or favorite slave ingeniously puts
himself into the position of actually running things, of being the
true master. So everyone is annoyed by the individual who
always insists upon being the master. These matters should be
shared, we feel. Nevertheless, one great source of weariness in
any human relationship, one reason why we cannot abide constant interaction with anyone, no matter how fond we are of
them, is the simple wear and tear of constantly having to shift
from one role to the other. This, in Hegelian terminology, is
what concrete freedom in ordinary social relationships amounts
to, and it is exhausting. Hence the temptation of negative freedom, and hence the temptation to maintain one role or the other
in sadism or in masochism, or far more likely, in sadist-masochist
pornography, both written and pictorial.

The need for flexibility in social interaction is, therefore, inconsistent with the need for stabilization. Yet for survival both
are necessary. This is what makes Hegel's analysis so subtle.
Absolute freedom is necessary to examine the incoherence of a
culture's explanatory and validational and social management
concepts; yet it is but preparatory for action. Negative freedom
is violent and destructive; yet at times it is necessary to break
up institutions which have outlived their historical usefulness.
Concrete freedom is the condition of experience, of actually
engaging the world in its forms of concrete universals; yet it is
exhausting, tension-laden, and frustrating, and it cannot even

249

exist without restraint, restraint by others, restraint of others, and restraint of oneself. Moreover, the intellectual consequences of absolute freedom can be absurd, and perhaps usually are. Not all cognitive resyntheses are by any means of any significance. Likewise negative freedom can easily destroy institutions which are still of the greatest possible value. So absolute and negative freedom can be vacations from the exhausting problems of concrete freedom. Perhaps in the totality of human behavior this is quantitatively their principal function.

I have ventured on this analysis of sadism and masochism because the problem was originated at the threshold of the nineteenth century, and I have employed a Romantic philosopher's insights into the problems of mastery, slavery, and freedom because they give nineteenth-century tools to analyze one of the most extraordinary figures of Victorian England, Algernon Charles Swinburne. It is not a fashionable thing to say, though it is a little more fashionable than it was a decade ago, but to my mind Swinburne is one of the great poets in the English language. He is also in style and in content one of the most puzzling and most difficult. He wrote the first intellectually serious works on eroticism in English literature, and for good reason. He was a masochist, and not a paper masochist either. He was the real article. As late as 1895, when he was nearly sixty, he continued to visit a *maison des supplices,* a brothel devoted to the special interests of sadists and masochists. He was intensely curious about the Marquis de Sade, and before he had access to his works he had written a superb poem about him. When a friend loaned him the Marquis, he wrote to his benefactor letters of wild excitement. Undoubtedly the example of de Sade gave him some cultural support in exploring sadism and particularly masochism in poetry.

This was the subject of *Poems and Ballads,* which caused such a storm when it was published in 1866. In fact the original publisher withdrew it from publication, and to keep it in print Swinburne had to turn to a publisher just on the edge, or a little beyond the edge, of respectable publication. John Camden Hotten was a thoroughly unscrupulous man, and the great editor of Swinburne's letters, Professor Cecil Y. Lang, thinks that Hotten actually blackmailed the poet. Hotten had done a considerable amount of pornographic and semipornographic publication, and his sexual interests seem to have been a little like those of Swinburne himself. At any rate, they collaborated in writing and publishing several under-the-counter or "privately published" volumes on sadistic and masochistic themes. For years Swinburne kept adding to a series of poems and stories which he called *The Whippingham Papers*, and some of these, too, were eventually privately published in a volume of that title. These works make it easier to understand some of the *Poems and Ballads*, but they also raise a problem.

Between works like *The Whippingham Papers* and *Poems and Ballads* there is an obvious difference. The one type has the function of all pornography and quasi-pornography; it presents as vividly as possible the particular kind of sexual experience the writer takes his pleasure in, for whatever reasons. The other explores the cognitive aspect of such interests in the attempt to locate their psychic source. The one presents; the other organizes toward an explanatory end. These two functions come out clearly when one notices that the first type is not presented to the culture for validation or invalidation, but that the second is. Swinburne was in fact furious over the reception of *Poems and Ballads*, its invalidation by reviewers as filthy fleshliness, as shocking self-indulgence in the vicious and the forbidden. Partly he was furious over the hypocrisy of a society which damned his work, and at the same time encouraged an army of prostitutes, some of whom actually were leaders in setting the styles in clothes, and in supporting two streets in London entirely devoted to the sale of literary and pictorial pornography of the most uncompromising sort.

After all, he knew the difference. He had written both kinds. *Poems and Ballads*, he insisted in a pamphlet he wrote in self-defense, was not only a serious work but a moral one. Yet before he published, he knew perfectly well that a great many would be shocked; he hoped they would be shocked. Nevertheless he was convinced and insisted that there were principles of valida-tion available in the culture which could be successfully applied to his poems. "And if literature indeed is not to deal with the full life of man and the whole nature of things, let it be cast aside with the rods and rattles of childhood." Later in his book on Blake he defended the principle of *l'art pour l'art* on similar grounds. The morality of poetry, he claimed, was precisely that the poet was above the common morality of his culture. *His* morality was to treat anything he chose with uncompromising honesty. He knew, of course, that such principles were not available in the culture, that such a mode of validation was not a fact. Moreover, it is a dangerous principle to appeal to. It can be turned the other way. Those who object to the claim for public validation of forbidden subjects—or disapproved sub-jects—can invariably say that the trouble with the work is that it does not deal with the full life of man, but only with a very partial aspect of that life, nor does it deal in terms of the whole nature of things, but from a very limited and special point of view, not valuable to the community at large. This is the sense of the Supreme Court's demand that if it is not to be censored, a work must have redeeming social value. Swinburne's position was that any work which treats of whatever subject, even the most shocking, has redeeming social value if the treatment is serious.

What, then, did he mean by serious? The contrast between the erotic poems of *Poems and Ballads* and his pornographic works—which were, after all, pretty mild as pornography goes

—gives us some hint, as does a letter to Hotten outlining his strategy for his defense of *Poems and Ballads.* Even though, he admitted, the atheism of some of them was scarcely to be differentiated from atheistic sentiments he had uttered, no reader had the right to impute such sentiments to *him,* for the poems were dramatic. At first glance this merely means that the speaker of the poem is not to be identified with the poet, but is an imagined speaker. After all, he pointed out, the volume contained poems which were as Christian and pious, though medieval and Catholic, as anyone could hope for. These certainly were not to be ascribed to him. Anyone who knew him knew that such poems were dramatic.

The book, he claimed in his pamphlet, was "dramatic, many-faced, multifarious." And when we add to this another sentence, it is possible to see that another semantic function is at work. "Were each poem to be accepted as the deliberate outcome and result of the writer's conviction, not mine alone but most other men's verses would leave nothing behind them but a sense of cloudy chaos and suicidal contradiction." Here, then, is what he meant by dramatic and serious, at least when these words are used to justify the use of subjects currently forbidden in the culture. Today the dominant culture, at any rate, forbids the public validation of White hatred for Blacks, though it does not forbid, of course, public validation of Black hatred for Whites. Let us imagine a writer of genius—and it would take genius—who writes anonymously but with absolute sincerity violent anti-Black pamphlets to be distributed by the Ku Klux Klan, but who also writes a novel in which the moral conflicts such hatred entails in him are expressed and the sources of that hatred elsewhere are sought for and explored. If we should believe of William Styron the hatred for and prejudice against the Blacks which some of his Black critics accused him of, and if we believed that he secretly writes anti-Black tracts, then we would have a case analogous to Swinburne's. It is perhaps the difference between negative freedom and concrete freedom, as they are to be found in literature. The one attacks the validational system of the culture; the other explores the conflicts that must necessarily result when any validated morality is actually uncompromisingly applied.

Putting it this way makes more acceptable Swinburne's defense on the grounds that the current literary morality of his day required that a book be fit to place in the hands of children and girls. "Would you give it to your daughter?" Swinburne's position was that literature should be virile, not puerile and feminine, and he implied that the current attitudes were damaging to the English race. Thus the absolute application of the validational system of a culture, its approved morality, is as much negative freedom as attacks upon that system. Both seek to avoid the issues of concrete freedom. Here the distinction made in the discussion of Tylor between polarization and alienation will be of service. Since the belief system and the moral system, the explanatory mode and the validational mode, of any culture are always incoherent, polarization seeks to resolve the problem by selecting only one more or less coherent strand and acting upon that. So in Castro's Cuba and among our rebellious students alike the values selected, as most observers have noticed, are anything but innovative. They are, in fact, for the most part middle-class values, and when they are not, they are classless values. The negative freedom of the one, now the destructive period is over, takes the form of a demand for absolute submission to the state, the payoff to be a return to concrete freedom. Since the destructive phase of the other has scarcely begun, it is as yet impossible even to guess what the outcome will be.

Swinburne, at any rate was claiming that the literary morality of the day was threatening to become, in part had become, a negative freedom. The issue he was raising is a perennial one, since the problems of concrete freedom are perennial. He was in fact demanding not only the right to treat publicly, to submit to social validation, forbidden matters; he was demanding social validation for that which in fact had been invalidated. He was challenging the whole validational system, and with good reason. Just as Hegel's treatment of submission is inadequate—for it is not enough to say that the slave continues to engage in the concrete world and to develop new means of mastery, without discussing the delicious attraction of submission as a vacation from that engagement—so is his treatment of freedom. His position was that the individual in becoming civilized conforms his will to the ends of the state and so achieves his freedom.

Hegel has been bitterly condemned for this conclusion, and with some justice, for it certainly seems to leave concrete freedom entirely up to the state; and what is the state, Marx asked, but a collection of masters, to whom the rest of the society are slaves? It appears that Hegel's incomplete exploration of the charms of slavery led him to ignore the possibility that the citizen's identification of his interests with the state is a vacation from the subject–object tension, from exposure to the concrete. It appears to be the absorption of the subject into the object, but is in fact the absorption of the object into the subject, negative freedom. Hegel's citizen and state relationship reminds one too much of O and her master.

Hegel saw history as the struggle, increasingly successful, for human freedom. In his scheme absolute freedom could never be achieved in the concrete world, but concrete freedom was progressive. His sense of historical drama was that negative freedom is a matter of social crisis. The Terror occurred during such a social crisis, and there was an historical justification for it, even though it was negative freedom. Indeed, as a young man, still fully committed to the Enlightenment, he initially saw the French Revolution, as did Wordsworth and Coleridge, as a great and permanent leap forward into what he subsequently called concrete freedom. He may have changed his mind, but the drama-laden crisis as a model for understanding negative freedom remained with him. Because his exploration of submission was inadequate, he seems not to have been aware that the pull away from concrete freedom toward negative freedom is not a critical event but a social and cultural constant, of which his own conception of the citizen-state relationship could well be cited as an instance. Possibly because he felt the irresolvable tension between subject and object so attractive (perhaps because it appealed so much to his dramatic sense, with which he was richly gifted), he thought such delight to be normal among men. But it is not so; quite the contrary. Concrete freedom may be the line of human progress, but most people shrink away from it most of the time, and even a Hegel shrinks away from it some of the time. What man *wants* is negative freedom, a vacation—to do his own thing.

Such a vacation Swinburne himself enjoyed in *The Whippingham Papers* and its companions, but in his serious work he was challenging the validational mode of his culture. One of the puzzling things about Swinburne is that after writing the erotic works of *Poems and Ballads* he so soon turned to political poetry, poetry devoted to abstract freedom and to freedom as it was being grasped by the Cretans, by the Italians, by the Parisians in 1870. The shift has been said to be a complete mystery, or to be the result of a struggle against his father, resolved as soon as he had found a father–surrogate in Mazzini, or to be a temporary aberration. Nothing, however, from the point of view of the analysis proposed here could be more consistent than this shift. Moreover, as we have seen, there is every reason in the world for a masochist to be interested in freedom, for he commands at once a whole spectrum of freedoms: he has the concrete freedom of turning his body into an object; he has the illusory freedom of resolving the subject–object tension by perceiving himself and his body as object in relation to the subject, his master and torturer; he has the negative freedom of a vacation from concrete freedom. That Swinburne, a masochist, should have been passionately interested in freedom need occasion neither surprise nor difficulty.

But there is both surprise and difficulty in the fact that he used his own psychological peculiarity both for his vacation writings and his serious writings. And there is a further puzzle and surprise in his transition from the serious masochistic eroticism of *Poems and Ballads* to the political and speculative poems on freedom. Though his Greek tragedy, *Atalanta in Calydon* was published before *Poems and Ballads,* it was in fact written after most of the lyrics had been written. *Atalanta* was a great success, probably because its style was so innovative and difficult, and yet superficially so attractive, that nobody understood it. Besides it was a Greek tragedy, and everybody knew that was respectable, no matter what happened in it. But in fact it is a study of family relations, the most devastating comment on the family written before the twentieth century.

Why this strange path from erotic masochism *through the family* to the theme of freedom? To answer that question it is necessary to begin with the first difficulty, his use of his own masochism and his struggles with it as the subject to be explored in the first poems written in his mature style. Indeed, his mature style emerges only with these poems, an indication in itself that exceedingly profound interests were involved, as well as, what is perfectly true, an extraordinary and extraordinarily objective insight into his own strange and troubling eroticism. There is scarcely a parallel in English literature, at least before 1865, and not very many after it. An apparent exception is Byron's *Manfred,* but that is so mysterious that it was long after his death before anybody knew that Byron's own incest with his half sister was the source for the inexplicable suffering of Manfred. Even today, serious writing in Swinburne's sense about a sexual aberration by a sexual aberrant is rare. There is plenty of pornography, yes, but even when a serious effort is made public, validation is ordinarily withheld. Critics tend to invalidate such works, for fear perhaps that a sympathy with the struggles will be taken for a sympathy with the aberration. For validation, apparently, the critic and the reading public have to be convinced that the work is entirely dramatic, and that the author can in no way be identified with the protagonist.

The question amounts to the problem of the nature of the cultural support which enabled Swinburne to undertake so strikingly original and daring an experiment. The common theory that it was the expression of his compulsive erotic obsession is quite inadequate. For one thing, his vacation writings, as I have called them, were an adequate outlet; for another, these poems are not the expression of an erotic obsession—they are the exploration of it. They are attempts to come to grips with it, to understand it, to explain it. Swinburne's reaction to de Sade is instructive. Before he read him, he wrote a beautiful and highly inaccurate poem about him. When he read him, he did so with great excitement, as does anyone when he reads anything on a matter which is intensely important to him, whether it is sex or mathematics. But in time he came to mock him, to parody him, to patronize him.

It is clear that for all of de Sade's philosophizing, Swinburne classed his work with his own pornography, and that he rejected de Sade's explanation as no explanation at all. Either he saw de Sade's work as a justification for de Sade's own tastes, or he understood what de Sade was doing and rejected it; perhaps both. In any case, de Sade gave him no understanding of himself, beyond a very superficial level. Whether he was right in this or wrong, he had to work out his own comprehension. And in that need to work out his own understanding of the incomprehensible in himself lies the clue to his cultural support.

From the beginning of Romanticism writers—and philosophers as well—had two great themes, the ineffable and the mysterious, the incomprehensible, that for which the culture could provide no explanation, and this is what the ineffable and the mysterious have in common. The mystic, or the ecstatic, experience, which was Wordsworth's marvelous speciality, is one for which there can never be a language—or so the mystic and ecstatic prefer to believe. The mysterious is that for which the explanatory mode of the culture has no universals with which to categorize it. A special mode of the mysterious is the forbidden, of which the explanatory mode asserts that it could perhaps be explained but that it is too disgusting, too revolting, too inhuman to be worth the effort. This is yet another indication of the close bond between explanation, validation, and social management. Hence in these three areas of human experience, Romanticism tended to find its proper subjects.

It is interesting that Kant, who laid the foundations for Romanticism by sundering subject from object, should have defined the aesthetic experience—by which he did not mean the experience we have before works of art, but the experience before nature, or art as nature—as one in which the subject actually does know the object, the mysterious and elusive *ding-an-sich*. And this experience is ineffable, inexplicable; nothing can be said about it. To this day a school of aesthetics survives —and by some is even taken seriously—which says that this ineffable experience, this trance-like rapture, this ecstasy, this seeing into the heart of things, as Wordsworth put it, is the true aesthetic experience. Some members of this school also insist that though it is often triggered by works of art, not all art does so, nor for all individuals, nor need the triggering stimulus be a work of art. In his *Religion* Wallace considers something like this kind of experience as the center of the religious ritual, for which separation is an essential pre-condition. The outcome of that ritual is, as we have seen, cognitive resynthesis, sometimes temporary, sometimes long-lasting, sometimes affecting only the individual, sometimes his entire culture, which is thus re-modeled.

From this two useful hints may be derived. One leads to the

late nineteenth-century Religion of Art. The confusion of this experience with the artistic experience was powerfully reinforced by the doctrine; yet if Wallace is right, this attitude is not incorrectly called a religion. At any rate, early in the century the Romantic concluded that only two stimulus sources could produce the experience, nature and art. This is quite different from the nature worship of the eighteenth century. In that rationalistic religion, nature was perceived as the work of God, or, in non-Christian terms, the Goddess of Nature, the harmony of nature quite consciously personified. The Enlightenment experience before nature was fully explicable, and in fact derived from an explanatory system.

The Romantic worship of nature, on the contrary, was based not on seeing nature as exemplifications, so to speak, of either God or the harmony of the universe, but rather as the occasion for an ineffable experience which could not be explained. The purpose, the designed purpose, of the experience was that it should be inexplicable. This is one of the reasons why music became culturally so significant, so independent of controlling social situations, while the Romantic musical experience was often enough taken as the model of the aesthetic experience. There was a widespread conviction that music was meaningful, but there was no agreement on what it could mean. Inexplicable meaningfulness, meaning that does not mean—this became the Romantic ideal for the encounter with both art and nature.

The other hint comes from the theme of separation. The Romantic was alienated from his culture, and parted the self from the role. However, as we have seen, there is no way to act except by playing roles, so the Romantic either played roles ironically, as Tylor did, or he developed the anti-role, the Bohemian, the dandy, the historian, the anthropologist. Such role-playing undermined the validational mode of the culture, and sought either to escape social management or to control it, as did the historian Karl Marx.

260

One strategy for challenging the explanatory mode was that of philosophy, which set about simply to overthrow it by offering a more adequate one. The more subtle strategy was to locate an experience which the explanatory mode could not explain, either because it had never taken cognizance of it, or because it admitted its helplessness before it, a helplessness usually redeemed by invalidating it. Such a strategy accomplished what ironic role-playing and anti-role could not. It was not a social activity at all. On the contrary it was an intensely private experience, a separated experience. Thus today there are plenty of music lovers who are delighted with modern sound equipment since they no longer need attend concerts and can listen in absolute privacy. I cannot be certain, but I have the impression from my reading in the nineteenth century that closing one's eyes during musical performances is concert behavior which emerged in the course of the nineteenth century, and probably fairly late in it.

To the degree the ineffable experience gradually became in the course of the century stabilized and integrated within the tradition of Romanticism, it became of course a social role, but a social role that is played in absolute privacy is a pretty attenuated one. A fine example of what is involved here is to be found in an entry in one of Coleridge's notebooks. Having to arise in the night to urinate, he admired the play of the moonlight on and in the yellow urine in the white chamber pot. Certainly, though ordinarily private, the protocol of excretion is well-defined, too well-defined, according to Freudians, and one element in that protocol is the feeling of disgust toward excretory products, an attitude in which we are all trained at an early age.

Coleridge proceeded to play the excretory role ironically, by admiring what is supposed to be disgusting; thus he challenged the validational system. At the same time he undermined the explanatory mode by encouraging in himself an aesthetic experience which that mode could not account for, nor indeed had taken cognizance of. There is also more than a touch of engagement in the forbidden, for the tone of the notebook entry is one of high self-gratulation. He was obviously greatly pleased with himself when he made the entry, for even making it was a challenge to the system of social management—though a covert one—as well as having the aesthetic experience stimulated by a pot of urine in the moonlight. At work in this minor Romantic incident, then, is the ineffable, the mysterious, and the forbidden, as well as the seeking out of such material. It is evident that it was not merely permitted to happen; it was actively sought for. Wordsworth's *Prelude* is an active seeking for it, and it is about active seeking for it. It was, after all, the Romantics who invented the taking of psychedelic drugs as a means of accomplishing separation and achieving the ineffable experience. The message of the drug, it appears, turns out to be separation itself. As Wallace says, in the cognitive resynthesis experience, elements of that synthesis already must exist in the culture. Thus in the fascinating emergence today of the dropout commune, a last strategy of separation from the society and its culture having been innovated, drug-taking is beginning to be frowned on.

Now certainly in early nineteenth-century England drug-taking was not a particularly rebellious act. On the contrary, not religion but opium was the opium of the people. If you were too poor to get drunk on Saturday night, you bought opium instead of alcohol. As the factory system increasingly required a work force capable of social coordination early Monday morning, the social managers set out to dry up the British working population, which had been permitted in the eighteenth century to drink all it wanted to. It was to be a good many decades before the industrial requirements became sufficiently exacting to require a similar attack on opium and its derivatives and on marijuana. One can, in Romantic literature, find a steady rise in the interest in drugs as their fascination and dangers were explored, and as they were gradually moved into the area of the forbidden.

Indeed the curve of the Romantic exploration of the forbidden rises steadily throughout the nineteenth century, in all Europe, not England alone. Of all the spheres of the forbidden, nothing was so rich with promise and variety as the erotic sphere. Here was something which offered, first, privacy. Then, in the orgasm, it offered an ineffable experience. Coventry Patmore was to exploit this in his later writings. Behind his religious books in his library he kept his erotic ones, and a little examination revealed that his late nature writings were intensely sexual, but in such a way that sex and religion were identified through the ecstatic, the mystic, the ineffable. Furthermore, the sexual sphere was mysterious. The current modes for explaining it, even its ordinary varieties, were inconceivably feeble; even today they are not much stronger, now that the explanatory mode of Freud, once so promising, is turning into myth and vanishing into mist. As for the fancier varieties, there was no explaining them at all, except for such explanation as original sin and the corruption of man offered; and that had become little more than a validational mode. Finally, eroticism was forbidden. Not that the ordinary forms of heterosexual intercourse were forbidden. It was rather that public discussion of sex, either oral in mixed company and increasingly even in all-male groups, or written, was forbidden.

The obscenity laws came not long after the middle of the century. Moreover there was a rising tide of puritanism, whatever its sources; probably the industrial revolution was the principal one. In any event Mrs. Grundy became increasingly powerful, as Swinburne noted and protested, so much so that one of the meanings of "Victorian" came to be prudery and sexual repression, or at least the repression of the discussion of sex. As for the sexual deviations, they were invalidated with a steadily increasing intensity. Such a mild affair as masturbation was placed under increasing social management and invalidation; before D. H. Lawrence's, I know of only one poem on masturbation in the whole nineteenth century, at least by a serious writer. That was Rimbaud's. It was in fact a political attack on Napoleon III, through his son, and used masturbation as a sneer. It was daring to use it, but Rimbaud's attitude was anything but daring.

The nineteenth century saw the wholesale continuation of a practice that originated in the eighteenth, the publication of pamphlets on the horrors of self-abuse. It was not until the 1870's that in England prostitution began to be controlled, though it was looked on with increasing horror. As for homosexuality, Wilde was arrested in 1895 on a very recent law. Since eroticism was invalidated in more and more of its manifestations and with steadily growing intensity, through the century, the Romantic interest in eroticism follows the same pattern as the Romantic interest in drugs. The more it was forbidden, the more the Romantics were interested in it. Because it was ineffable, inexplicable, and forbidden, the Romantic felt a moral duty to explore it, since to do so was to challenge at once the explanatory, the validational, and the social management modes of the culture.

This was the cultural force that enabled Swinburne to undertake his daring experiment of writing serious poetry on his own erotic aberration. And it explains as well the curiously moral tone his defense of his poetry always took, for he published yet another one in 1872. In short, by his time Romanticism had developed with considerable richness its validational mode, the purpose of which was to establish its alienation and to facilitate cultural transcendence. Swinburne wrote about himself not only because it was also a well-established Romantic tradition to begin with oneself and move outward toward the object, toward man, society, and nature, but primarily because he could not understand himself. As I have suggested, this failure of self-understanding was responsible for his initial excitement over de Sade and his subsequent boredom with him. There was no explanation of any kind for masochism in his culture, nor is there yet. One of the reasons I have used Hegelian concepts as a way into the problem is precisely the lack of any other way. However, though this interest of Romanticism in the inexplicable, the ineffable, and the forbidden gives us an explanation for Swinburne's determination to explore sadism, it fails to provide us with an adequate explanation of why he chose to do so in poetry.

The Romantics sought for the inexplicable, but to undermine the explanatory system it was necessary not only to find it, it was equally necessary to present it in such a way that it remained inexplicable but became meaningful. That is, like music it had to be meaningful but its meaning had to resist verbalization. It had to be significant, but what it signified had to be beyond utterance. It had to be at once meaningful and without meaning. This is the Romantic paradox of the symbol. Furthermore, it had to have something called "organic unity," but no one to this day has been able to define organic unity in any useful manner whatever; no one has been able to generate a set of verbal directions such that one can tell whether a work has organic unity or not. The term "symbol" has been equally recalcitrant, though every literate person on the contemporary scene is pretty well trained to say "symbol" and "organic unity" on what he and often others judge to be appropriate occasions. The term "myth" is similarly used, and similarly resistant to analysis.

Yet this "meaningful meaninglessness" or "meaningless meaningfulness" can be understood.

One sense of the term "meaning" is that one can say what the meaning of an utterance is. That is, one can in response to it generate an utterance which will be validated as an acceptable substitute for it. This is the kind of "meaning" one finds in dictionaries, but also in all discourse. It can be of two sorts. One sort is to say what the meaning of a proposition is by giving an example. The other is to subsume it in more inclusive categories or universals. The utterance in question then becomes an example of these more general statements. Or in other words, one makes sense out of it by organizing it into the categories of the explanatory system of the culture. Why do men engage in aberrant sexual behavior? Because we all inherit original sin, the corruption of the spirit, the intelligence, and the flesh. Why is there original sin? Because it is the will of God. "Original sin" is an example of the explanatory "will of God," and "aberrant sexual behavior" is an example of "original sin." This was the explanatory system available for Swinburne, and it is not surprising he found it inadequate, having rejected the ultimate explanatory term, "will of God." This is, of course, the theory of explanation by subsumption originated by the Neoplatonists, remodeled by Hegel and independently rediscovered by Tylor, though perhaps he did not know it.

From this point of view meaningful meaninglessness is not too hard to understand. It is in fact a very common experience. Consider Swinburne's problem, masochism. He could not explain it by subsuming it progressively under "original sin" and "the will of God." He could not even subsume it under "masochism," a word not used in England until 1893. All that he knew was that his sexual drive took the form of the desire to experience pain, and that his fantasies of desirable women were invariably of dominating, masterful women who caused him humiliation, and that both the pain and the humiliation gave him ineffable pleasure

That pleasure first appeared when he was a schoolboy. The technique of social management in English schools, the best of which were virtually restricted to the aristocracy, of which he was a member, was frequent and violent flogging on the bare buttocks with birch rods, ordinarily softened in water to make them more supple and stinging. Flogging was a technique employed in the British Navy as well. This suggests, of course, that Swinburne, among his other difficulties, might also have been homosexual, and according to Professor Lang there is a persistent oral tradition that this was so. It may be. Certainly, some of Swinburne's most powerful poems took Lesbianism as their subject, and in spite of his claim that "Hermaphroditus" is a philosophical poem, it is unquestionably erotic. On the other hand, he could not have been exclusively homosexual, for his dominating women are too convincing to be faked. In any case Swinburne was perfectly aware that the whipping schoolmaster could take erotic pleasure from the act, as well as the boy. The harder the whipping, so to speak, the greater the affection—on both sides.

At any event in his poetry homosexuality between men is very rare, and between women, no matter how brilliantly presented, it is minor in bulk. Furthermore, homosexuality could be understood in the sense that there was at least a name for it, several in fact, but masochism was nameless. Even "sadism" was not to enter the language until 1888. So, Swinburne observed in his behavior and his feelings a repetitive pattern for which there was not even a name, let alone an explanation. Yet on the other hand his sexual experiences and his periods of erotic feeling were sufficiently similar for an analogous pattern to be readily observable.

This is precisely the source of meaningful meaninglessness. Hence another meaning of the term "meaning" is its subsumption of examples in language or instances (in the empirical world) sufficiently alike to be categorized together, but for which no universal term and hence no explanation exists; or in the case of homosexuality, a universal term exists, but no explanation. It would be hard to imagine, then, anything more mysterious and inexplicable for Swinburne to deal with than his own masochism.

To clarify this, consider a scientist whose theory has broken down under the impact either of a newly discovered internal or logical incoherence or under the assault of data which is sufficiently like the explained or theoretically organized data to be included or categorized with that data, but which presents inexplicable and aberrant features. His recourse is to go to his laboratory, to make observations, and to comb the reports of others. His hope is to be able to grasp new data by means of sufficiently demanding analogical relationships, to see a new pattern, and thus construct a new theory, or explanation; or it is to grasp how the inexplicable and aberrant features of the destructive data are analogically coherent with the explained data, and thus remodel and improve the disturbed theory. In the period between "understanding" the analogical relationships and creating or reconstructing the theory the scientist experiences the "meaningfulness" of the data, but is as yet unable to provide a verbal explanation. It is still, in that sense of "meaning," meaningless though nevertheless meaningful.

This can, I think, be made even clearer if we distinguish between two quite different meanings of "understand." On the one hand "understand" means to be able to make an appropriate response to a situation; on the other hand it means to be able to explain the situation verbally. Consequently, to say, "I understand it but I can't explain it" is to make a perfectly reasonable remark, and similar to the one so often heard in the scientific enterprise, "I've got it but can't yet put it in words." This was precisely Swinburne's position.

Now just as a scientist in pursuit of his elusive analogical relationships explores by means of reports, observations, and experiments, so Swinburne explored his masochism by putting it into a great variety of imagined situations, and by subjecting it to the strains of dramatic conflict. This is what has come to be called, since the arrival of Romanticism, "poetic thinking," but there is nothing poetic about it at all. It is the normal, indeed the only possible method when explanations have broken down or are unavailable. Nevertheless, to understand why the Romantics called it "true poetry" or "the essence of poetry" (by which they also meant drama and fiction, and indeed, in time, all the arts) is to understand why Swinburne explored his masochism in poetry.

The first clue comes from Schopenhauer and Hegel, both of whom rejected traditional Aristotelian logic. To change his language a little but not his concept, Schopenhauer began with the notion of overlapping ideas. By this he meant that each universal or category is differentiated from other categories by attributes; yet the same attribute can be found in two categories, thus linking them. This, he maintains, is what makes discourse possible: we get from one category to another by means of an attribute common to both, as a horse and a dog are both domesticated placental animals. Now, he says, it is obvious that we can proceed in several directions, either in the direction of nondomesticated placental animals, or in that of domesticated placental animals, and so on.

His main example is that of traveling. One path from traveling leads to "dispelling boredom, exhilarating, pleasant, and good." Another leads through "expensive, causing losses, cause of becoming poor," to evil. Another leads from traveling through "ample opportunity for storing experience, increasing knowledge, enhancing prestige, earning universal trust, rendering fit for public duties, promoting to public office, enriching, useful," to good. Or one can branch from enhancing prestige and move through "yielding honor, exciting envy, incurring hatred, pernicious," to evil. One must read the whole section in *The World as Will and Idea* to see how cleverly and amusingly—and devastatingly—he exploits this notion. And it is devastating, because he points out that is is not logic that leads one through these various paths, but human will, or, if one wishes, adaptational interests. But whatever it is, it is not logic.

Similarly Hegel rejected Aristotelian logic and constructed in its stead something far more elaborate than Schopenhauer did. As we have seen, he constructed a subsumptive logic, which leads backward from the world into what he called the "absolute," as in absolute freedom. All he meant by "absolute" was that as a concept it was unmodified by the concrete world. But it was not an absolute in the sense that it was final. On the contrary, it was merely the limit of the consciousness, the explanatory limit. Behind this absolute and the whole subsumptional hierarchy of explanation or reason by which one reached it lay human interests, needs, desires. This, as in Schopenhauer, was inaccessible to reason. He saw, it is true, a place for traditional logic, but a minor place. A very recent philosopher has claimed, interestingly enough, that formal logic is merely a set of directions for manipulating sentences, and that it has nothing to say about either the adequacy of those sentences or about their relation to the world outside of language.

One of the few living philosophers who has troubled to master Hegel has called his logic highly original. It certainly is a highly Romantic logic, and we have seen how Tylor, without the aid of Hegel and scarcely knowing what he was doing, used very much the same kind of thinking in constructing historical and cultural anthropology. But whether Hegel and Schopenhauer were on the right track or not—and of course I think they were—they both made highly original breaks with the whole course of European philosophy, to which Aristotelian logic was central. Both, of course, derived from Kant, who made the first break when he demonstrated that traditional logical or causal thinking leads to antinomies, rational incoherence. Thus on the grounds of logic and causality it is equally demonstrable that the world is infinite and that it is finite

What was going on in philosophy was going on in a superficially different way in literature. The alienated Romantic writers also perceived that the rationalism of the Enlightenment had led to incoherence and an internal breakdown of explanatory modes and consequently of validational modes. The traditional modes of logical and causal explanation had, for them, failed. They have been accused over and over again of turning to the irrational, to, it is claimed, the purely emotional. But this accusation is an error and has led, in fact, to the profound misapprehension of Romantic culture. As far as emotion is concerned they insisted that the degree to which a cognitive act is emotionally weighted determines the outcome of that act. Wordsworth's *Prelude* can be quite thoroughly understood as an exploration of this situation. It is, of course, remarkably similar to the claims that Hegel and Schopenhauer were to make in the next, second decade of the century about what really controls the reason. It is refreshing to observe that a few modern psychologists are at last coming around to this position. Cognition, whatever it is, cannot be identified with "reason" and "cause."

But this, of course, was not nearly enough for the cognitive resynthesis they so desperately needed. What they were looking for was a new kind of thinking, since the old causal and logical kind had, so far as they were concerned, failed. There was, we are assured by a brilliant recent philosopher, good reason for their conclusion. C. M. Turbayne in his *The Myth of Metaphor* has demonstrated that the notion of causality which arose in the seventeenth century and dominated the physical sciences until the twentieth century was actually a metaphorical projection upon the empirical world of the nexus of traditional logic. As has already been suggested, "cause" is a word that connects statements about the world, not events in the world. Properly rewritten, a causal statement is a predictive statement about the outcome of nonverbal behavior, effective for someone who knows the cultural conventions for responding appropriately to that predictive statement. "Causality" then is a metaphorical myth, a way of relating and organizing logically statements that purport to be about the world. Ironically, the Romantics seem not to have perceived this.

It was ironic precisely because the Romantic writers found in myth what they were looking for. In undermining the content of the explanatory system of their culture, they turned to the mysterious, the inexplicable, the forbidden; in undermining the form of that system they turned to pre-seventeenth-century poetry, particularly Shakespeare and his contemporary dramatists, to classical mythology, and to quasi-mythical philosophy, such as the Neoplatonists. In Germany, they also turned to folklore. What they were looking for was the structure of cognition that underlies "rational," that is, causal-logical thinking, which they regarded as superficial, deceiving, or at best relatively trivial. What they discovered, to put it baldly, is that cognition does not proceed from point to point by a logical process but instead proceeds by integration, disintegration, and reintegration of patterns.

As Coleridge put it, this deeper power, the imagination, "dissolves, diffuses, dissipates, in order to create." The application of this perception can be found in Wordsworth's *Prelude*. There, by observing his boyhood behavior at certain moments of imaginative integration, he shows that there was a common cognitive structure although the situations were different. The experiences were analogous because their pattern or structure was identical. Thus the mind, so to speak, creates the world by organizing it according to patterns preexistent in the mind to any given experience. But also, as Coleridge implies, under the impact of experience, these patterns are restructured.

A few later developments of this strain of Romantic thinking about the character of cognition will make this a little clearer. I have already pointed out that is the way Tylor's *Primitive Culture* is structured and that this book brings out the cultural significance of what the Romantics were doing in their new theory of the structure of thinking. The impact of cultural anthropology, as established by Tylor, is this: So long as one is unaware of any possibilities other than those learned from one's own culture, one has an irresistible tendency to know those possibilities as determined, ineluctable, necessary, natural, in the order of things. And so long as one thinks logically and causally, any information about possibilities outside one's culture can be absorbed without changing one's cultural assumptions. Thus information about other cultures had no impact on the degenerationists because they could explain them causally and logically. However, if one sees in terms of patterns—if one sees imaginatively, as Coleridge would have put it—one perceives the way Wordsworth did. The material and the situation and the content of a fraternity initiation are different from the initatory puberty rites of primitive cultures, but the form, the pattern, is identical. Once this is grasped, the possibilities of one's own culture are no longer determined, ineluctable, necessary, natural, in the order of things. One is not condemned to them. The mind, given its imaginative freedom, can transcend those possibilities and create new ones.

There is, I think, little or nothing to be said in favor of Freud's theory, but nevertheless he accomplished one great intellectual feat and service. As a boy and as a young man he was steeped in Romantic philosophy and literature. When he came to the creation of psychoanalysis, he did so because he had observed that if you point out to a patient the similarity of structure in his reports of his behaviors, he can generate similarly structured behavior in free association and even in dreams. And having learned those structures he can, sometimes, transcend them. As Philip Rieff has so brilliantly pointed out, Freud's effect was to create a covert culture of a tiny group of human beings who have transcended their culture—that is, Romantic aliens.

Actually, of course, what Freud and subsequent analysts have principally done is to shift the patient's behavior from unacceptable behavior to acceptable behavior, or if they cannot do that, at least to get him to accept privately his publicly unacceptable behavior so he can stop tearing himself apart. In short, Freud continued the Romantic theory of cognition by showing in his case histories that the mind indeed does think analogically, by patterns, creatively, imaginatively, in Coleridge's sense, and his therapy was aimed, though only rarely with success, at getting the mind to dissolve, diffuse, dissipate, in order to create. His difficulty was that he did not realize what he had done and constructed his theory causally. As a theory it shows the complete bankruptcy of causality.

Two recent developments in anthropology are likewise to the point. One is the demonstration by Lévi-Strauss that myths are not random fantasies but are in fact structured, not by logic but by patterns. It is not surprising that his philosophical source is Hegel, to whom he came through Marx. To be sure, he, or at least his followers, give one the impression that the structures of myth are structures for the sake of structuring, and not explanatory in function as well, but there is no reason why they should not be both. Thus Professor Wallace in his *Religion* analyzes myths to show their patterned analogy, and his whole method of working out his definition of religion is by the examination of similarly structured sequences of behavior leading to the cognitive resynthesis, which is almost Coleridgean in its phraseology and quite Coleridgean in its concept.

To the imagination Coleridge opposed the fancy, which, he claimed, is characterized by fixities, and eighteenth-century poetry was to him a mere matter of the fancy, working by "associations." If for that term we substitute "cultural conventions" what he was after is clear enough. What is involved is the distinction often quite bewildering he and so many Romantics attempted to make between "allegory" and "symbol." Allegory is a mere matter of the fancy. In allegory the explanatory terminology is incorporated into the exemplary narrative, and the course of the narrative is controlled by the logically structured explanation. Thus the relation between Uncle Sam and the government of this country, or, to be more modern, between pigs and policemen, is fixed by cultural convention. The exemplary material can only, Coleridge thought, illustrate the concept, and the best the fancy can do is to find new illustrations.

In symbolism, on the other hand, the explanation can only be arrived at by studying the patterned structure of the work, or by comparing, as the cultural anthropologist does, patterns in various works. Of course Coleridge himself combined the notion of the symbol with a quite different notion, the inexplicable and mysterious. Consequently in *The Ancient Mariner* he created a symbolic structure which could not be then explained, though now there is increasing agreement on its general meaning: roughly, Wallace's pattern of separation, contact with the spirit world, and cognitive resynthesis. A literary work, then, which is not logically coherent but analogically coherent has the unity which is organic, just as in a tree the trunk bears the limbs, the branches bear the twigs, and the twigs bear the leaves, which themselves show the same pattern repeated in the veining. The functions of the various parts are different but the various structures are analogically identical; they exhibit the same pattern.

The Romantic writers found in myth and in pre-seventeenth-century poetry and drama a kind of thinking which could undermine the explanatory systems of their culture and which was at the same time peculiarly adapted to exploring the mysterious, the inexplicable, and the forbidden, because it is, as the subsequent history of science has shown, the logic of discovery. But because they found it in literature, and especially in poetry, they called it poetic thinking. This has led, of course, to a pseudo problem. What is the difference between the scientific imagination and the poetic imagination? And, of course, there is none.

Here was the cultural support and tradition which justified Swinburne in pursuing his investigations into his own strange psyche by writing poetry. Wordsworth discovered the pattern of his life and its imaginative center—using the word just as Coleridge did—by seeing the structural similarity in certain events in his life, events which he called spots of time. Swinburne saw only too clearly the pattern of his erotic needs and satisfactions, but could not explain them. Wordsworth and Coleridge together worked out the preliminaries of an explanation —which Coleridge took much farther—and they were activated by a need for discovering a new way of thinking about their own and about the human past. This guided Wordsworth in his investigations into himself. In writing the *Prelude* he already had some idea of what he was looking for. Even so it took him a good many years. For Swinburne there was only the pattern; there was no guiding explanation. That had to be sought. He exhibited that pattern in a sequence of poems, written over about five years, which were partly based on his own experiences, partly imagined situations analogically similar to his own experiences, and partly examinations of such insights as he had managed to achieve.

Poems and Ballads opens with a mysterious, conflict-ridden, bitter, and ecstatic poem. It is a vision of a beautiful woman, "fervent as a fiery moon," whose eyelids are sorrowful and whose mouth is sad. She sings of charity, tenderness, pleasure, sorrow, sleep, sin, and lovingkindness, "that is pity's kin and is most pitiless." The only hint of an explanation for this confusing and paradoxical fusion of pity and pitilessness is that the woman's name is Borgia. It is Lucrezia, whose infamous reputation had not yet been tamed by Renaissance historians; she has turned out to be a rather commonplace woman, virtuous and a patron of the arts at the Este court. However, her flaming reputation had not yet been damaged when Swinburne took her as an emblem of the dominating and destructive woman the masochist craves.

276

She is accompanied by three men, Fear, Shame, and Lust, the three attitudes of the male masochist. Fear is what is behind the mask of pity. To the masochistic man, pity has no valid life in it. If it is pity for the sorrow and sadness of the sadistic woman, then pitilessly she uses lovingkindness to entrap the man so that she may humiliate him by revealing that her pretended love is pity. If it is pity for himself, then the woman reveals to him that his self-pity conceals a fear of his own nature. The mask of shame is sorrow comforted. That one needs to be comforted for what one is is a further humiliation, the humiliation of shame. And Lust is really what passes for Love. This unexplained identification is explained later in the volume, in "Hesperia"; "For desire is a respite from love." Thus the Borgia type reveals to the masochistic type that three acceptable feelings are but masks for three unacceptable ones.

Yet the poem is equivocal, for there is no suggestion that the speaker, having learned all this, ceases to be inflamed with love for her, or does not see her as perfect and redemptive of sin and sorrow and death. Of the serious poems in the book, those Swinburne later wished to include in a revised edition, with his juvenalia omitted, this seems to be the first or one of the first he wrote. The major poems in the collection all come later. Thus, we may guess, Swinburne began to explore his mysterious and explicable and forbidden problem. The title of the poem, strangely, is "A Ballad of Life." The question he is addressing himself to is a genuine puzzle, one that is rarely met head on. It is this: "Is the victim of an erotic aberration one whose cognition of human relationships is so distorted as to be invalid, or does his aberration give him a subtler, profounder, and more valid insight into the nature of human relationships than the inaberrant individual can possibly have?" Certainly this poem is a masochist's insight into human life, but should it be dimissed for that reason?

No doubt the current culture would answer that the insights of the erotically aberrant must be invalid, and the answer would come with the brusque condemnation characteristic of those critics who dismissed Swinburne for his indecency and his corrupted fleshliness. The two judgments are, in fact, equally moral judgments, though the first is masked as a psychological judgment. The reason for this identity is that the modern judgment is a Freudian judgment. Though it may be that Freud, particularly in his later years, saw psychoanalysis as an instrument for cultural transcendence, his earlier work, as it has been developed and therapeutically applied, is unquestionably an instrument of social management, which it accomplishes by validating and invalidating behavior according to the current validational mode, whatever it may be.

This basis for invalidating the insights of masochism may be dismissed. Furthermore, what is validated as an inaberrant erotic mode, true love leading to happy marriage, is just as clearly a mode of social management. This is moral love, and the culture validates it. Its function is to provide a model for resolving the domination-submission incoherence within any person and between any two persons by identifying dominance with the man and submission with the woman. Of course, it is only a model, and it never works as smoothly as anybody would like. Nevertheless, any society must have models of resolving dominance-submission incoherence—general or universal directions, we might call them—identified as necessary and natural. It has even been recently suggested by Lionel Tiger in *Men in Groups* that the basis for this particular resolution is genetic. It may well be. Certainly, it has been established for so many millions of years and by now is so deeply ingrained into all but a few cultures that it might as well be genetic.

What sex offers is orgasm, the total release and resolution of tension, preceded by a progressive exclusion of all other stimuli as the sexual tension mounts. The tension release is, to be sure, only too brief, but it is better than none at all. What love offers is the promise of total tension release, the resolution of all internal and interpersonal incoherence and conflict. Hence it is one of the most powerful and appealing and seductive human cognitions. I say "cognition" quite purposely. If love is thought of as an emotion it can never be understood. If it is understood as a cognitive act that is emotionally most heavily weighted, comprehension is theoretically possible. In "The Ballad of Life" total tension release and conflict resolution is seen as precisely the promise of the visionary woman. Love, or eroticized sex, is, for these reasons, obviously superbly designed to be an instrument of social management. An indication of this is that it appears, historically, to have become an important, even a central, cultural factor only with the rise of the higher civilizations, cultures that require more complex and subtle modes of managing themselves than primitive life needs.

Moreover it is worth pointing out that any inaberrant sexual relation, if passion leads it beyond the bounds of decorum, very commonly leads to the infliction upon the sexual partner of mild tortures which the standardization of the sexual role indicates are not to be taken seriously nor as comment on the desirability of the sexual object. And for the same reason these mild tortures are enjoyed by the receiver. The moments before the orgasm itself are, besides, an extraordinary fusion of pleasure and pain.

The analysis at the beginning of this speculation came to the conclusion that sadism and masochism are metaphors of social management, and here I have proposed that inaberrant love is a model for social management which uses love to reinforce the social validation of that model. It is a very nice instance of conditioned therapy. Sadism and masochism, then, are metaphors which select out of inaberrant love the social management factor or attribute. They are ways of selecting out one ingredient in the extremely complex and many-factored sociopersonal cultural convention of love-and-marriage. This function for an erotic aberration may, indeed, be the function of all the aberrations. If this line of reasoning is at all adequate, it

279

follows that the insights of a masochist into eroticism are not necessarily invalid. On the contrary, if he has all his wits about him—as Swinburne certainly did—his insights may be considerably more valid than those whose eroticism is not aberrant. After all, to engage in any culturally validated activity is not likely to lead to any insights except those of the mode of explanation which supports and is knotted together with the culture's mode of validation and social management. It was the Romantic position that the outsider can see more clearly than the insider, and the Romantics were surely right, as Tylor demonstrated.

Swinburne's insights into eroticism, therefore, should not be dismissed because they are the insights of a masochist. Rather the reverse. They are worth paying attention to because of that, and particularly because Swinburne, masochist though he may have been, was highly intelligent. So it is instructive that the second poem in the volume is "A Ballad of Death." Together the two poems imply that the essence of life is love, that the essence of love is suffering and humiliation and lust, and that the consequence of this is the desire for death. Swinburne was writing not long after a period, the 1830's and 1840's, in which advanced thinking saw love as redemptive. From that period the notion has deeply penetrated into the culture, down to the comic-strip and movie and soap-opera level. Yet already in the 1850's a different attitude toward love was emerging, though not yet in England.

Swinburne was the first English writer to begin the attack on love. Extramarital love and lust had been traditionally attacked for as long as Christianity had lasted. Transcendental love, however, asserted that redemptive love could be found even outside of marriage. The story of Camille is an early popularization of this notion, and its appeal seems to be perennial. Swinburne, however, learning much from Baudelaire, asserted that love is lust, that erotic pity is fear, and that erotic sorrow is shame.

Love, then, is a humiliating bondage, at least to the masochist, who finds his freedom in that very humiliation. What Swinburne is asserting is that socially invalidated eroticism and socially validated eroticism are subjectively identical; only the sociocultural judgment marks a difference between them. It is like theft. You may steal, but you are not a thief if you do not define yourself as a thief and if nobody else does. Indeed, there is a strong cultural validation for some kinds of theft—stealing towels from hotels, or tablecloths and silver from restaurants, or cheating on the income tax. That there is stronger invalidation for any kind of theft—though not, it would seem very much stronger—is merely witness to the internal incoherence of any culture's validational system, as Hegel pointed out.

So, from Swinburne's point of view, it is with love. Aberration is, like theft, not a matter of the character of the aberrant act but a matter of social definition and social role. Love is at once a bondage and a promise of freedom. This conflict can be resolved only in death so long as love in any form is a cognition the individual judges to be essential to his life. Absolute freedom can be experienced only rationally, or, to be a little more careful, only in verbal behavior, and only by the philosospher, be he good or bad at philosophizing. The attempt to realize absolute freedom in the world itself properly results in concrete freedom, the tension between the subject's absolute desire for freedom and the object's absolute recalcitrance. Negative freedom is a vacation from the tension of concrete freedom. Love, with its promise and its momentary orgasmic realization of the resolution and reduction of all tension, is the promise of negative freedom; but it is a freedom never finally realized. Hence the agony of being in love, and hence the desire for death, which is the only experience that can promise the realization of negative freedom and fulfill that promise.

Swinburne was not unaware that love is bondage from the sadistic as well as from the masochistic point of view. Lucrezia

281

Borgia is as sad and sorrowful as the three men who accompany her, the three aspects of her lover. Whether one's attitude toward the object is that of domination or that of submission, of mastery or slavery, the consequence is the same: bondage to the object, for the object is cognited as promising to offer the realization of abstract freedom in negative freedom. Just as the primary source of submission is a concealed desire for mastery, so sadism and masochism are ultimately identical. The one offers the illusion of conquering the world, the other the illusion of being conquered by it. Both are in bondage to an illusion. Love is the illusion of resolving the tension of concrete freedom as it manifests itself in social management.

Inaberrant love is in the service of social management. Some kinds of aberrant love, particularly sadism and masochism, are revelations of the political significance of erotic desire and the erotic relation. Love is bondage to negative freedom. The more violent and bloody a revolution the more it is likely to emphasize that all is being done for love of mankind. It would be foolish to doubt for a moment the sincerity of this. So it appears that Hegel was right about the intimate connection between revolution, negative freedom, and bloodiness and violence. The climax of erotic freedom is the death of oneself, if only the momentary extinction of consciousness or, more subtly, one's sense of identity; while revolutionary negative freedom finds its climax in the death of others.

There are only two ways out of the seductive and enticing humiliation of love: death, and the transcendence of love into concrete freedom. In one poem in the volume, "Hesperia," Swinburne considers the possibility of love as redemptive, as leading to concrete freedom. It concludes with a wild and magnificent flight on horseback from love, masochistic and sadistic love, as bondage. But it ends with a query: "Ah love, shall we win at the last?" The kind of love he imagines in this poem as redeeming from bondage love is surprising for Swinburne, for it is the traditional notion of a healing, helping, and altogether desirable love, the kind developed by the transcendental concept of the 1830's and 1840's, a period in which the love for mankind was particularly rampant. What is it doing here? Why did Swinburne consider it? Why is he so doubtful about its viability?

There is one traditional way love can be transcended, a way validated by the very system of social management that uses it for its own purposes. That way is marriage, or its equivalent. Within the traditional western cultural system marriage is considered to be a relationship higher in value than love. In marriage, love is transcended because two people become cooperative partners in realizing concrete freedom. Hegel may have been too optimistic in thinking of the state as the instrument of concrete freedom, since it tends to preserve its subjects in a condition of abstract freedom, of masochism, while it tends to convert the people who run it into sadists. That is no doubt why it is so easy for the state to persuade men to die for it.

Had Hegel seen the state not as *the* instrument of social management in the interests of concrete freedom, but one of many such instruments, in more or less incoherent relation to each other, he would have put far less trust in it. In his confidence in the state he seems to have fallen victim to the kind of error he condemned: his state tends to become an abstraction, not a concrete universal. This is certainly a weakness in his thinking that Marx saw, though Marx's own remedies are ultimately sentimental, a form of abstract or negative freedom. Since, as Hegel was perfectly aware, the belief-system of a culture is inevitably incoherent, validation must have force, brutal power, to support it; and to provide that power is the function of the state. One of the devices of social management the state maintains by force is marriage. To transcend love by marriage is, therefore, to enter into the system of social management which uses love as one of its means for maintaining itself.

Consequently, love is validated by marriage, and though marriage can be used to transcend love, the validation ensures generally an intermittent regression. From this point of view marriage is an unmistakable model for domination and submission as well as the self-destruction of the orgasm, a useful model for the self-limitation and self-maiming without which no society can exist. Further, in any Christian culture, such as Swinburne's, the theological explanatory mode also explains love-and-marriage by using it as a metaphor for all kinds of nonsexual relationships, as in the love of Christ for his bride the Church, the allegorical explanation of The Song of Songs, or in the Mystic Marriage of St. Catherine, or in the fiction that the nun is the bride of Christ. Thus it is integrated into the explanatory system and simultaneously validated.

For one, like Swinburne, who was working backward from his cultural support of questioning and denying the adequacy and validity of the culture's modes of explanation and validation and social management (one of his earliest serious interests was revolution and republicanism), the significance of love-and-marriage in the social system was not difficult to arrive at. Or rather, he proceeded from both ends toward the middle. His Romantic cultural tradition was echoed at the other end of the continuum by his aberrant erotic nature. The latter meant that he could not transcend love by marriage; the former meant that he rejected the culture's modes of explanation, validation, and social management.

Between the political structures of society and the intrapersonal structures involving two people lies a social structure at once private and public—the family. To transcend love by marriage is to establish a family, and to do so is to enter fully into the process of participating actively in the current modes of social management. To say that the family is the foundation of society is a remark as dubious as it is commonplace. The restricted family seems to have emerged only with the industrial revolution, while the nuclear family of today, the two-generation family, is something that has appeared in this country only in the last few decades and as yet by no means in all the rest of the European culture area, only in its highly industrialized and urbanized areas. It seems more adequate to say that society is the foundation of the family since the family appears to change in response to the interest of a changing society, or more precisely, of changing modes of social management. The family is the foundation of society only in the sense that social management uses the family for the purposes of educating the young in social structure—hierarchical and peer relationships.

Above all, society uses the family to train the young in the seductive sadistic and masochistic, triumphing and humiliating, enticements of love, thus preparing them to accept willingly self-limitation, self-maiming, and self-destruction. We learn to risk death and to die for love, for love of erotic objects, other men and women, for love of parents, of home, of country, even of the army itself, or any institution. The social task of parents is to train children through frustration and disorientation until they yearn for the total tension release of the enveloping parental bosom. Thus they are softened up for easeful social management.

The logic of his Romantic tradition, his cultural support, and the logic of his erotic aberration, led Swinburne to converge his public impetus and his private upon the one social structure which is both public and private, the family. He saw with utmost clarity one direction in which love leads, death and the desire for death, and his finest exploration of that theme is the famous "The Garden of Proserpine," one of the last poems written for *Poems and Ballads*. The first climax of the poem is reached with:

> And well though love resposes,
> In the end it is not well.

The paradox of love is uttered in:

> And love, grown faint and fretful
> With lips but half regretful
> Sighs and with eyes forgetful
> Weeps that no loves endure.

And so:

> From too much love of living,
> From hope and fear set free,
> We thank with brief thanksgiving
> Whatever gods may be
> That no life lives for ever;
> That dead men rise up never;
> That even the weariest river
> Winds somewhere safe to sea.

The poem ends with:

> Only the sleep eternal
> In an eternal night,

as the one human end to be desired.

It is directly after this poem that Swinburne places "Hesperia," the one poem in which he conceives the possibility that there is a redemptive love, but it ends with a question, "Ah love, shall we win at the last?" But the answer is already stated in "The Garden of Proserpine." "To think so, is to suffer an illusion." The escape from aberrant eroticism into inaberrant, "normal," love is but to change the decor of hell. With this insight, for Swinburne the way of transcending love through the path of marriage was closed.

In a poem early in the volume, the apparently autobiographical "The Triumph of Time," he saw the only possibility of
erotic happiness in a relation in which the woman recognized
fully his aberrant nature and permitted him to express it. But
who, he asks, can even believe in, let alone accept, "such fellows as I am?" Here already is the theme of the identity of
aberrant and nonaberrant love, for the poem flickers back and
forth between a recognition of his aberrant nature and attitudes
of adoration of the beloved by the lover and submission to her
which had long since been conventionalized in the culture.
Hence the cultural shock, the delightful shock, of the early
1930's, when Jimmy Cagney pushed a grapefruit into his beloved's face. But the woman in "The Triumph of Time" cannot
understand him and accept him as he is. He turns then and goes
"back to the great sweet mother, Mother and lover of men, the
sea." It is true that Swinburne took extraordinary pleasure in
swimming, swimming far out to sea, alone, so far he sometimes
had to be rescued by fishermen. And in this poem it is clear what
the charm of the sea was for him. He was *alone* in it. The sea
is his metaphor for complete personal disengagement.

> Thou art fed with our dead, O mother, O sea,
> But when has thou fed on our hearts?

He becomes one with the sea in a total relaxation of tension,
propelled and moved by the sea's currents, and the verses, as
they unroll, reveal a gradual extinguishing of individual identity.

It has been suggested by a noted psychiatrist that there is
such a thing as partial suicide, of which one manifestation is the
steady reduction of interpersonal relations to the minimum
necessary for life, the cutting off of all others in one's life, even

when, or perhaps especially when, those others are the source of gratification. Gratification is a temptation to live; an individual may commit a kind of psychic semisuicide by eschewing gratifications and actively seeking out frustrations. This is the pattern of "The Triumph of Time," and of Swinburne's love for the sea. Yet he calls that sea "mother," and also "lover of men." The identification is, of course, disturbing, and I believe he meant it to be so. It was probably one of those details in the volume which the hostile reviewers found even too shocking to mention.

Christianity has done all in its power to emphasize the sacredness of mother love, and no wonder, considering the educational function of the family. The mother is the first to offer that tension-destroying abstract or negative freedom, to use the Hegelian terms, to offer the comfort of surcease of the struggle to maintain one's identity in the face of frustration and disorientation, to make the child amenable to social management. No wonder mother love is sacred! As he matures, the child, having learned to exploit this stimulus for the sake of the supreme gratification it offers, has only to find other stimuli to serve the same purpose. Having learned the role of eroticism, the role of sweet submission unto death, he has only to find occasions to play it, of which one is sexuality, discovered by some during puberty, but not by all. The man who can love nothing is incapable of socialization. Socialization is the price we pay for life, and love is the fearful price we pay for socialization. It is a fearful price because its seduction and enticement form the promise of negative freedom. It commits us to a life of intermittent yearning.

Hence it is not to be overlooked that although Swinburne at first glance seems to be using the conventionalized concept of mother love, though in a rather strange way, to be sure, and although like a kind of proto-Freudian he seems, and indeed is, tracing love to the child's being comforted by the mother, who is the one, after all, who ordinarily has made the comforting necessary, nevertheless he associates mother, love, and death. And so we need not be too surprised that when he undertakes his first major work, *Atalanta in Calydon*, he should choose a Greek legend in which a mother kills her son. "For there is nothing," says Meleager, the son, "terribler to men/Than the sweet face of mothers, and the might"; and at the end of the play, "Mother, I dying with unforgetful tongue/Hail thee as holy and worship thee as just/Who art unjust and unholy; and with my knees/Would worship, but thy fire and subtlety,/Dissundering them, devour me."

Family Relations could well be the title of *Atalanta*, for rarely has the family been so devastatingly attacked. I know of no instance before *Atalanta*, with the partial exception of Jane Austen's *Persuasion*, in which at the end of her writing life her hitherto lightly concealed intellectual brutality is at last allowed to express itself. Moreover the paradoxical character of Meleager's judgment on mothers in general and his mother in particular is found elsewhere in Swinburne's thinking, and not merely in love. It is found in his conception of God. Swinburne was no believer, and one may be reasonably certain that his judgment on God was in fact a judgment on what society, that is, mankind, uses "God" for, explanation and validation and social management.

His attack on God first appears in *Poems and Ballads.* In the throes of frustrated love Sappho, in "Anactoria," cries out how she would like to make the faithless Anactoria suffer: She would

Make thy life shudder in thee and burn afresh,
And wring thy very spirit through the flesh [.]
Cruel? but love makes all that love him well
As wise as heaven and crueller than hell.

Me hath love made more bitter toward thee
Than death toward men;

And now comes the judgment on God and the link between love and God.

      but were I made as he
Who hath made all things to break them one by one,
If my feet trod upon the stars and sun
And souls of men as his have alway trod,
God knows I might be crueller than God.

"God is love, say the Christians. "Yes indeed," says Swinburne, "but that doesn't mean quite what you think it means. Rather—"

      who bade exceed
The fervid will, fall short the feeble deed,
Bade sink the spirit and the flesh aspire,
Pain animate the dust of dead desire,
And life yield up her flower to violent fate?
Him would I reach, him smite, him desecrate,
Pierce the cold lips of God with human breath,
And mix his immortality with death.
Why hath he made us? what had all we done
That we should live and loathe the sterile sun,
And with the moon wax paler as she wanes,
And pulse by pulse feel time grow through our veins?

And she goes on to utter her final challenge:

But, having made me, me he shall not slay

In *Atalanta*, Althaea, the mother, is the most pious of women. She fears the gods, and obeys them, and she justifies her actions by that obedience. But Meleager, her son, places his trust in life, and in the gods; moreover he loves Atalanta, a foreign woman, dedicated to virginity and Artemis, who has thus, by the standards of Althaea and her brothers, defeminized herself, who is "unnatural"; Meleager attempts to transcend the values of his family; and finally he kills his uncles because they have murderously attacked Atalanta. For all these crimes Althaea kills him, and it is clear that the death of her brothers is but her excuse, her justification, or better still, the trigger that has set her off on the course she wishes to pursue, the death of her son.

But this is too crude for the subtlety Swinburne has offered. Althaea kills Meleager because he is attempting to escape her control. A more salient instance of social management reaching for its ultimate weapon, power over life and death, would be difficult to imagine. It is the reason, I believe, Swinburne seized upon this legend; but not the only reason. Meleager calls his mother terrible, but also he calls her sweet. He calls her just and holy; and he calls her unjust and unholy. And this last at the moment of his death. His cultural incoherence is never transcended. It is, in fact, only polarized. His mother says we must fear the gods; he proposes the antithesis—that we should trust the gods. She says they are jealous of our happiness; he says that they wish us well and want us to be happy. In these two generations Swinburne has ingeniously juxtaposed the two Christian conceptions of God—the God of wrath and divine vengeance of the Old Testament and of the Puritans, and the God of perfect adaptation to environment which the Enlightenment deists put in place of Him, colored by the New Testament conception of the God of love.

To assert a God of wrath, and to assert a God of love, then, amount to the same thing. They are two sides of one coin. They are to ask the wrong question of life: "What is an ultimate, final, explanation?" It is the explanatory system that is responsible for this incoherence. Thus, as the chorus concludes in the great climax of one of its lyrics, after contrasting these two positions,

291

None hath beheld him, none
Seen above other gods and shapes of things, ...
The lord of love and loathing and of strife
   Who gives a star and takes a sun away;
Who shapes the soul, and makes her a barren wife
   To the earthly body and grievous growths of clay; ...
Who makes desire, and slays desire with shame; ...
Smites without sword, and scourges without rod;
      The supreme evil, God.

Althaea and Meleager have been talking about the gods. But this God is above those gods. He is the high God. He is evidently the Christian God, who is indeed the lord of love and loathing and of strife. Therefore, the chorus continues,

   ... each man in his heart sigheth, and saith,
      That all men even as I,
   All we are against thee, against thee, O God most high.

So Swinburne asks, "What is the instrument with which this high God tortures man?" And his surprising answer is, "Language." And the chorus concludes,

   For words divide and rend;
   But silence is most noble till the end.

This is their answer to the question with which they began.

   Who hath given man speech? or who hath set therein
   A thorn for peril and a snare for sin?
   For in the word his life is and his breath,
      And in the word his death,
   That madness and the infatuate heart may breed

From the word's womb the deed
And life bring one forth ere all pass by,
Even one thing which is ours yet cannot die—
Death.

The allusion to the opening of the Gospel According to St. John
is unmistakable. "In the beginning was the Word, and the Word
was with God, and the Word was God."

The language of men, then, is the source of their suffering, for
in language Meleager and Althaea seek to justify their positions
and validate them by appealing to the gods; but behind those
gods is the ultimate language of explanation. To Swinburne the
explanation of human affairs available to the culture was a theological explanation, and it was an ultimate, final explanation.
God is indeed the word, for men make of their explanatory
systems a God, which validates their behavior and which justifies the most extreme use of power—life and death—in social
management.

So Meleager only imagines that he is transcending the values
of his family and his mother. And a further manifestation of this
same pattern is his love for Atalanta. Dedicated to Artemis, to
the hunt, and to virginity, she is inaccessible. Thus Meleager's
justification—that the gods are beneficent and want us to be
happy, his Enlightenment religion and morality—is denied by
his actions, for he chooses as a sexual and erotic object a woman
who is committed to a life that necessarily denies him the
beneficence of his deities, denies his happiness by condemning
him to unfulfilled yearning, denies him any perfect adaptation
to nature. In choosing Atalanta he chooses for himself a self-
limitation, a self-maiming, a partial suicide. Swinburne, through
the chorus, provides the explanation in his marvelous evocation
of the birth of Aphrodite from the sea-foam, nor is it to be
forgotten, nor does Swinburne want us to forget, the occasion
of that birth. Cronus castrated his father, Uranus, and threw the

VICTORIAN REVOLUTIONARIES

bleeding genitals into the sea. From the wound itself fell drops
which gave birth to the Furies of the earth; the genitals floating
on the sea turned into foam from which was born Aphrodite—
the fury, to Swinburne, of the sea.

> For an evil blossom was born
>   Of sea-foam and the frothing of blood,
>   Blood-red and bitter of fruit,
>   And the seed of it laughter and tears,
> And the leaves of it madness and scorn; ...
> ... a wonder, a world's delight,
> A perilous goddess was born; ...
> For all they said upon earth,
>   She is fair, she is white like a dove, ...
>   For they knew thee for mother of love,
>   And knew thee not mother of death. ...
> For bitter thou wast from thy birth,
>   Aphrodite, a mother of strife; ...
> What ailed thee then to be born?
> Was there not evil enough,
>   Mother, and anguish on earth ...
> That thou must lay on [man] love?
>
>
> Thou shouldst not so have been born:
>   But death should have risen with thee,
>   Mother, and visible fear,
>   Grief, and the wringing of hands,
> And noise of many that mourn; ...
> For against all men from of old
>   Thou hast set thine hand as a curse, ...
>   And made ... kingdoms and races
>   As dust and surf of the sea.

294

Here once again we find the constellation of love, mother-
hood, death, and the sea, now specifically used to explain the
behavior of Meleager. Once again his apparent attempt to escape from and transcend the values of his family is only a repetition of family relations, specifically the sado-masochistic
relation of dominance and submission between mother and
child, the terrible face of dominance—the sweet face that en-
tices the child to submission. These are the two faces of
Lucrezia Borgia described in "The Ballad of Life," but Swinburne has penetrated much farther into the source of that duplicity and incoherence, and he has seen its relation to family
and to social management and its associated modes. This he has
done not by generating new explanations in the Romantic manner, by organizing his lyrics and his tragedy to bring together
analogically identical structures of incoherence at all levels of
behavioral analysis, from the mother–child relationship through
the family, love, politics or social management, to metaphysical
and theological explanation and justification. Nor does he put all
the blame on dominance, for Althaea suffers in her act of dominant vengeance upon her son even more terribly than Meleager
himself.

She has control over his life because when he was born she
was warned that his life would last only as long as the brand
then burning on the hearth should not be burnt out. She
snatched it from the fire and preserved it. Here again one sees
the appeal of the story for Swinburne, for a better symbol of
social control could scarcely be imagined. Freud's notion that all
men wish to marry their mothers was both in error and incomplete. He confused the source of the strange cognitive act we
call love with the occasion of its first appearance. Moreover, he
should have added that all mothers wish to kill their children,
and all fathers too. The number of parents I have heard express
that wish either forthrightly or barely veiled is surprising, or

rather, not surprising at all. If the child is condemned to the sweet bondage of submission, the parent is condemned to the terrible bondage of domination. The occasions on which parents long to be rid of their children, and the language used on such occasion, reveal that it is not their children they long to be free of but the slavery of having to dominate and to control, of having to be the instrument of social management. Althaea makes her decision in a frenzy in which she seems to be burning up, and after the fact is done, and the brand thrown again upon the fire, she retreats into silence. She too commits a partial suicide. The silence indicates the nature of such suicide just as Meleager's literal bodily withering away indicates the same factor. It is an error to think of partial and complete suicide as an emotional act. Like love, it is a cognitive act, a deliberate reduction of the range of experience over which the individual attempts to exert cognitive control. As psychologists are beginning once again to discover, and even a few psychiatrists— those moral policemen of our culture—people *think*, and they think all the time. All behavior is cognitive behavior, more or less emotionally loaded. Althaea confirms the chorus's utterance that "silence is most noble till the end." In the face of the fundamental incoherence of social life, what is there to be said?

To that fundamental incoherence of human existence Swinburne sees that man, or at least the culture that he knew, had so far made available two resolutions, the desire for death and death itself, reached through the path of erotic love, and the two forms of bondage, sadism and masochism, masterhood and slavery, dominance and submission. If one rejects eroticism and the way of death, and turns instead to life, the price of life, one finds, is the bondage of dominance and submission. Moreover, there, too, love is to be found, for what in private relationships is love is in public relationships negative freedom, the freedom of submitting to the state or the freedom of destroying the state, the state being the most inclusive institutionalized instrument of social management.

In such a scheme a man's life is seen as bouncing back and forth between private and public life. To escape the suicidal path of private eroticism he turns to public life, only to find there, concealed behind social institutions, the same path toward death, the denial of the fullness of life, that is, the attempt to exert cognitive control over ever-expanding ranges of experience. Here is to be found the tension between subject and object, true concrete freedom, and it is why, as Hegel said, the history of man is the history of increasing freedom. But denied that fullness by social or public life, the individual turns back once again to private life, to eroticism, in the attempt, necessarily doomed, to find there a way out of the situation to concrete freedom. In *Atalanta*, Swinburne moved from the private to the family sphere of life, thus making the transition to the problem of social management, validation, and explanation, as the great speculative choruses reveal. And the final chorus is:

> Who shall contend with his lords
>   Or cross them or do them wrong?
> Who shall bind them as with cords?
>   Who shall tame them as with song?
> Who shall smite them as with swords?
>   For the hands of their kingdom are strong.

Clearly the next step was to come to grips with the formalized institutions of social management, the state and its adjunct, institutionalized religion.

And that next step he made with the publication in 1867 of *A Song of Italy*, begun only a few months after the publication of *Poems and Ballads*. There is, therefore, no puzzle in why Swinburne turned from the eroticism of *Poems and Ballads* to political poetry. The actual course of writing was from *Poems and Ballads* to *Atalanta* and then to the political poems. The erotic lyrics and the tragedy of family relations were no inexplicable interlude in his intellectual course, something dictated by his strange and aberrant sexual character which, by reason of the aberrancy, must be considered as discontinuous from his political verse. On the contrary, his aberrancy made it possible for him to transcend his cultural values, to see into the true character of eroticism, and to see its continuity into family life and thence into the structure of society. His encounter with the great and visionary Italian Republican Mazzini was not the cause of his redirection but merely an incident, or at best a milestone, in the direction in which he was already moving. As a youth he had been a passionate republican and, as we have seen, he had now created in *Atalanta* a meaningless meaningful myth of personality, culture, and society. The Hegel-like logic of his development *required* him to proceed from the family to politics, the problem of state and church, then inseparable throughout Europe, but especially in Italy, where the Pope was a secular ruler and the principal hindrance to the unification of that fragmented nation. It was a logic of subsumption; the family subsumes eroticism, and the state subsumes the family, the attribute common to all three categories being love, the doomed effort to resolve the incoherence of dominance and submission, also common to all three categories.

Hegel once again can give us a guide into Swinburne's political thinking. As we have seen, Hegel saw the state as the instrument for achieving concrete freedom, and hence the individual was absorbed into the state. But according to the analysis of the situation toward which Swinburne was working, this is simply to repeat on a more inclusive level the dominance, submission, and love which are all manifestations of negative freedom. Hegel conceived the state on the model of a person, indeed as a person, and he saw concrete freedom emerging in the struggle between person-states.

298

For this there is some justification. The personality is most empirically conceived as a ragbag of behavioral patterns, validated and invalidated by the culture. Our cognition of a person, however, tends, like all cognitions, to stabilize itself. The result is that the personality is cognited as an entity. The state, likewise, is cognited as an entity; language itself turns the state into a person. "The United States has engaged in a war in Vietnam," turns this society's instrument of social management into an entity, which is then praised or reviled as if it were a person. Actually, the United States has done nothing at all, for there is no entity "United States." Certain members of the government, in opposition to other members of the government, have sufficient power over the instruments of social management, the patterned intrapersonal relationships in which dominance and submission and love are the central attributes, to use other people in fighting a war in Vietnam.

Hegel, in deciding that the state is a person, has in fact simply fallen into a common linguistic trap. For though to have a cognition of the state as a person is the same kind of cognition as that of having a cognition of an individual personality as an entity, the individual person is, after all, a biological organism, and the state is not. It is only metaphorically an organism. Hegel, in his organic notion of the state, has been trapped not only by a common linguistic error but also by the myth of a metaphor.

Far from transcending Hegel's position—and his error—Marx merely polarized himself in antithesis to Hegel, demanding that the state should be destroyed, and asserting that by the inner necessity of the historical process the state would wither away. To be sure, he said that this withering away would come about from the economic necessity of the historical process, but this abandonment of the Hegelian term "inner" merely serves to conceal that "economic necessity" and "historical process" are both verbal constructs. Thus, just as Hegel, in asserting the state as the human instrument for concrete freedom, denied the individual organism any freedom but negative freedom of revolution against the state or devotion to it, so Marx in getting rid of the state merely asserted a negative freedom, or abstract freedom, for the individual organism. The cognition of both grasped the state as a person, and both deprived the individual organism of concrete freedom.

The difficulty, of course, is that there is no such empirical entity as the "state." The word serves merely to categorize those intrapersonal behavioral patterns the common attribute of which is that there is no higher level in the social hierarchy; there is no appeal beyond them except to the brute force of power, which is in fact their common attribute. The only way to appeal beyond those individuals who are occupying the roles of terminating the hierarchy of appeal by the application of power is to displace them. Whether the revolution of displacement is accomplished by violence or by voting makes little difference.

In moving beyond the family, therefore, Swinburne was bound to engage with the more inclusive political problem, the state. His meaningless meaningful analysis of social structure was more subtle and more thoroughgoing not only than the primitive efforts of de Sade but also than the infinitely more sophisticated efforts of Hegel, and certainly far more than Marx's. Yet since it was "meaningless," that is, since it was generated analogically and mythically, rather than in explanatory language, the question arises as to whether or not he was able to construct an abstract explanation of what he had analogically grasped by means of exemplary cognition.

His earliest political poem, written in 1852, "A Song in Time of Order," was an attack on Napoleon III, who in the name of order had persuaded Frenchmen to elect him Emperor of France. Swinburne was then an adolescent, and it is not surprising that he should have applied a purely Enlightenment ideology to the analysis of Napoleon's behavior. He uttered

once again the old cry of "tyranny and priestcraft." The Enlightenment, at least its radical and optimistic wing, was convinced that could we but do away with organized religion and
its adjunct, tyrannous state power, mankind could be genuinely
free; and of freedom they held a fairly naïve notion. In returning
to politics in his maturity, and after an extraordinary feat of
social analysis, though nonexplanatory in its construction,
would Swinburne be able to go beyond this Enlightenment
position?

Well, he went to the notion of brotherhood, a metaphor for
that relationship among men best defined as friendship, a relationship in which, supposedly, there is neither dominance nor
submission. For such a relationship Swinburne again used the
term "love," but in quite a different sense from that of the erotic
lyrics or *Atalanta*.

Now it becomes "Love, the beloved republic." It is a political
love, the love between equals. Is it a genuine concrete freedom
or a negative freedom? In a sense, to that question there is no
answer. Absolute freedom, abstract freedom, negative freedom
can be discussed in language; their attributes can be listed; their
requirements can be legislated. But concrete freedom can only
be experienced. It necessarily eludes language, for since it
enacts the irresolvable tension between subject and object, its
attributes are unpredictable. All that language can do, ultimately, is give directions for behavior, and if meanings are
adequately conventionalized, it can predict the consequences
of such behavior, but only if the behavioral responses to its
directions are so rigidly conventionalized that no significant
innovation intrudes.

But concrete freedom necessarily yields constant innovation.
At best it can be said that Swinburne, like Marx and the Enlightenment before him, saw the necessary precondition for a socially realized concrete freedom in friendship, in the
disappearance of dominance and submission and suicidal love.

Like so many revolutionaries he saw the cooperative seizure of power from the state and the destruction of the state as the occasion in which that republican love would be established among men. But it seems to be clear that if the state is an abstraction, then the destruction of the state can only be an abstraction; as Hegel maintained, in actual practice revolution only destroys an abstraction, and is then only negative freedom. Certainly, human experience with revolutions so far seems to confirm Hegel's analysis. Consequently, the beloved republic achieved in the act of overthrowing the state can at best be a negative freedom, cannot, therefore, last. And so this new love which Swinburne had conceived would take the place of erotic love is in its turn merely an illusory escape from domination–submission, and is named "love" only too aptly. The beloved republic is Lucrezia Borgia in a new mask. Swinburne apparently was no more able to go beyond the Enlightenment position than was Marx.

In the political poems Swinburne wrote for six years, beginning in 1866, his attacks were directed against specific oppressive tyrants—the Turks in Crete, the Papacy, Napoleon III—and against the church, particularly the Catholic church in Italy. His efforts were an application of Enlightenment categories, and his proposed resolutions of social conflict were liberty, equality, and fraternity. He failed to comprehend the significance of de Sade's analysis, or that de Sade's position was like his own, in that both saw eroticism as ultimately politics. Thus he missed de Sade's devastating attack on Enlightenment optimism. He understood clearly enough that man—by which he meant European man—is seduced into the dominance-submission–eroticism complex by societies' modes of explanation, validation, and social management. At least he understood it mythically and exemplarily, if not abstractly and philosophically. He also saw almost as clearly, as have all revolutionaries, that a true human freedom which transcends the dominance–

submission–eroticism complex must be free of explanation, validation, and social management.

But, to be Hegelian again for a moment, is a society possible without these three factors? Hegel's conclusion was that in the infinite it was possible; that is, not at all. He thought that freedom was progressive, but never final; Swinburne and Marx thought that it could be final. Historically, in falling back upon an Enlightenment ideology, Swinburne regressed from a Romantic position. In "Hertha" Swinburne, inspired by Darwin, saw all evolution as leading to the achievement of absolute freedom in the concrete world, the last act of achieving freedom being the throwing off of religion and accepting man as fully natural. Thus at last man realizes that he is one with nature, and this is his freedom. It is of course an Enlightenment conclusion.

Swinburne, then, was himself involved in a cultural incoherence. His cognition of the incoherence of social structure was Romantic; his resolution of that incoherence was Enlightenment. Two things now occurred in his life. The first was that he ceased writing political poems. For the rest of his life the freedom he talks about is the freedom of separation from mankind, the freedom of the sea. In a poem of 1880, "Thalassius," he writes a kind of allegory of his life, and sees his error in thinking that he could ever to his profit mingle with mankind. His alienation becomes complete. But the abandonment of his political poetry meant a return to eroticism. He was caught in that oscillation between the public and the private mentioned above. In that sphere of behavior he was still to write magnificent poems, particularly his greatest single effort, *Tristram of Lyonesse*, a work of almost intolerable psychological penetration and intelligence, his greatest study of the destructive power of erotic love.

However, in his personal life, the practice of his aberration, though apparently continued, was no longer sufficient. He turned to a more powerful means of tension resolution than sex can offer, for it is more lasting, and in fact can be maintained almost indefinitely, as Swinburne did, almost to the point of death. He became a severe alcoholic.

And now came the most astonishing turn in an astonishing life. In 1879 he collapsed completely under the impact of continuous drinking. At the request of his mother, and with her financial support, the lawyer Walter Theodore Watts, later Watts-Dunton, came to the rescue and carried him off to a suburban villa in Putney. There he submitted entirely to the social management of his rescuer, even, at his urging, abandoning his efforts to write further novels, a literary enterprise for which he was superbly gifted. Instead he wrote rivers of poetry, much of it, in spite of those who have not read it, up to his highest standards. And he wrote a number of biographical and critical essays for the *Encyclopaedia Britannica* and various journals on Elizabethan playwrights and French and English nineteenth-century literary figures. He published constantly, for he needed the money, and his reputation was such that he could get some money out of everything he wrote. Watts-Dunton protected him, kept off unsuitable visitors, pretty thoroughly controlled what very little drinking he did, made him respectable.

Politically, Swinburne became a fairly typical late nineteenth-century English Imperialist, a full-blown patriot. This is not surprising. Throughout the nineteenth century, nationalism was seen as the avenue to political freedom, a position supported, of course, by Hegelianism. That much of his political interests he preserved. Given his submission to Watts-Dunton and to dominating women who would whip him, it is not surprising that he surrendered to an Hegelian submission to the state, in that he saw freedom as a function of the Imperial Power of England.

There is a melancholy question to be asked as the consequence of studying Swinburne's career. He achieved an insight into the character of European society which was surpassed in the nineteenth century only by Wagner's. He genuinely transcended the attitudes of his culture, but that transcendence was incomplete, for his mythical, his meaningless meaningful comprehension was Romantic, but his proposed resolution for the incoherence he had discovered was, as has been noted, Enlightenment, since that was the only explanatory mode he knew. This need neither surprise nor distress, for it was not until Nietzsche that Romanticism fully transcended the Enlightenment. Swinburne demonstrated that the explanatory, validation, and social management modes of a culture can be transcended. The question he forces us to ask is this: That may be the case, but can the dependence of society—the predictable patterning of human interaction—upon explanation, validation, and social management be transcended? Can the human need for tyranny and priestcraft, no matter what guise they appear in, crude religion or subtle analytical philosophy, ever be dispensed with?

During Swinburne's later years another Englishman, equally devoted to human freedom, made a famous statement that power corrupts and absolute power corrupts absolutely. Very good, and a noble assertion of the moral purity of freedom. But can the proposition not be developed in a different way—thus: All power corrupts; all societies depend for their continuance upon power; therefore all societies are and must be corrupt? And is not love the most exquisite manifestation and consequence of that corruption?

Index

INDEX

op art, 21
Orr, Mrs. Sutherland, 86, 116
Ortega y Gasset, José, 184
Orwell, George, 15
Oxford University, 179, 186, 210

painting, 130–174
Pater, Walter, 26, 217
Patmore, Coventry, 263
personality, 61, 64, 66, 76, 78, 80, 82, 98, 105, 114, 118, 147, 148, 151, 219
Picasso, Pablo, 136, 139, 165, 166
picturesque painting, 157
Plato, 6
polarization, 223–224, 254, 291
pop art, 141, 152–153
Pope, Alexander, 10, 20–21, 227
pornography, 252–253, 257–258
post-impressionism, 135
Poussin, Nicolas, 131
Pound, Ezra, 103
power, 50, 53, 54, 64, 180–183, 185, 186, 190, 210, 283, 293, 305
Pre-Raphaelitism, 130–174
Prescott, William H., 217
Proust, Marcel, 45
Purchas, Samuel, 200
Puvis de Chavannes, Pierre, 165

Ranke, Leopold von, 122
Raphael, 156, 164
realism, 105–108
Reform Act of 1832, 109
religion (*see* myth)
Renoir, Pierre A., 139
Richards, Ivor A., 91
Rieff, Philip, 184, 273
Rimbaud, Arthur, 264
Ripa, Cesare, 164
role, 27, 28, 78, 110, 114, 116, 128, 166, 192, 224, 260, 261, 281
romanticism *passim*
Rosetti, Dante Gabriel, 140, 154–155, 159, 162–166
Rubens, Peter Paul, 20
Ruskin, John, 139, 151, 157, 158, 159–160, 163

Sacher-Masoch, Leopold von, 245, 265, 266, 268, 276–282, 285, 295–296

Sade, Marquis de, 236–250 *passim,* 258, 265, 267, 279, 281, 282, 285, 295–296, 300, 302
Saint-Simonians, 227
Schiller, Friedrich, 67
Schoolcraft, H. P., 178
Schopenhauer, Arthur, 33, 49, 70, 269
Schumann, Robert, 133
Schwitters, Kurt, 154, 159
science, 180, 183, 194–205, 212, 215, 231–232, 241, 267–268, 271, 275
Scott, Sir Walter, 8, 9, 10, 48, 106, 150–151, 228
Scott, William Bell, 164
self, 27, 28, 76, 166, 169, 223–234 *passim,* 260
sentimentality, 65, 125, 160–161
sexual behavior (*see* love)
Shakespeare, William, 36, 82, 114
Shaw, George Bernard, 112, 209
Shelley, Percy Bysshe, 14
signs, 14, 25–26, 166–172, 200
slavery, 47, 240–241
Soane, Sir John, 88
social management, 11, 23, 28, 47, 92, 144, 145, 179, 181–183, 186, 190, 192, 194, 202, 204, 210, 216, 223, 224, 231, 232, 234, 239, 249, 259, 260, 264–305 *passim*
sociology, 144, 148
Sophocles, 131
Spengler, Oswald, 74
Spenser, Edmund, 85
state, 298–300
statistics, 144
Stephens, John Lloyd, 217
Sterling, John, 13–14
Sterne, Lawrence, 45
Stevens, Wallace, 16, 77
Stewart, Dugald, 63, 212
Story of O, 246–247, 255
Sturm-und-Drang, 67–68
Styron, William, 253–254
subject-object relation, 14, 21, 28, 33, 35, 41, 42, 58, 66, 102, 105, 118, 123, 124, 126, 159, 171, 189, 203, 212, 216, 222, 230, 231, 232, 242, 246, 249, 255, 281, 297, 301